639.92

P
N

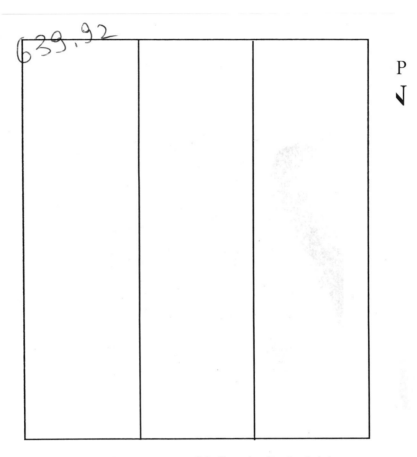

Please return or renew this item by the last date
shown.

Libraries Line and Renewals:     **020 7361 3010**

Web Renewals: www.rbkc.gov.uk/renewyourbooks

**KENSINGTON AND CHELSEA LIBRARY SERVICE**

# THE BEST PLANTS TO ATTRACT AND KEEP
# WILDLIFE IN YOUR GARDEN

## MAKING A BACKYARD HOME FOR ANIMALS, BIRDS & INSECTS

## ENCOURAGE CREATURES INTO YOUR GARDEN BY GROWING WILDLIFE-FRIENDLY PLANTS, SHOWN IN 420 PHOTOGRAPHS

### CHRISTINE AND MICHAEL LAVELLE

Photography by Peter Anderson
Special wildlife photography by Robert Pickett

**southwater**

This edition is published by Southwater
an imprint of Anness Publishing Ltd
Hermes House
88–89 Blackfriars Road
London SE1 8HA
tel. 020 7401 2077
fax 020 7633 9499

www.southwaterbooks.com
www.annesspublishing.com

If you like the images in this book and would
like to investigate using them for publishing,
promotions or advertising, please visit our website
www.practicalpictures.com for more information.

UK distributor:
Book Trade Services;
tel. 0116 2759086; fax 0116 2759090;
uksales@booktradeservices.com;
exportsales@booktradeservices.com

North American distributor:
National Book Network;
tel. 301 459 3366; fax 301 429 5746;
www.nbnbooks.com

Australian distributor:
Pan Macmillan Australia;
tel. 1300 135 113;
fax 1300 135 103;
customer.service@macmillan.com.au

New Zealand distributor:
David Bateman Ltd;
tel. (09) 415 7664;
fax (09) 415 8892

Publisher: Joanna Lorenz
Senior Editor: Felicity Forster
Photography: Peter Anderson
Special Wildlife Photography: Robert Pickett
Illustrator: Liz Pepperell
Copy Editor: Richard Rosenfeld
Jacket Design: Nigel Partridge
Designer: Lisa Tai
Proofreading Manager: Lindsay Zamponi
Production Controller: Christine Ni

## ETHICAL TRADING POLICY

At Anness Publishing we believe that business should be conducted
in an ethical and ecologically sustainable way, with respect for the
environment and a proper regard to the replacement of the natural
resources we employ.

As a publisher, we use a lot of wood pulp in high-quality paper
for printing, and that wood commonly comes from spruce trees.
We are therefore currently growing more than 750,000 trees in three
Scottish forest plantations: Berrymoss (130 hectares/320 acres),
West Touxhill (125 hectares/305 acres) and Deveron Forest
(75 hectares/185 acres). The forests we manage contain more
than 3.5 times the number of trees employed each year in making
paper for the books we manufacture.

Because of this ongoing ecological investment programme,
you, as our customer, can have the pleasure and reassurance of
knowing that a tree is being cultivated on your behalf to naturally
replace the materials used to make the book you are holding.

Our forestry programme is run in accordance with the UK
Woodland Assurance Scheme (UKWAS) and will be certified
by the internationally recognized Forest Stewardship Council (FSC).
The FSC is a non-government organization dedicated to promoting
responsible management of the world's forests. Certification ensures
forests are managed in an environmentally sustainable and socially
responsible way. For further information about this scheme, go to
www.annesspublishing.com/trees

Previously published as part of a larger volume,
*How to Create a Wildlife Garden*

## PUBLISHER'S NOTES

Although the advice and information in this book are believed to be
accurate and true at the time of going to press, neither the authors
nor the publisher can accept any legal responsibility or liability for any
errors or omissions that may have been made nor for any inaccuracies
nor for any loss, harm or injury that comes about from following
instructions or advice in this book.

Great care should be taken if you decide to include pools, ponds
or water features as part of your garden landscape. Young children
should never be left unsupervised near water of any depth, and if
children are able to access the garden all pools and ponds should
be fenced and gated to the recommended specifications.

# CONTENTS

| | |
|---|---|
| Introduction | 6 |
| | |
| **GARDEN WILDLIFE** | **8** |
| Insect-eating birds | 10 |
| Omnivorous birds | 12 |
| Seed-eating birds | 14 |
| Fruit-eating birds | 16 |
| Carnivores and insectivores | 18 |
| Herbivores | 20 |
| Omnivores | 22 |
| Reptiles | 24 |
| Amphibians | 26 |
| Aquatic life | 28 |
| Spiders and scorpions | 30 |
| Butterflies and moths | 32 |
| Beetles and bugs | 34 |
| Bees and wasps | 36 |
| Earwigs and flies | 38 |
| Grasshoppers and crickets | 40 |
| Dragonflies and damselflies | 42 |
| Worms | 44 |
| Other invertebrates | 46 |

| | |
|---|---|
| **PLANTS TO ATTRACT** | |
| **GARDEN WILDLIFE** | **48** |
| How plants are named | 50 |
| How to use the plant directory | 51 |
| Annuals and biennials | 52 |
| Bulbs | 62 |
| Perennials | 66 |
| Herbs | 84 |
| Shrubs | 90 |
| Mixed hedges | 102 |
| Single-species hedges | 104 |
| Trees | 106 |
| Climbers | 112 |
| Pond and bog plants | 116 |
| Fungi and decomposers | 120 |
| | |
| Suppliers | 122 |
| Index | 124 |
| Acknowledgements | 127 |
| Plant hardiness and zones | 128 |

# INTRODUCTION

*Gardens give the opportunity to help a wide range of creatures – from birds and butterflies to frogs and dragonflies; and by planting the right types of flowers, herbs, shrubs, hedges, trees, climbers and pond plants, gardens can become wonderfully rich in wildlife. The aim of this book is to help you to encourage all sorts of animals, birds and insects into your backyard by choosing wildlife-friendly plants. Doing this will not only create a beautiful area, but will also help to keep your garden healthy.*

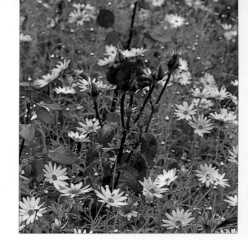

Above: *Roses are often attacked by aphids, but brightly coloured daisy flowers attract beneficial insects that will eat the aphids.*

### WHAT IS WILDLIFE GARDENING?

The idea of gardening for wildlife has become popular, even fashionable, in recent years, with many high-profile gardeners and organizations hailing it as a new approach. The simple truth, though, is that there has always been a huge variety of wildlife living in, or visiting, our gardens, although conventional gardening techniques and materials have led to a decline in their numbers.

### A NATURAL PARTNERSHIP

Gardens and wildlife have always shared the same space. The ants that forage, the worms that mix the soil and the bees that pollinate flowers are the most obvious examples. But some gardeners with an overly fastidious view of nature don't want to know about anything else, purging homes and gardens of anything verging on the "unclean" or "unhealthy".

While the idea of cleanliness is fine indoors, outdoors it causes a problem. The outside world is a living, functioning system, rich in many types of organism that depend on diversity and balance. In the quest for a sanitized environment, many gardeners have targeted some wildlife species on the grounds of plant health or simply because they don't want to share their space with them. A war began against creepy crawlies involving an array of noxious chemical agents whose effects were – and indeed still are – felt well beyond the confines of the garden. In addition, the combined forces of urbanization and industrial-scale agriculture have diminished the numbers of many other once common creatures.

It is only when birds and butterflies cease to visit the garden that the damage is noticed. Gardeners now realize that not only are we in danger of losing considerable natural diversity from our gardens, towns and cities, but that gardens are actually an ideal place for solving the problem. Domestic gardeners have a huge role to play in the future of many species of wildlife, especially now, as the traditional countryside in so many continents is under threat from the pressures of modern living.

Left: *With a little thought, even a relatively small garden space can provide variety and interest for both people and wildlife.*

Below: *Birds often rely on trees as perching and nesting sites. Holes in trunks are also used by insects, mammals and amphibians.*

## THE LOOK OF A WILDLIFE GARDEN

To some, the idea of being wildlife-friendly might mean forsaking the perfect lawn, trimmed borders and rose beds. Others might even assume that a wildlife garden means a disordered, untidy eyesore. Nothing could be further from the truth.

True, some of the early wildlife gardeners did look to the countryside for ideas, attempting to make tiny, overgrown pockets of "wilderness" in their backyards. Increasingly, though, wildlife gardeners have taken a more fundamental approach, applying the model of nature – a dynamic, self-balancing and regulating system – when designing their own gardens. So, with a bit of know-how, every garden, however small, can act as a private nature reserve with its hedges, trees, flower beds and even sheds, walls and paths providing wildlife habitats. In fact, many gardens need only a little adjustment to vastly improve their wildlife credentials. Whether your passion is for herbs, flowers or vegetables, your garden has the potential to provide a habitat for many different wildlife species.

## WHAT CREATURES NEED

The most important requirements in a wildlife garden include providing creatures with shelter from the elements and a measure of protection from predators, while also providing food, water and nesting materials and, ideally, an environment in which to conduct their day-to-day lives, including mating and raising their young. Even those without a garden can help. Pots, window boxes and hanging baskets can all provide excellent feeding sites.

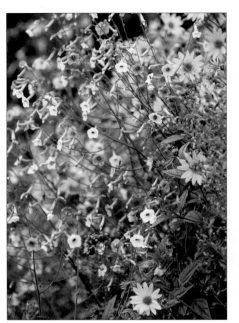

Above: *Flowers are an extremely significant part of many wildlife gardens, and give a stunning display, as well as being functional.*

In most cases, the types of plant used are an extremely important part of making your garden wildlife-friendly. Animals feed in a variety of ways, so ensuring that you have a range of plants, chosen to suit these varying needs, will help to maintain a healthy, thriving population of different animals. These in turn will attract carnivorous species, many of which may take up residence in your garden.

## IN THIS BOOK

This book is divided into two sections. The first gives an overview of the most common creatures that you'll see in a garden, with notes on recognition, how to attract them into the garden and what habitats they need. Understanding why they visit and their needs are key aspects to the success of a wildlife garden. The second section is an extensive directory covering over 200 of the best wildlife-friendly plants. The plants are grouped into standard categories –

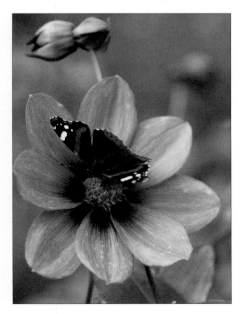

Left: *Butterflies prefer single-flowering dahlias, such as the* Collerette Group, *rather than the showy blooms of other dahlia types.*

Right: *Dragonflies will visit a garden to feed, and if a suitable pond is present, they will readily lay their eggs in it. They are superbly agile fliers with excellent eyesight, and are able to capture fast-moving insects on the wing – a truly spectacular sight.*

Above: *Knowing which particular flowers provide food for garden creatures is an important aspect of wildlife gardening.*

annuals and biennials, bulbs, perennials, herbs, shrubs, hedges, trees, climbers, pond and bog plants, and fungi and decomposers – with each entry explaining how to grow the plant, where to position it, how to propagate it and which types of wildlife will benefit. There are also suggestions for closely related plant species, and the wildlife they will attract.

Whether you want your garden to be an outdoor living space, a dazzling array of colour or a place to grow food for the kitchen, the application of the following principles will help you achieve this, and create a rewarding wildlife sanctuary.

# GARDEN WILDLIFE

This part of the book focuses on the more common types of wildlife found in a variety of garden habitats. Each group is described and its benefits to the garden are clearly outlined. Advice on how you can provide for the creatures' needs, as well as essential facts regarding their conservation status, habits and lifestyle, are all included. For species that may cause alarm or become a nuisance, tips are added on the best way to deal with them. This directory is only a sample of common species; for more information about the wildlife in your area, consult a local guide.

Left: *There are many species of beautiful butterfly, such as this painted lady, that visit gardens to feed on the nectar from flowers.*

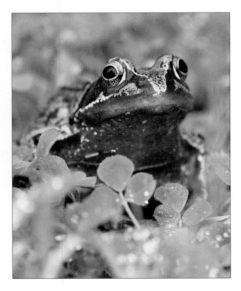

Above: *Amphibians frequently venture into gardens, and knowing which is which can help you to cater for their requirements.*

Above: *Bumblebees are just one of the types of wild bees that will travel to your garden and perhaps take up residence there.*

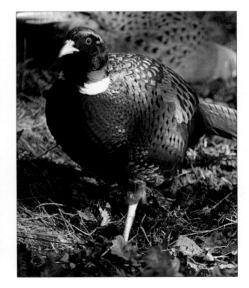

Above: *Pheasants are a semi-wild species, often introduced as game-birds, and are sometimes seen foraging in gardens.*

# INSECT-EATING BIRDS

*Insectivorous birds are a familiar sight in the summer garden, and their activities help to control pests. Many of the species seen, though, are seasonal summer migrants that visit to feast upon the abundance of insect life that appears at this time. In addition to this, certain species develop insect-eating tendencies during periods of summer abundance because this offers the richest source of protein and fats for their young, allowing them to raise a family quickly and successfully.*

Above: *Wrens are among the smallest of garden birds, but are voracious predators of insects in the summer months.*

### ROLE IN GARDENS

In garden settings, birds take insects and small invertebrates, many of which are regarded as pests. They constitute an important food source, especially in regions where insects are most plentiful. Swallows, martins and swifts pursue their insect meals while flying, often swooping down in pursuit, and woodpeckers can sometimes be seen – and more often heard – making holes in wood to find grubs. Even the flocks of starlings that walk across your lawn are systematically searching for insects.

### HABITAT PREFERENCES

Whilst some birds are entirely insectivorous, others, including many common songbird species, eat insects only when raising young. Some of these feed the offspring entirely an insect diet, but only a small percentage of their own food is insects. This habit has the obvious advantage that they do not have to change their preferred habitat and can remain in a garden all year.

Some larger birds also eat insects as part of their diet when these are plentiful but revert to other animals at other times of the year. Swallows, on the other hand, are a well-known example of a species that feeds only on insects and so must make radical shifts in its habitat preferences within a single season by migrating vast distances to follow seasonal "gluts" of their prey in different countries.

### FEEDING STRATEGIES

Although there are many different species of insect-eating birds, they often adopt similar strategies for catching their prey. Most have fine, narrow beaks, although even this can vary greatly according to species. Ecologists therefore tend to divide insectivorous birds according to their hunting habits, or guilds.

These guilds consist of groups of species that, although not necessarily closely related, behave in similar ways.

Below: *Barn swallows migrate vast distances to follow seasonal abundances of insects.*

Leaf gleaners, such as warblers, pick insects off leaves, whereas bark gleaners, such as nuthatches, pick them off tree trunks. Woodpeckers are wood and bark probers because of their ability to dig out their prey from within the branch.

The air salliers, including flycatchers, sit on a perch waiting for their prey to pass, whereupon they fly out and catch insects

### PROFILE

**Garden benefits** The insect-eating habit of birds should be a delight to most gardeners because their prey includes many potential pests. Incoming migrants also help tackle the rocketing summer population.

**Migratory species** For insectivorous birds, with their high mobility, migration is the rule rather than the exception. For some, such as swallows and swifts, the journey covers thousands of miles.

**Natural diet** Insectivorous birds do not only eat insects but will often take a range of invertebrates. Because they gain most of their moisture from these, they drink less frequently than seed-eaters.

**Resident species** Very few insectivores remain as residents in higher latitudes. Mostly small birds such as the wren, they are very susceptible to cold and limited to mild regions as a consequence.

**Supplementary diet** Mealworms are an excellent supplement and can be offered in a simple dish or a specialist feeder. In addition, many food suppliers now provide dried food for insectivores.

Left: *There are numerous species of woodpecker that may visit gardens, all of which prefer to feed on wood-boring grubs.*

Right: *Lavender is an excellent plant for attracting insects such as bees and butterflies, which flock to the flowers in search of nectar. In turn, these creatures often become food for many bird species.*

on the wing. The final guild includes the swallows, martins and swifts – gleaners of aerial plankton. In other words, they eat a large number of small insects while on the wing. In reality, however, most birds opt for more than one strategy, particularly if food becomes scarce.

Most insectivorous birds consume several different kinds of insect, often switching their preferences through the season according to the abundance of species available.

## MIGRATORY SPECIES

Birds that feed exclusively on insects often face seasonal food shortages if they remain in one place, and that's why they travel in search of food. Swallows and flycatchers in north-western Europe fly south in autumn to spend winter in Africa. It is easy to see why they do so because the cold, dark months offer little reward in terms of insects. What is less easy to understand is why they should return. The simple answer is that countries in high or low latitudes have a large seasonal glut of insects in summer. The birds move from place to place, so that it's always summer, and there's always plenty of food.

Migrating insect-eating birds also prosper because there are often not many resident insectivorous birds in their summer feeding grounds. This means that the migrants have an abundant food supply without facing competition from too many residents. Furthermore, feeding and raising their young in high or low latitudes means that they can use the longer hours of

daylight to gather plenty of food, so they can potentially raise more young. A final, if less obvious, advantage for migratory birds is that they avoid specialist predators trying to feed on them, because few of their predators make the same migratory journey. They and their chicks do, though, suffer from parasites, like any other bird species, and often these parasites have adapted to hibernate in nests where they wait for the host to return.

## PLANTS TO ATTRACT INSECT-EATING BIRDS

Evening primrose (*Oenothera biennis*)
Fern-leaved yarrow (*Achillea filipendula*)
Flowering rush (*Butomus umbellatus*)
Golden rod (*Solidago virgaurea*)
Honesty (*Lunaria annua*)
Lavender (*Lavandula angustifolia*)
Lemon balm (*Melissa officinalis*)
Tansy (*Tanacetum vulgare*)

**Evening primrose**

**Golden rod**

**Honesty**

**Tansy**

## THREATS

**Pesticides** The increased use of pesticides in both urban and rural settings means that insects are now relatively scarce. In addition, many surviving species carry small traces of these poisons, and they can accumulate in the bodies of insect-eating birds.

**Predation** Small birds are vulnerable to predation from larger species, both birds and mammals. Domestic cats are a big danger in urban gardens, and both squirrels and large birds, such as magpies, will take eggs and the young in the breeding season.

**Territory** If food becomes scarce, small birds are generally less able to compete with larger birds and become seasonal insectivores. Many need larger territories as a result, and the effort of defending this may use up a large amount of daily energy.

**Urbanization** Insect-eating birds often find it difficult to find the required amounts of food in very built-up areas. The lack of suitable vegetation and the human tendency to kill insects means that insect prey is often relatively scarce. Vehicular pollution can also limit the insect population because toxins can eventually build up in the urban habitat and ultimately in the insects' bodies.

# OMNIVOROUS BIRDS

*The changing seasons bring times of alternate plenty and shortage for birds that have highly specialized diets, and unless they are able to migrate, they can face starvation when food is scarce. For the majority of resident garden birds, their need to survive has driven them to adopt an omnivorous diet, thereby allowing them to exploit various foods as they become available. It is a highly successful strategy, and the chief reason behind the success of many species in colonizing our towns and gardens.*

Above: *A familiar sight in many European gardens, blue tits exploit numerous food sources, especially during the winter.*

## ROLE IN GARDENS

Birds that eat anything digestible/edible are known as omnivores. This is not to say that an omnivorous bird will eat any item of food that is put in front of it, and in most cases omnivores have specific feeding needs that may vary seasonally or perhaps because of local variations in their habitat. In fact the vast majority of birds tend to be somewhat omnivorous, although the tendency is usually most pronounced when their normal food source is in short supply. Being an omnivore is usually the most successful survival strategy in rapidly changing environments, or in places subject to extreme seasonal variation. Also note that many larger birds are omnivores because their body size makes specialization difficult unless a habitat – and therefore food supply – is very consistent all year round.

In time, successful omnivorous species can become very numerous. Members of the crow family, such as magpies and jays, will eat smaller birds and immature chicks. This results in an unusually high number of these large birds while the smaller species are often rarer than might be expected.

## HABITAT PREFERENCES

Because omnivores will eat both plant and animal matter, they survive well in many environments and often prove highly adaptable. Some, like the seagull, have no problem adapting to living near humans and have recently started scavenging landfill sites and city streets. This shouldn't be so surprising because modern cities are similar in many ways to tall, rocky cliffs, and as the seagulls often nest or roost on top of tall buildings, safe from predators, it is only natural that they should feed nearby.

As habitats change, those creatures that best adapt to them tend to prosper. Urban bird populations have changed over time, and pigeons now seem to have reached epidemic proportions. Surprisingly, garden birds are often quite urban in their distribution, with higher densities in towns and cities than in the surrounding countryside. The most common species of these urbanized populations are often omnivores, and the garden is an ideal habitat.

## FEEDING STRATEGIES

Being omnivorous has obvious advantages, but different foods often require adaptations to the digestive system. Some omnivorous bird species lengthen the digestive tract in winter to get more out of the relatively poor quality food. This allows them to be mostly vegetarian in winter, switching to an insectivorous diet in summer.

The beaks of omnivorous birds are usually relatively long and unspecialized, although this can vary considerably according to their evolutionary history. Feral ring-necked parakeets in the UK, for example, are much more omnivorous than

Left: *Originally from Europe, chaffinches have also been introduced elsewhere. Their varied diet has contributed to their success.*

## PROFILE

**Garden benefits** Omnivores can be a mixed blessing in the garden, particularly if you have a vegetable patch. On the other hand, their varied diet includes many garden pests, and resident omnivores will often begin feeding on them much earlier than migratory insectivores.

**Migratory species** The vast majority of omnivores are able to avoid the necessity of migrating vast distances, and many – including members of the thrush family – just travel short distances to escape harsh winter weather, and often take up temporary residence in gardens.

**Natural diet** Many omnivores have set patterns regarding exactly what and when they will eat. Birds are often insect eaters in the summer months, for example, before their digestive tracts adapt for their winter diet of berries and seed.

**Resident species** Resident species of omnivorous birds often face a bleak prospect during winter. Food shortage, exacerbated by other resident competitors and incoming winter migrants, means that there is a naturally high mortality rate as a consequence.

**Supplementary diet** Omnivores should be provided with a varied diet. Numerous mixes exist, and the best idea is to provide a full range of food types, including grain, small seeds, suet, fruit and even some live food.

Near right: *The American robin, much larger than its European namesake, eats a mix of insects, worms and many fruits.*

Far right: *The Australian pied currawong has a wide and variable diet, adapting well to both towns and gardens.*

the original wild populations in Africa and Asia that eat fruit, berries, nuts and seed. This is likely to be a result of their foraging in domestic gardens where meat and bacon rinds are often left out on bird tables.

It is this ability to adapt, learn new tricks and exploit unfamiliar food sources that differentiates omnivores from other birds with more restrictive diets.

## MIGRATORY SPECIES

Omnivores, like most birds, will migrate if food becomes scarce. They rarely undertake the huge journeys so characteristic of insectivores, however, with starlings or European robins simply travelling a few hundred miles and, even when they do migrate, it will not always be the whole population that does so. In fact the most likely migrants in a normally resident bird population are invariably the females and young. Many common species move from one country to another, while others simply move into the towns from the countryside. Some species regarded as non-migratory will sometimes move large

distances when faced with harsh winter conditions, and because these newcomers look just like the residents, their arrival often goes largely unnoticed.

Robins, thrushes, skylarks and blackbirds all tend to undertake short flights to warmer areas, and blackbirds that live in Scandinavian countries fly south-west to spend the winter in countries with a less severe winter. In fact blackbirds often change their habits and distribution over the year, raising families and feeding in gardens

during the spring and summer where they can raise up to three broods. After the breeding season, they must "feed up" for the coming winter, and move out into the surrounding countryside to do so.

Below: *The sweet, edible fruits of juneberry (Amelanchier) mature in midsummer and are eaten by a wide variety of birds.*

### PLANTS TO ATTRACT OMNIVOROUS BIRDS

Blackthorn (*Prunus spinosa*)
Bramble (*Rubus fruticosus*)
Evening primrose (*Oenothera biennis*)
Gooseberry (*Ribes uva-crispa*)
Hawthorn (*Crataegus monogyna*)
Ivy (*Hedera helix*)
Juneberry (*Amelanchier lamarkii*)

Blackthorn

Bramble

Gooseberry

Hawthorn

### THREATS

**Competition** Omnivores are adaptable and able to exploit new situations, but this brings them into contact with new competitors. Some urban birds are highly aggressive, and often chase away or even kill newcomers.

**Disease** Any increase in population raises the chances of disease spread. Omnivorous birds often congregate where there is a food source, and disease becomes more prevalent than for birds following a more solitary life.

**Habitat changes** As changing habitats favour certain incoming species, others are less favoured and some omnivorous birds that were formerly common in cities – such as the raven in London – are now scarce or absent, having been unable to adapt to modern city life.

**Predation** All birds face predators in either the garden or their natural habitats, and they are usually numerous enough to cope with any losses. In gardens, cats are usually the main threat, although other birds (including birds of prey) also take their toll.

# SEED-EATING BIRDS

*Once very common, changes in agricultural practices caused a decline in many seed-eating bird species. Fortunately, the increasing popularity of garden feeders has thrown these birds an essential lifeline, and many species now prosper in a domestic setting. These include some of the most engaging of garden birds, many of which are migratory species that flock into towns to escape harsher conditions elsewhere. For many of these species, gardens form an essential part of their continued survival.*

Above: *Goldfinches eat mostly seeds but will sometimes peck at and eat buds, sap and occasionally insects through a season.*

## ROLE IN GARDENS

The majority of birds using garden feeders will be seed-eaters for at least part of the year, although there are comparatively few that are exclusively seed-eating (most seed-eating species hunt nutritious insects when they are feeding and raising their young). The main problem with being a seed-eater, though, is that the majority of seeds ripen in summer and autumn. By the following spring, seed is in short supply and the birds must switch to a substitute or face a shortage. Feeding seed-eating species therefore helps them through this period, and ensures that they will be in peak condition, ready for the breeding season in spring.

## HABITAT PREFERENCES

Recent years have seen a serious decline in many formerly common seed-eating birds. Intensification of agriculture has borne most of the blame, although realistically the shortage of food is the root of the disaster. The seed-eaters' numbers were previously probably artificially high as they prospered under traditional agricultural practices.

If that sounds puzzling, note that large flocks of seed-eaters were often seen feeding on winter stubble before moving on to land that was ploughed in late winter to find weed seed that had been thrown on to the surface. Before the widespread use of herbicides, crops had many weeds that left seed in the soil. It was these weeds that the seed-eating birds depended on, and modern agricultural efficiency has largely removed them. A second problem is that seed-eaters can no longer feed on spilt grain in the stubble because fields are now ploughed soon after the autumn harvest.

Another traditional agricultural habitat that has declined is the hay meadow. Many were rich in species, but it is actually how they are managed that is important. In fact they do not have to have a great variety of plants to be important for birds, and those that contain dandelion and sorrel are especially useful for seed-eating birds, such as linnets, in summer.

Ironically, housing developments that spread over what was once farmland may yet help save some of these birds. The increasingly popular habit of feeding seed-eating birds has thrown them a lifeline, and many now prosper as a result. It is not the same for all species, though, and the house sparrow, found in many towns and cities, was first attracted to our streets when the only form of transport was horse-drawn. The sparrows fed on the spilt grain in the streets and lived around the stables, common all over the city. The arrival of the car saw the decline in their numbers across much of their original range, although ironically they remain a pest in other countries where they were introduced by European settlers.

Always try to provide as much natural food as possible to ensure that you preserve their natural behaviour patterns. Plants such as sunflowers (*Helianthus*), and a patch of wildflowers that includes thistles, knapweed (*Centaurea*) and teasel (*Dipsacus*) will help to attract seed-eating birds.

Left: *Although they have a variable diet, great tits are mostly dependent on seeds throughout the year, especially in winter.*

## PROFILE

**Garden benefits** Seed-eating birds are potentially beneficial when they switch to hunting insects in order to feed their young. Their habit of foraging seed from the soil in winter also helps to reduce weed growth the next season.

**Migratory species** The corn and snow bunting, brambling, siskin and many other finches, for example, tend to migrate in short hops in search of food. They do not always choose a regular destination, and often only a proportion of the birds in an area migrate.

**Natural diet** Seed-eating birds will eat a whole range of seed, including grain, wildflower and nuts. They prefer oil-rich seed, and will switch their preferences as a season progresses according to the availability of food.

**Resident species** Resident breeding populations of seed-eating birds are extremely dependent on the availability of food, and almost all non-migratory species move between breeding and wintering areas in order to forage.

**Supplementary diet** Many seed-eating birds are choosy about what they eat, and prefer oil-rich, high-energy food. The best includes black sunflower hearts (seed with the husks removed), white proso, millet, niger (thistle) and good-quality peanuts.

Above: *Siskins have smaller bills than other finches, this being ideal for extracting seeds from birch, alder, spruce and pine cones.*

Traditionally, feeding birds was limited to the winter, although recent evidence suggests that serious shortages are experienced in summer by many species when they are rearing their families. Summer feeding with sunflower hearts and other seed can help the birds to lay more eggs and rear a healthier brood. Always make sure you buy from a reputable supplier because commercial bird food brands can be quite variable, and may not be formulated or intended to meet all the nutritional needs of the seed-eaters.

### FEEDING STRATEGIES

The seed-feeders generally have short, thick, strong beaks that are good for crushing or cracking open seed, and they can take some time to learn which foods are safe or good for them to eat. They often have an instinctive wariness about any change in their habitat, and you will need to be patient when you try to feed them. They will always prefer their natural food sources, and when they come to the garden for the first time they may not actually recognize supplementary foods.

Try offering black sunflower, white proso, millet, niger (thistle) and peanuts, but remember that most of these foods are supplements and can't always meet all of the bird's nutritional needs. Gradually add variety once they become accustomed to feeding at the site. They will soon overcome their caution and start to experiment.

### PLANTS TO ATTRACT SEED-EATING BIRDS

Amaranth (*Amaranthus caudatus*)
Dandelion (*Taraxacum officinale*)
Fat hen (*Chenopodium album*)
Field forget-me-not (*Myosotis arvensis*)
Millet (*Panicum miliaceum*)
Red clover (*Trifolium pratense*)
Sunflower (*Helianthus annuus*)
Teasel (*Dipsacus fullonum*)

Amaranth

Red clover

Sunflower

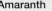

Teasel

The seed-eaters are naturally more gregarious in winter, probably because of their tendency to form large flocks at this time (though in summer they'll defend their territory). This often helps them locate food and feed more efficiently than when alone, also making them less vulnerable to predators.

### MIGRATORY SPECIES

Seed-eaters tend to be resident species, but some of the buntings and finches do migrate in search of food, moving to areas

Below: *Dunnocks have a variable diet through the seasons but depend heavily upon small seeds during the winter months.*

### THREATS

**Competition** The winter is a time when birds naturally flock, and this can cause aggression and tension. Birds at a winter feeder are forced together, and aggression is likely. Try to spread food around, and for aggressive species such as robins, you should put food out separately to avoid conflict.

**Habitat loss** Intensification of farming has meant that many species of once common birds are in serious decline due to loss of habitat and food sources. Oil-rich wildflower seed is vital for these species, and many now remain abundant only in gardens.

**Herbicides** Weedkillers have been used with increasing regularity in many countries, both to control crop weeds and to improve the look of the garden. But letting some weeds flourish is vital for foraging seed-eaters.

**Predation** The seed-eaters' habit of feeding on the ground makes them vulnerable to attack by cats, especially where the latter can hide and wait under garden bushes.

where the climate is milder and food more accessible. These winter migrants return to their breeding grounds in spring, although in some bird populations (e.g. goldfinches) only part of the population migrates. Other species simply move to lower ground.

Below: *Dandelions are generally regarded as weeds by gardeners but their seed is an ideal food for smaller seed-eating birds.*

# FRUIT-EATING BIRDS

*Fruit is an abundant and nutritious source of natural food, and one that many bird species have learned to exploit. In cooler climes, fruit tends to be a seasonal bounty, and so in these regions there are very few birds that exclusively eat fruit. Those that do tend to be limited to the tropics where this food source is available all year round. Most fruit-eaters alternate their diet, eating insects or other protein-rich foods in summer, and switching to fruit in the cooler months.*

Above: *Redwings eat insects in summer, but migrate to gardens in autumn, when their dietary preference changes to fruits.*

### ROLE IN GARDENS

Berries grow on a wide variety of plants including trees, bushes, climbing plants and even some herbaceous and ground-cover plants. When they are ripe, birds often descend on them and can clear a bush in a matter of hours, with some species (such as thrushes) switching almost totally to a fruit diet in late summer and autumn.

Birds and berries are a remarkable example of how plants and animals have evolved together, with one exploiting the other. The fleshy pulp of a berry is surprisingly nutrient-rich, and contains a good deal of starchy carbohydrate or sugars that conceal and protect the seed within. Most berries are also full of vitamins. The trade-off is simple. The birds benefit from the nutrients contained in the soft flesh, and spread the seed in their droppings.

The major limitation for most birds with a fruit diet, however, is that it is not available for enough of the year. Late winter to midsummer is a time when there is precious little fruit around, and the birds must find an alternative. Even when fruit is plentiful, many fruit specialists still supplement their diet with insects or other animal protein to ensure that they have a balanced diet.

Left: *Yellow warblers are a migratory species in North America that fatten up on fruit before heading south for winter.*

### PROFILE

**Garden benefits** It is rather difficult to say exactly what benefit fruit-eating birds actually have in the garden. They have an important role ecologically in dispersing seed, but are most useful in the summer when they switch to insect eating.

**Migratory species** While there are fewer migrant fruit eaters, many bird species that move short distances in winter will eat fruit in winter. Waxwings, on the other hand, are unpredictable in their movements but travel long distances in search of food.

**Natural diet** Fruit is rarely the sole part of any bird's diet for the whole year, but it does form an important part of some species' diet from midsummer into the colder months. Even fruit specialists occasionally take alternative food types.

**Resident species** Birds will often widen their territories to forage, and may even defend them to protect their fruit. Many species flock together in winter and adopt a methodical feeding approach that is different to their summer behaviour.

**Supplementary diet** Fruit-eating birds will quite happily take substitutes for fruit, provided they are able to recognize what it is. Pieces of broken apple and dried raisins may prove popular, and specialist suppliers now sell dried fruit especially for these birds.

### HABITAT PREFERENCES

Fruit availability varies according to the season and, in most temperate climates, is available from midsummer until late winter. The fruit of the guelder rose (*Viburnum opulus*) or currants (*Ribes*) are quite short-lived and, if not consumed immediately, will fall from the plant and rot. However, fruit of the cotoneaster and holly (*Ilex*) remains on the plant for many months, being a vital food reserve for much of the winter.

Always choose a range of plants that produce fruit over a long period. Remember that most species of fruit-eating birds have their favourites that they will take first, and that some fruit will remain on the plant for a long time before it is taken. Early fruiting bushes, such as currants and wild strawberries, are just as important as the late berries, and even a small garden can accommodate some of these plants.

### FEEDING STRATEGIES

Fruit is extremely important for many songbirds that switch from a summer invertebrate diet to a winter one based on berries. This is especially important when cold weather arrives and frozen ground prevents resident species foraging for worms, grubs or fallen seed. It is at these times of year, when food is short, that nourishing fruit is most vital.

Some birds tend to descend en masse to take berries when ripe, with starlings, for example, being highly systematic in their approach, methodically stripping bushes and trees from the top down. They also crop far fewer berries than other birds, and leave bushes picked clean. The thrushes, on the other hand, are well known for their tendency to defend their territory, and will often defend a berrying tree or shrub against all-comers. This acts as a larder that will see them through the winter, and if hard

Above: *Elderberry is an excellent source of berries in midsummer. The berries are especially liked by blackbirds and thrushes.*

times do not materialize the birds gain a great advantage in having food to the end of winter, enabling them to nest early.

## MIGRATORY SPECIES

As with most bird species, harsh winter weather is often a trigger for them to move south. While most only move short distances, there are a few that cover much greater distances and the movements of berry-feeding birds are always inextricably linked to the availability of the fruit itself.

Possibly the most famous migratory berry-eaters are the waxwings. In both Europe and North America these beautiful birds leave their forest homes and move to warmer climes, often descending on

gardens to feast on berries. They are communal feeders with individuals eating up to 500 berries each day, and in Holland they are called *pestvogel*, meaning invasion bird, due to their habit of appearing suddenly and clearing away all the fruit.

The cedar waxwing of North America is also migratory and equally fond of berries. Flocks of these birds show a high degree of cooperation when they feed, and when the end of a twig holds a supply of berries that

### PLANTS TO ATTRACT FRUIT-EATING BIRDS
Blackcurrant (*Ribes nigrum*)
Elderberry (*Sambucus niger*)
Herringbone cotoneaster (*Cotoneaster horizontalis*)
Holly (*Ilex aquifolium*)
Guelder rose (*Viburnum opulus*)
Mezereon (*Daphne mezereum*)
Rowan (*Sorbus aucuparia*)
Wild strawberry (*Fragaria vesca*)

Cotoneaster

Holly

Mezereon

Rowan

### THREATS
**Competition** Even if there is plenty of food at the start of winter, harsh weather may force the birds to eat more of it and shorten the supply. In addition, migrants moving into the area compete for resources and visiting flocks may even strip an area clean.

**Habitat loss** Changes to the countryside caused by agriculture have meant that many native berrying shrubs have been destroyed, particularly when hedgerows are removed from field margins, and bird numbers often fall as a consequence.

**Poor fruit years** In some years the amount of fruit that sets on a tree or shrub will be considerably less than usual, mainly because the weather damaged blossom or deterred pollinators. The following winter shortages may therefore occur.

**Predation** The tendency to seasonal fruit-eating among many bird species often attracts them to settled areas where domestic cats are common predators. Ironically, the very shrubs they are feeding on often give cover to these ambush specialists.

only one bird can reach at a time, members of a flock will even line up along the twig and pass berries from beak to beak down the line so that each bird gets to eat.

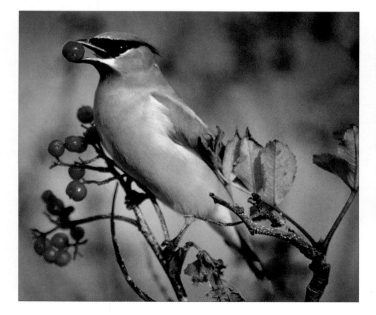

Left: *The American cedar waxwing eats berries and sugary fruit all year, but takes insects during the breeding season.*

Above: *Although naturally migratory, the availability of supplements in gardens means that some blackcaps overwinter.*

# CARNIVORES AND INSECTIVORES

*Carnivorous mammals are rare and exciting garden visitors and, although smaller insectivores are more numerous, these too are rarely seen, being shy and often nocturnal. Mammals that capture and eat other animals or insects in order to feed themselves are important elements of many habitats, and if you keep your garden wildlife-friendly you should be rewarded with a glimpse of one of these exciting, if reclusive, animals.*

Above: *Polecats are mainly carnivorous, feeding largely on frogs and voles, but they will also catch rats and other small prey.*

### ROLE IN GARDENS

Mammals, like any other group of animals, have developed into those that eat plants and those that eat other animals. The latter are carnivores, and they play a vital role in controlling the number of plant-eaters in a habitat. A surprisingly high proportion of mammals eat other animals, and it is widely believed that the earliest mammals may all have been carnivores. Fossils of ancient mammals are those of small, insect-eating creatures known as insectivores, and indeed a great many mammals still pursue this strategy.

When we refer to carnivorous mammals, it usually means those species that capture and eat other vertebrates, including other mammals. Some carnivores are large and dangerous mammals like bears, but there are a number of smaller carnivores, such as stoats and small cats. They are no less fierce than their larger counterparts, and some of the smaller mustelids such as stoats, weasels and minks often attack, kill and eat prey that is even larger than they are. Ultimately, though, it is their small size alone that means we can live in close proximity to them.

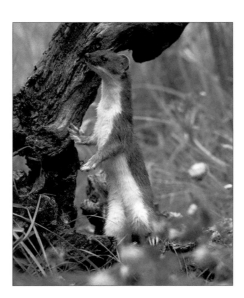

Above: *Stoats, common throughout Europe, Canada and the United States, often catch prey that is larger than they are.*

The most common mammals found in gardens eat insects, and also worms, woodlice and other small invertebrates. The garden therefore often represents an ideal hunting ground, and the abundance of insects can limit the mammals' need for a very large territory. Shrews are commonly found in gardens and, though rarely noticed, consume vast amounts of invertebrates, often 125 per cent of their body weight each day. Others, such as the hedgehog of Europe and Asia, are more obvious.

### HABITAT PREFERENCES

Most predatory mammals do not have very specific preferences, and all that is required is dense cover for them to shelter in or possibly to mount ambushes from. Long grass and thickets are essential if you want

to encourage insectivores, such as hedgehogs or shrews, and of course the greatest asset in encouraging a predatory mammal into the garden must be an abundance of its preferred prey.

You can always give some species a helping hand, though, and bats in particular need roosting sites in which to stay during daylight hours. They naturally occupy a crevice in rocks or trees, but may be helped by positioning bat boxes in the garden that keep them safe and allow them to sleep soundly, well out of the way and hidden from larger day-hunting predators.

Left: *Hedgehogs are common visitors to European gardens, feeding on a range of invertebrates, including some pest species.*

### PROFILE

**Garden benefits** The most obvious advantage of carnivores and insectivores in the garden is their ability to control pests. Many mammal predators are at, or near, the top of the food chain and, as such, help maintain a balance of nature.

**Nuisance behaviour** Many smaller carnivores can become a problem because they forage for food. Moles are a prime example, their excavated earth mounds ruining a smart lawn.

**Risk to people or pets** Remember that any wild animal can, and often will, bite if threatened. Carnivores are specially adapted to bite and tear flesh. Some species may also attack pets if given the chance.

**Supplementary diet** Carnivorous and insectivorous animals are best left to their own devices. Feeding them can result in their becoming too habituated and possibly aggressive.

## WHAT IS A MAMMAL?

Essentially warm-blooded, the skin of a mammal is virtually covered in hair. With the exception of one small group of Australian egg-laying mammals, all give birth to more or less fully developed young that are then fed milk by their mothers. Also, mammals live in most places, and although most are ground-dwellers, many habitually climb up rocks or trees, and most are capable of swimming. One group, the bats, has even evolved the ability to fly in pursuit of their prey.

Mammals are extremely variable in size, with the pygmy shrew being so small it weighs just 2–4g (½-⅙oz), while the blue whale reaches almost 200 tons. Among them are numerous carnivores (e.g. cats and stoats), omnivores (raccoons and hedgehogs), and herbivores (rabbits and squirrels). While most gardens will harbour relatively few (if any) mammals, a number of species are likely to visit, with a few usually smaller species of herbivores even becoming residents.

Above: *Overgrown areas with plenty of decaying vegetation and logs provide both shelter and hunting ground for carnivores.*

## THREATS

**Competition** Many mammal species face increased competition, partly due to shrinking habitats, but more often because they face a threat from an introduced species. Feral domestic cats in the United States and Australia and mink in Europe are examples of such invasive competitors.

**Habitat loss** Many hunting animals need to maintain a territory in order to have access to sufficient numbers of their prey. Larger mammals need larger territories and, as humans encroach upon them, the predatory species often suffer as a result.

**Pesticides** The use of insecticides in gardens and the wider countryside has meant that many species have become rare. This is partly because prey species are in short supply, but also because animals higher in the food chain accumulate these toxins from prey species to lethal levels.

**Persecution** Many predator species have been persecuted by humans. Often this is because they are seen as vermin or a threat to domesticated animals. They have also been relentlessly pursued both for their fur and as trophies, leading to some species becoming rare or endangered as humans encroach upon their natural habitats.

## FEEDING STRATEGIES

Many carnivores are stealth hunters and tend to capture their prey by ambush. Insectivores, on the other hand, are rarely ambush predators, usually preferring to locate their prey by a combination of smell, sound and sensitive whiskers. Their hunting might appear erratic to us, but their progress through their territory is usually systematic and effective. They consume prey as soon as they find it, and are often either nocturnal or tend to live and hunt in dense vegetation and, as a consequence, are less reliant on sight than some of the other larger carnivores.

Moles are also insectivores but have evolved a highly specialized lifestyle, spending almost all their life underground, digging long, deep tunnels and, as a result, they are almost blind. Their tunnels act as a trap for many invertebrates, especially worms that fall into them and are quickly located and eaten by the patrolling mole.

Not all the insect-eating mammals are ground-dwelling, and the night brings forth the bats, a group of mammals that are widely misunderstood and much maligned. There can be few garden creatures that polarize our views as much as these small but useful creatures. Bats have been around for over 50 million years, and have developed the ability to "see" at night. While the expression "blind as a bat" is inaccurate – they have eyes and can see – they do not use them at night. Instead, they use a complex system of high-pitched sounds called echolocation to navigate in flight, as well as to locate and capture their prey.

Below: *Bats like this pipistrelle are often seen in gardens, pursuing insects feeding on plants such as honeysuckle at dusk.*

## PLANTS TO ATTRACT BATS

Common honeysuckle (*Lonicera periclymenum*)
Common jasmine (*Jasminum officinale*)
Evening primrose (*Oenothera biennis*)
Heliotrope (*Heliotropium arborescens*)
Night scented stock (*Matthiola bicornis*)
Tobacco plant (*Nicotiana affinis*)

Honeysuckle

Jasmine

Heliotrope

Tobacco plant

# HERBIVORES

*In direct contrast to the shy and secretive carnivores and insectivores, the plant-eating (herbivorous) mammals are often more easily seen, although many of the smaller ones remain hidden in dense vegetation and are often nocturnal. Herbivores are extremely important in many habitats because many carnivorous animals depend upon them as a food source, and while the idea of them consuming your valuable garden plants may seem alarming, the majority are relatively non-destructive.*

Above: *Water voles mainly eat grass and plants near flowing water, but occasionally eat fruits, bulbs, twigs, buds and roots.*

### ROLE IN GARDENS

It is widely believed that herbivorous mammals evolved from omnivorous ancestors. They are an extremely successful group and occupy almost every habitat on the planet. They are often more numerous in gardens than other mammal types, although the only evidence you might see is the damage they have done to your plants. Of the herbivorous mammals, rodents are the most likely garden visitors, being by far the most numerous of all mammals, comprising around 41 per cent (or 1,750 species) of all mammalian species. Unfortunately, many are regarded as pests, both in the garden and in the home. They are characterized by highly specialized, chisel-like, gnawing incisors and have extremely strong jaw muscles, allowing them to chew through even the toughest plant material. These incisors grow continuously throughout their life.

There are many more herbivores on the planet than there are carnivores, and the vast majority are small and inconspicuous.

Below *Deer are large herbivores that only visit gardens near countryside. They can cause considerable damage in a short time.*

Above: *Brown hares, and their relatives the jackrabbits, feed mainly on herbs during summer, and grasses in the winter.*

Their success and large numbers have made them important species when it comes to shaping and maintaining habitats.

It is hard to see the value of herbivorous mammals in the garden because their habit of eating prize plants can instantly turn them into pests. They are, however, an important link in the food chain with predatory mammals, birds and reptiles, such as snakes, depending on them for their survival.

The majority of smaller herbivorous mammals are relatively non-destructive in the garden, and prefer to forage only for the richest foods. The result is that they are mostly seed- or fruit-eaters and do little harm, particularly if a wild area is left for them. They also help to cycle nutrients (via their droppings), and may even help control certain kinds of weed.

### HABITAT PREFERENCES

The sorts of herbivorous mammals you find will vary with the type and design of your garden, as well as the range of nearby habitats. Gardens bordering woodland, for example, will doubtless get mammals such

### PROFILE

**Garden benefits** All herbivores are termed primary consumers, and their feeding helps shape habitats and cycle nutrients. They can help control certain weed species, although their true value may be in supporting populations of predatory mammals.

**Potential for nuisance behaviour** Certain plants may be repeatedly targeted, and it is probably easiest to avoid growing them rather than persecute the responsible animals.

**Risk to people or pets** Any large animal can be potentially dangerous, but smaller mammals are relatively benign. They are all wild, though, and will react if threatened or cornered. Squirrels are often quite aggressive if frightened, and will bite.

**Supplementary diet** Herbivorous mammals don't generally need a supplementary feed, and often ignore most items left out for them, preferring wild food. Squirrels are a notable exception, and some suppliers produce food mixes for them.

as squirrels and wood mice, although many former woodland species now have a permanent home in city gardens and parks. Remember, though, that they will only stick around – and indeed continue to visit – if there is food and shelter.

Rabbits and hares are examples of slightly larger herbivores that sometimes visit rural gardens. They will not only eat plants – preferring young and freshly planted ones – but will dig holes, destroying

## HERBIVORES AND FOOD CHAINS

Herbivores are a vital part of all terrestrial habitats, and many mammals have adopted this feeding strategy. As primary consumers they turn plant nutrients into animal matter, and their droppings are quickly recycled and may even be exploited as a niche by certain invertebrates and microbes.

The vast majority of the world's mammals are herbivores. Most are small mammals, with rodents (rats, mice and squirrels) accounting for over two-fifths of all mammal species. Many of these small herbivorous mammals are liable to be eaten by birds or other predators because their sheer numbers make them a valuable food source. They are often most vulnerable to attack when feeding. Consequently they are extremely fast runners and often have keen senses, employ camouflage, and live in dense cover or are nocturnal.

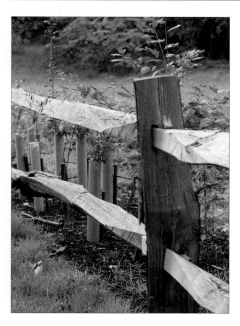

Above: *Where herbivores are likely to be problematic, newly planted areas like this hedge will need adequate protection.*

other plants in the process. In small numbers, and with the proper protection for young or treasured plants, they can be tolerated although many gardeners would prefer not to see them at all.

Larger herbivorous mammals are much rarer and hardly ever visit gardens because they mostly range over extensive areas, and are shy of humans. Deer, on the other hand, are an example of a large mammal type that is becoming increasingly common, and are now often found on the fringes of urban and suburban areas. They often enter inhabited areas at dusk to feast on garden plants and drink from a pond before retreating early the next morning. Despite their grace and beauty they can be destructive, and although repellents can dissuade them, their numbers are increasing and the damage can be extreme. Fencing is often the only solution.

## FEEDING STRATEGIES

Just about everything except leaf litter and mature tree bark is eaten by herbivorous mammals and, in common with most mammals, they tend to be opportunistic. They will often exploit different food sources at different times of year due to changing availability. This allows them to survive fluctuations in the numbers of different plants, and often allows many species that are common in gardens to adapt to changes in their habitat. There are exceptions to this, of course, with Australian koalas having restricted feeding habits, consuming only the leaves of a few eucalyptus species. Such specialized diets are rarely catered for in gardens due to the diversity of plants.

Herbivores must consume a large amount of plant material each day because it mostly consists of cellulose with water and some carbohydrates, but very few fats

### PLANTS TO ATTRACT SQUIRRELS

English oak (*Quercus robur*)
Hazel (*Corylus avellana*)
Scots pine (*Pinus sylvestris*)
Sweet chestnut (*Castanea sativa*)

**English oak**

**Hazel**

**Scots pine**

**Sweet chestnut**

## THREATS

**Disease** Animals moving into urban areas can catch diseases from domestic or introduced species and, in some cases, lack any immunity, resulting in plagues that can wipe out populations.

**Habitat loss** Certain mammals are extremely specialized in their habitat requirements for food, shelter and nesting sites. The loss of any one of these factors, as a consequence of development, can mean that they are unable to live in an area.

**Introduced predators** Herbivores have evolved behavioural traits in the presence of particular predators. When faced with introduced predators – such as domestic cats in the United States – they often lack the ability to escape, and their numbers decline as a result.

**Pesticides** Plants often accumulate a variety of environmental toxins, including pesticides, in their tissues. Herbivorous mammals must consume large amounts of vegetation to satisfy their food requirements, and these poisons can accumulate in their bodies to lethal levels.

and proteins. This renders it considerably lower than meat in energy content, which is why most herbivorous mammals spend more time eating than carnivores. To overcome these problems, smaller herbivores often feed on seeds or fruits as both of these provide a far more nutritious diet than leaves.

Below: *Red squirrels naturally eat tree seeds in forest regions and may visit gardens to forage where tree seeds occur.*

# OMNIVORES

*Mammals that eat both animal and plant matter are called omnivores. They are generalist feeders, and some will hunt and kill prey when it is available. However, all have the common ability to adapt to new surroundings, including our gardens. This has led to many omnivorous species becoming highly successful town-dwellers, and many are now more numerous in areas of human habitation than they were formerly in their original "natural" habitats.*

Above: *Raccoons are adaptable American omnivores, renowned for being clever and mischievous, and are often seen in gardens.*

### ROLE IN GARDENS

Omnivores are capable of consuming both animal and vegetable matter as part of their diet. Their teeth are often less specialized than those of herbivores and carnivores, and are a mixture of sharp cutters and flat grinders, allowing them to deal with a wide range of foods. Being an omnivorous species, however, does not necessarily mean that their diet is in any way indiscriminate, and neither does it mean that the animals eat equal amounts of meat and plants. It does mean, though, that mammals with this trait can live on different types of food according to what's available throughout the year, and this is especially useful where seasonal variation means that food sources are variable.

Omnivores have typically descended from carnivorous ancestors, and their varied diet may well reflect changes that occurred in their habitats over time. Raccoons, skunks and badgers are all examples of mammals called mustelids that were originally predators. Their ability to consume many different types of food has meant that they can exploit a range of different habitats, and these creatures have adapted well to changes in the landscape wrought by humans. They are frequent visitors to

### PROFILE

**Garden benefits** Omnivores can be a mixed blessing in the garden, particularly in the case of larger animals, such as foxes and raccoons. However, they hunt and kill certain pests, and play a vital role in the absence of other predators.

**Potential for nuisance behaviour**
Most of the nuisance behaviour you are likely to encounter will be destructive activity that is associated with foraging for food or nesting, although this is not always particularly serious.

**Risk to people or pets** This depends largely upon the mammal. Raccoons and badgers are extremely strong and will take on domestic dogs or even people if cornered.

**Supplementary diet** Deciding whether to feed an omnivore is tricky, though most species don't need it. Occasionally feed titbits, such as grated vegetable, raisins and pet food mixed with water, if conditions are very harsh.

gardens, and are often far more common than similar-sized carnivorous mammals both in and around gardens.

Not all omnivores are descended from carnivores, however, and some, such as the rat, obviously have a herbivorous ancestry. In fact many carnivores and herbivores take other types of food where the opportunity arises, and this type of "opportunistic omnivorousness" is common in mammals, although those species that can truly be classed as omnivores are in the minority.

It is too tempting to see omnivores as "nature's dustbins", although for some species – such as the rat – the term does seem appropriate. In the majority of cases, however, omnivores are opportunists that can switch their feeding habits according to the availability of food. In gardens they will do the same, and often their presence is the result of your providing a habitat or food source to their liking.

Omnivores are often a mixed blessing in the garden because their foraging activities can be both useful and highly destructive, and even exciting creatures, such as badgers, are sometimes reviled due to their habit of digging in lawns, stealing root crops, and – if they learn the habit – overturning dustbins. Other omnivores, such as raccoons

Left: *The red fox is the most widespread member of the dog family, owing its success to its adaptability and wide-ranging diet.*

Right: *Rats are very common omnivores which have spread widely in association with human habitation and agriculture.*

Above: *Gardens with plenty of tall plants and some open space provide an excellent foraging ground for most omnivores.*

and skunks, often cause similar problems, and larger types (e.g. pigs and some bear species) could become downright dangerous if they take a liking to your garden. Having said that, they are a part of a natural ecosystem, and they can hardly be blamed for following their own instincts.

## HABITAT PREFERENCES

As generalists, many omnivores are not particularly fussy about their surroundings. This is borne out when we see creatures such as foxes taking up residence even in heavily built-up inner-city areas, and other creatures, such as raccoons, living in and around domestic dwellings.

As a rule, most gardens are too small to act as the total territorial area for either individuals or groups of omnivores, although some of the smaller rodent omnivores may be perfectly content in your garden for their whole life. But, in general, most mammalian omnivores are small to medium-sized creatures that will visit, rather than reside in, a garden. Having said that, they will need to live somewhere. If they decide to live in your garden and you are concerned, seek advice from your local wildlife society.

## FEEDING STRATEGIES

The extent of an omnivorous mammal's territory may depend a lot on the environment. Most omnivores naturally forage over quite a large area, in keeping with their adaptive tendency, but may disappear shortly after appearing if food is sparse. In addition, solitary omnivore species have often evolved to live in changing and variable habitats, moving on when the pickings become slim.

Animals that have moved from a herbivorous to an omnivorous existence often eat more vegetable matter. They are often quite eclectic in their tastes, and are not natural hunters. Omnivores that are descended from carnivores, however, are quite able to capture, kill and eat prey, and many omnivores, such as foxes, badgers and raccoons, will readily do so. These animals have a wide gape to their jaw structure and well-developed musculature and teeth that enable them to kill and consume prey, even though the majority of their diet is comprised of plant foods and killing is a rare part of their behaviour.

Below: *Badgers are shy, nocturnal creatures that eat earthworms, insects, small animals, berries, nuts, roots, and other plant matter.*

# REPTILES

*A very misunderstood group of animals, reptiles are often met with fear or trepidation when encountered in the garden, or indeed elsewhere. They are an important and ancient group of creatures, though, that fulfil a significant role as "pest controllers" in many habitats. Whilst most common in warmer climates, a number of species make their homes in places that have a marked variation in the seasons, where they tend to hibernate in winter and are thus only seen in the warmer months.*

Above: *Common lizards hunt insects, spiders, snails and worms, which they stun by shaking before swallowing them whole.*

### ROLE IN GARDENS

Reptiles are mostly very beneficial in gardens, provided that they are of a non-venomous type. Lizards often eat insects and help control the number of pests in a garden, and many snakes are specialists in hunting small mammals. They are often especially sensitive to their habitats, and their presence is a clear indication that your garden habitat is both balanced and healthy.

Many reptile species face an uncertain future, chiefly because their habitats have been lost, fragmented, neglected or unsympathetically managed. They are mostly creatures of the wild, although certain species regularly visit or even take up residence in gardens. There is little to fear, and you should consider yourself fortunate to have spotted what will usually be a shy and retiring creature.

Reptiles are fascinating animals, and play an important part in the ecology of some habitats. Their somewhat secretive

Below: *Sand lizards mainly feed on slugs, spiders and insects, but will also feed on other foods, such as fruit and flower heads.*

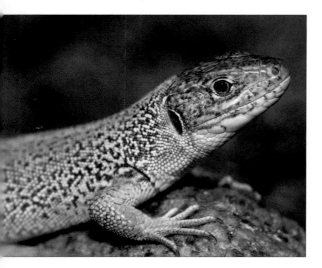

behaviour in gardens means that they often go largely unnoticed or, at best, are only glimpsed fleetingly before they disappear into the nearest cover. They are a somewhat misunderstood group of animals, and this often leads to a needlessly fearful response when they are noticed.

There are three types of reptiles that you may encounter in a garden – the lizards; the legless, snake-like slow worms or glass lizards; and true snakes. In addition, you may more occasionally encounter a turtle or tortoise, although they are much rarer and more specialized in their habitat preferences and, because they rarely venture into gardens, they are not dealt with here.

### LIZARDS, SLOW WORMS AND GLASS LIZARDS

The largest group of reptiles, with more than 4,300 species worldwide, these resemble salamanders but have dry, scaly skin, external ear openings and usually clawed feet. Most lizards are small, with four legs and a long tail.

The legs of some lizards are greatly shortened, or vestigial, making creatures such as the slow worm or glass lizard rather snake-like, although they are easily distinguished from true snakes by their movable eyelids (snakes have no eyelids and cannot close their eyes).

### SNAKES

An exciting and important part of many habitats, snakes are the only group likely to harm people. Despite their fearsome reputation, though, most snakes are harmless and will quickly slither away, although all are best treated with caution

Right: *Slow worms are not snakes but legless lizards. They hunt slow-moving prey, such as slugs and earthworms, at dusk.*

---

**PROFILE**

**Diet** A few reptiles, such as iguanas and tortoises, are herbivorous but the vast majority are carnivores or insectivores that capture, kill and eat live prey. Lizards mostly eat insects whilst snakes take larger prey such as small mammals, birds or other reptiles.

**Garden benefits** Most lizards are harmless to the plant life in your garden and prove beneficial by controlling insect populations. In turn, some of the commoner types are a source of food for larger mammals and birds, and are therefore a part of the garden food web.

**Potential for nuisance behaviour** Reptiles are generally no trouble in the garden but can prove alarming. The best answer is usually to avoid contact with them, and they'll invariably keep out of your way.

**Risk to people or pets** There are comparatively few reptiles that pose a significant threat to people or pets, but poisonous snakes can occasionally be dangerous, particularly if cornered or threatened.

## WHAT IS A REPTILE?

Reptiles have lived on the Earth for over 300 million years. All have dry, scaly skins and rely on external heat sources to maintain their body temperature (hence the term "cold-blooded'). Unless they are warm, they tend to be very sluggish and make a surprisingly easy meal for cats, foxes, badgers and birds of prey.

All reptiles regulate their temperature by basking, particularly in the morning, first finding a warm site to heat up their bodies before moving away into the shade. This behaviour prevents them from overheating and, during hot periods, particularly in summer, many species then seek a cooler, shadier site.

Most reptiles continue to grow throughout their lives and periodically shed their outer skin. Also, all have eggs with a waterproof shell, although a few species – such as vipers – retain them internally until they hatch. The four surviving groups of reptiles are turtles and tortoises, snakes and lizards, the crocodile family, and the tuatara from New Zealand.

Above: *A pile of dry wood provides a good sheltering place for many reptiles, particularly in hot summer weather.*

and respect. Indeed, many snakes are actually very vulnerable and have particular environmental needs, and a number of species have legal protection for this reason. There are also some venomous types and, while few will harm you, they should not be provoked.

## HABITAT PREFERENCES

The needs of reptiles vary, but in general all need a place to shelter, nesting and hibernation sites (in cooler locations), and a ready source of food. The ideal habitats provide a good mixture of cover and open, sunny areas for basking, such as rough grassland or patches of shrubby vegetation.

Rock and log piles provide excellent shelter and basking sites, and also serve as an excellent habitat for many of the reptiles' preferred prey. On cloudy or wet days, reptiles may well shelter in these retreats and avoid coming out in the open because cool weather slows them down and makes them vulnerable to predators. Reptiles are often easiest to see in the mornings, warming up by basking on rocks or on top of vegetation. As the day becomes hotter, they often return to their shelters or other shady places.

## FEEDING STRATEGIES

The diet of lizards varies depending on species, although most of the species you will encounter in gardens are insectivorous. They ambush their prey and eat them quickly there and then, and rarely attack prey that is so large that it cannot easily be overpowered. For snakes, on the other hand, catching and eating prey would seem to be potentially more problematic. They have no claws with which to grab, tear or hold their food, and are unable to chew because their teeth and hinged jaws aren't designed for that purpose. Instead, they either poison or crush their prey.

Venomous snakes strike suddenly and inject venom into the victim, which first paralyzes it, and later assists the digestive processes. Most snakes have no venom, though, and use strength alone to immobilize their victims, having first grabbed their prey with their mouth. Constrictors wrap their body in tight coils around the victim to suffocate it, whereas others start swallowing immediately so that the animal is eaten alive. Snakes habitually catch and kill quite large animals because they are able to dislocate their upper and lower jaws, and spread their mouth and throat open to swallow them.

## PLANTS TO ATTRACT REPTILES

Bilberry (*Vaccinium myrtillus*)
Cranberry (*Vaccinium oxycoccos*)

Cross-leaved heath (*Erica tetralix*)
Ling (*Calluna vulgaris*)

Bilberry        Cranberry        Cross-leaved heath    Ling

# AMPHIBIANS

*Amphibians are very widespread and are often quite common across much of their range, being frequent garden visitors and even residents. There are three types of amphibian that you are likely to encounter in the garden: frogs; toads; and salamanders and newts. As their name suggests, amphibians are almost equally at home on land or in water and, although the adults of many species are almost entirely land-based, all must return to water to lay their eggs.*

Above: *Adult frogs often stay quite near to water, where they hunt insects or small animals that they catch with a sticky tongue.*

### ROLE IN GARDENS

Amphibians perform a vital role because they are predators of invertebrates, including many that might eat your prize plants. All amphibians are particularly sensitive to environmental stresses, and their presence is a sure sign of a healthy, natural garden. By encouraging them, you are also paving the way for other forms of wildlife. Ultimately, a plentiful population of amphibians could be just what your garden needs.

### HABITAT PREFERENCES

While you don't actually need a pond to have amphibians living in your garden, they do need a pool in which to breed. Although the pond does not need to be large, always make the largest one possible so that plenty of species can use it. More important than size, though, is its maximum depth, and that's ideally 60–90cm (2–3ft). It should have at least one side that shelves out gradually, allowing good access, preferably into surrounding rough vegetation for feeding and hibernation. Use a good mix of native pond plants, but avoid too many overhanging trees; many amphibians prefer to breed in ponds that receive full sun and warm up more quickly in the spring, thereby speeding up the development of the young.

Left: *Newts live both in and out of water, eating anything small enough to swallow, such as slugs, worms and beetles.*

### FEEDING STRATEGIES

Most amphibians eat anything that is small enough to fit into their mouth, although distasteful objects may be spat out again. They are extremely efficient hunters and

### PROFILE

**Climate change** Warming temperatures across the planet are affecting many amphibians. It is widely believed that climate change reduces the effectiveness of immune response to disease in many species, and it may also affect their habitat in other ways.

**Diet** All amphibian adults are carnivores or insectivores, and capture and eat a wide variety of prey. The tadpoles, on the other hand, begin life as herbivores and gradually switch to meat as they change into adults.

**Garden benefits** Frogs, toads, salamanders and newts enhance the environmental and aesthetic value of the garden. They also perform a vital role in hunting and eating many common garden pests.

**Potential for nuisance behaviour** Amphibians tend to be fairly problem-free. Their vocalizations may become quite loud in the evening, particularly around the breeding season.

**Risk to people or pets** There are very few dangers associated with garden amphibians and, in most cases, they are the vulnerable ones. Some toads and salamanders do exude a toxic poison, however, and it is best to avoid handling any amphibian if possible.

### LIFE CYCLE OF A FROG

*Frogs undergo an amazing change, or metamorphosis, from tadpoles into adults, a process that takes several weeks. The eggs are laid by returning adults in the spring and hatch into the fish-like tadpoles that quickly grow and ultimately transform into miniature adults.*

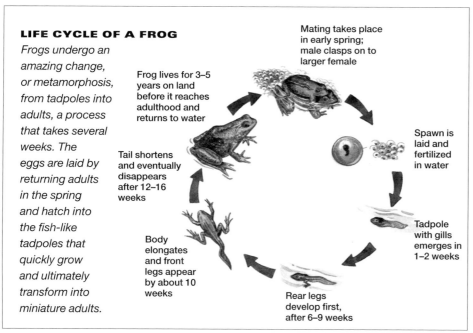

Mating takes place in early spring; male clasps on to larger female

Frog lives for 3–5 years on land before it reaches adulthood and returns to water

Spawn is laid and fertilized in water

Tail shortens and eventually disappears after 12–16 weeks

Tadpole with gills emerges in 1–2 weeks

Body elongates and front legs appear by about 10 weeks

Rear legs develop first, after 6–9 weeks

## WHAT IS AN AMPHIBIAN?

Amphibians are cold-blooded animals that differ from reptiles because they lack scales, do not produce eggs with a waterproof shell, and generally return to the water to breed. The three types of amphibians are the frogs and toads, salamanders and newts, and the strange and rarely seen caecilians – mostly tropical, worm-like amphibians that live underground.

Generally eggs are laid in a big mass in the water and fertilized externally. Without water, their eggs (which are not protected by a shell) would quickly dry out and the young would die before they hatched. The small, fish-like young (tadpoles) are completely unlike the adults and metamorphose over a period of a few weeks into a tiny replica of the adult. Once the metamorphosis is complete, the young adults leave the water and disperse into the surrounding vegetation, where they remain until it is time to breed.

Above: *Amphibians are vulnerable when they leave the water so they prefer to inhabit ponds with plenty of bank-side vegetation for cover.*

are extremely fast when capturing prey, often doing so in a fraction of a second using a long, sticky tongue.

When in water, salamanders and newts are voracious feeders and will snap at any small passing creature with lunging body movements. Frogs and toads, on the other hand, feed almost entirely on land, catching prey with their tongue.

## FROGS, TOADS, SALAMANDERS AND NEWTS

Probably the best-known of all amphibians, frogs are popular with gardeners for their ability to capture and eat insects, and many people derive immense pleasure, if not pride, from watching "their" frogs return to breed year after year. As wild habitats become increasingly scarce, our gardens (especially those with a suitable pond) provide a vital refuge for these fascinating creatures.

Though similar to frogs, toads differ in having a warty skin – frogs have a smooth, shiny skin – and they generally walk rather than leap. Having said that, toads do resemble frogs in their appearance and life cycle, and often eat the same prey.

Salamanders and newts are considerably different and much more reminiscent of the first amphibians that were the original vertebrate life forms to colonize the land, some 375 million years ago. When encountered for the first time, salamanders and newts can cause quite a stir because people often mistake them for lizards. Despite their looks, however, these common little amphibians are quite harmless to us, and are useful because they eat garden insects and invertebrates.

## A LIFE CYCLE IN TWO HALVES

All the amphibians you are likely to encounter in the garden must return to water in order to breed and, although the exact time and way in which this takes place may vary according to the species and geographical location, the life cycle is basically the same for all of them. The adults return to breed in ponds, usually in late winter or early spring and, once they arrive, a frenetic spate of breeding usually ensues. Breeding is often synchronized so that the spawn (egg masses) in a pond is laid over a short period. This ensures that there is too much for predators to eat, so that some eggs will hatch.

### PLANTS TO ATTRACT FROGS

Flag iris (*Iris pseudacorus*)
Duck weed (*Spirodela polyrhiza*)
Marsh marigold (*Caltha palustris*)
Water mint (*Mentha aquatica*)
White water lily (*Nymphaea alba*)

Flag iris

Marsh marigold

Water mint

White water lily

Once they do hatch, the young amphibians are considerably different from their parents. These tadpoles are born and live entirely in water, and have tails that allow them to swim like a fish. They also have gills so that they can breathe under water. As the tadpoles grow into adults, they lose their gills and, in the case of frogs and toads, their tails. All develop legs for moving on land and, like their parents, spend much of their time on land, although they'll also swim in water.

### THREATS

**Disease** Amphibians all over the world have been falling prey to a disease called *Amphibian chytridiomycosis* that is an infection of their skin cells by a microscopic fungus. The reasons for its spread are still unclear but many species are affected.

**Habitat loss** The loss of wetlands for both agricultural and urban development has taken a very heavy toll on amphibian breeding grounds. In addition the habitats occupied by adult amphibians are also under threat in some cases and many species are rare as a result.

**Pesticides** Many amphibians have very sensitive skin that is not entirely watertight, and is protected by a layer of mucus. This enables them to absorb oxygen when submerged, but also means that they tend to absorb poisons easily.

# AQUATIC LIFE

*Ponds are an important part of any wildlife garden, although few of us ever see or appreciate the true richness of the habitat that lies just below the water surface. Aquatic habitats are some of the most interesting and diverse habitats that it is possible to create in a garden. Their murky depths hide a constant and ongoing struggle between species to survive and breed, with many of these being highly specialized – often with a colourful, sometimes strange, and occasionally unique appearance.*

Above: *Ramshorn snails generally eat the most delicate plants, preferring algae, although they may also eat decaying matter.*

### ROLE IN GARDENS

Many of the creatures that live in a garden pond are from familiar groups of animals, and the aquatic realm has creatures from almost all the major groups of land animals. Consequently, a great many of them must rise to the surface to breathe, and some have adult forms that live as dry-land dwellers.

Freshwater habitats are very fertile and, as with many land habitats, are extremely rich in microscopic life. This is of vital importance in sustaining those larger creatures that exist further up the food chain. Often the rich soup of micro-organisms in ponds serves to make these habitats somewhat cloudy, so that all that can usually be seen are the more sizeable creatures, and even they are small and flea-like. The larger creatures are much more visible, though, and can sometimes be seen as they move around in the murky shallows.

Creatures that live in fresh water are essentially divided into two types: those that live in still water (e.g. a pond) and those that must have flowing water (and live in streams or rivers). There are relatively few creatures that fall into the latter category, and many of the creatures that will commonly inhabit a garden pond may also be found in streams and slow-flowing rivers.

### PROFILE

**Algal bloom** This condition particularly affects ponds with raised nutrient levels or an imbalance in the ecosystem. Pond environments must be balanced, and a small pond should have plenty of floating-leaved plants and not contain fish that eat small algal feeders.

**Garden benefits** A pond is always a positive benefit because it provides a source of drinking water for many land animals, and because many of the species that dwell in the water emerge when adult, enriching the wider habitat.

**Potential for nuisance** Summer mosquitoes are a major nuisance, as breeding females suck animal blood before laying eggs in shallow pools. Encourage bats, which will eat the adults, and wear mosquito repellent.

**Risk to people or pets** The main source of danger is the water itself, with its inherent risk of drowning, especially to young children.

### HABITAT PREFERENCES

Aquatic life is, in many ways, a completely separate habitat from the rest of the garden. Its most obvious benefit may be that larger terrestrial garden visitors can get a quick drink, and a few, such as herons, can feed here.

Many of the species in the water are only aquatic for part of their life, with some insects, for example, having entirely aquatic larvae that become entirely land- (or air-) dwelling adults. Mosquitoes hatch on the water surface and then take to the air, being the preferred prey of many smaller night-flying bats, such as the little brown bats of North America or the pipistrelle of Europe and Asia. Pregnant females of these species actually come close to eating their own body weight in mosquitoes in a single night.

Other species form part of a seasonal glut when they emerge from the water. Young amphibians, for example, emerge in their thousands although most of them fall prey to larger land animals in their first couple of years. Insects, such as the mayfly, emerge in synchronized "hatchings", usually over just a few days, in which time they fill the air and cause a feeding frenzy among birds and larger flying insects. The pond is also a breeding

Left: *Sticklebacks are extremely widespread fish that feed at night upon worms, insect larvae, small snails and water fleas.*

Above: *Backswimmers swim upside down near the surface of the water, eating tadpoles, small fish and aquatic insects.*

## THREATS

**Climate change** This threatens many species worldwide, including a vast number of aquatic organisms. Gradual changes in temperature and rainfall patterns over time may well result in the loss of certain key species that may, in turn, affect the populations of other pond-dwellers.

**Habitat loss** As natural wetlands and ponds disappear, so the numbers of animals that depend on them diminish. While some are able to relocate, others are unable to migrate as a land-living relative might, and have often become rare.

**Invasive species** Some species, whether deliberately or accidentally introduced, are termed "invasive" because they tend to grow rapidly, spread easily, and frequently out-compete native species. If they escape into wild habitats they may wreak havoc.

**Pesticides** These often accumulate in a pond if the water that drains from the surrounding land into them becomes contaminated. Over time, pesticides can reach toxic levels, and it is often the smallest animals at the base of the food chain that are the first to suffer the consequences.

ground, and occasional refuge, for many useful species including amphibians and the spectacular dragonflies that are excellent predators of garden insects and pests.

A new garden pond is often quite devoid of life, and it can take a couple of years before the ecology builds up. The complexity will develop over time and, as it does, more creatures will take up residence, so that after just a few short years the pond becomes an important element in both the garden and the wider habitat. The best ponds for wildlife have a variety of habitats, including deep and shallow shelves where the water can warm up during the day. In addition, there will be plenty of vegetation to give cover and oxygenate the water, whilst offering a variety of cover for the animals to hide in, make shelters, lay their eggs and raise the next generation.

## BENEFITS OF HAVING FLEAS, LICE AND SNAILS IN THE POND

All three are a sign of a well-balanced, healthy habitat. For a pond to have clear water, free of mats of floating algae (algal bloom), these creatures are a "must".

Many are very small crustaceans, belonging to three important groups - the water fleas, the ostracods, and the copepods, with the water fleas, such as *Daphnia*, being the largest. They are extremely important in the food chain of a pond because they are very numerous, they harvest tiny, floating algae, and clear the water before being eaten by larger animals. Water lice are also crustaceans, being closely related to the familiar land-dwelling woodlice that they resemble, although they have a flatter body. Water snails often breathe air, and can be seen coming up to the surface. They feed on the tiny algal "meadows" that often coat the plants and pond sides, and therefore help keep the water clear, which in turn keeps the plants healthy.

## FEEDING STRATEGIES

Pond-dwelling creatures can be grouped into three types of feeders: herbivores; filter feeders that eat detritus (all the semi-decayed fragments of plants or animals); and predators.

Many herbivores, such as pond snails, unlike their land-based relatives, do not actually eat the pond plants, but graze on the algae growing on them and on the pond sides, when the water gets sufficient light. The filter feeders, or detritivores, are often slow-moving creatures at the pond bottom that usually escape our attention, and include a variety of worms, molluscs and crustaceans, such as the water lice and so-called "water fleas" that move around in the water with jerky movements. They are very important in keeping water clear and are, in turn, eaten by larger creatures, thus forming an essential part of the pond's food chain.

The most exciting and often the most visible aquatic creatures are the predatory ones, such as backswimmers. These will pursue and overpower prey that is significantly larger than themselves,

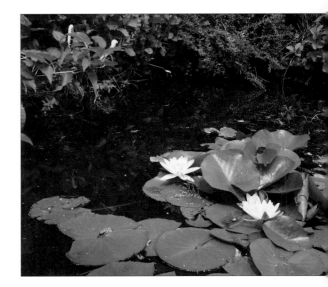

Above: *Pond water will stay clear when daphnia, or water fleas, are present. These will also provide food for larger predators.*

including tadpoles and small fish. Not all predators are as noticeable, however. Dragonfly larvae, though rarely seen, are super predators that catch prey with lightning speed, using their unique mouthparts to ensnare their hapless victims.

## PLANTS TO ATTRACT AQUATIC LIFE

Use the following plant types to attract different aquatic species. A range of plants is essential to provide different habitats for as many different species as possible.

Marginal/emergent plants, e.g. water mint
Water lilies and deep water aquatics

Oxygenators, e.g. *Elodea*
Free-floating plants, e.g. water soldier

Water mint     White water lily     *Elodea*     Water soldier

# SPIDERS AND SCORPIONS

*Probably some of the most feared creatures in the garden, spiders and scorpions can invoke severe bouts of arachnophobia. Despite this, both are important in nature, with spiders being particularly beneficial because they feed on insect pests. The hunting prowess of both spiders and their distant relatives, the scorpions, means that they help to control the numbers of other species and so play a vital role in the garden habitat.*

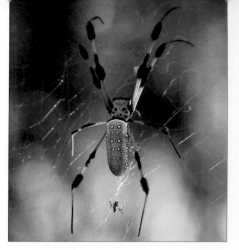

Above: *Golden silk spiders, common in the southern USA, spin large webs to catch flies, bees, wasps, moths and butterflies.*

### ROLE IN GARDENS

Spiders and scorpions are distantly related, and are among the oldest of all land animals, belonging to a group of creatures called the *Arachnids*. Both have four pairs of walking legs and fangs (called *chelicerae*) that are adapted for liquid feeding.

Spiders are extremely diverse and have the distinction of being the largest group of predatory animals. Some of the most familiar types are the big-eyed jumping spiders, small sheet-web spiders, orb-weaving spiders, cobweb spiders, non-web-weaving wolf spiders and crab spiders. Scorpions are the largest arachnids, with some tropical species reaching over 20cm (8in) long. The long body ends in a narrow, tail-like structure with a curved stinger held up over the back that delivers venom and paralyzes larger prey. They are mostly nocturnal, and all tend to have the peculiar property of fluorescing at night under an ultraviolet lantern.

While both spiders and scorpions are important predators, spiders are the most abundant and most ecologically important group, being found in almost every habitat.

One Eurasian spider family (*Argyronetidae*) even lives underwater in ponds and lakes where it makes silken "diving bells" that it fills with air brought from the surface.

Because of their abundance, spiders rank among the most important predators in many ecosystems, and their numbers can often exceed 100 per m$^2$ (sq yd). In short, their combined weight in a habitat often exceeds that of larger predators, albeit fewer in number, such as birds.

As all spiders are predators, mainly eating insects, they are a great benefit in the garden, controlling many pests and balancing insect populations. Despite this abundance however, spiders cannot reproduce faster than their insect prey, and so if populations are damaged by insecticides, the surviving insect pests often grow to larger population sizes than before the insecticide was applied – a phenomenon known as resurgence. Of course many spiders also become a meal for others, and they can be an important food source for birds, lizards, wasps and other creatures. Spider silk is also an important material for

some birds when building nests, with many songbirds, and nearly all species of hummingbird, heavily dependent on it.

### HABITAT PREFERENCES

Spiders occupy just about every habitat in the garden, and if you keep your garden pesticide-free their numbers soon grow, with many newcomers actually parachuting in by ballooning. This involves attaching long strands of silk to a firm anchor point before

Below: *Garden spiders are common on bushes and other vegetation, where they feed on flying insects caught in a sticky web.*

Below: *Harvestmen, only distantly related to spiders, have many omnivorous species that eat insects, fungus and decaying matter.*

## ARACHNOPHOBIA

Though many people fear spiders, the majority are too small to bite and are completely harmless. In fact, any spider whose body length is smaller than about 8mm (¾in) cannot break human skin with its tiny fangs. As most spider species are smaller than this, the majority are no problem and of those spiders that are large enough to bite, only a few are dangerous to humans.

It is also worth remembering that spiders only bite humans as a last resort when threatened, for example when disturbed. Occasionally they may hide in items of clothing and bite when pressed against the body. Spiders never attack humans unless they can help it, although defensive postures may cause alarm. Some notorious species, such as the black widow spiders of the United States and southern Europe, and the related redback of Australia, all have painful but non-lethal bites. The American brown recluse spider and Australian funnel web spiders can also cause painful if non-lethal bites.

Above: *Many spiders and scorpions need an area of dense undisturbed vegetation in which to hide from larger predators.*

Above: *The desert hairy scorpion, native to the southern USA, is a burrowing species, but can also be found under stones or logs.*

rising air currents lift the spiders up and into the breeze, dispersing them to new habitats. These spiders are usually small and immature, and are the familiar "money spiders" seen in the summer and autumn.

Scorpions tend to move more slowly than this, but if they are common in your area and you have a garden that is to their liking, they soon colonize it. They are rarely seen, typically preferring cool, shady areas where they hide in the day. A drystone wall, rock or log pile is often the best site, whence they emerge at dusk to commence a night of hunting.

## FEEDING STRATEGIES

All spiders and scorpions are predators, and the majority are generalist predators, eating many different kinds of insects and other small animals. Most rely on their venomous bite or sting to subdue their prey. The greatest variety is seen among the spiders, with some feeding on certain types of prey. Most use a web of carefully constructed sticky silk fibres to ensnare their prey, while others – the wolf and jumping spiders – do not use a web but subdue their prey by pouncing on them.

Crab spiders are experts at ambush and often hide in flowers, from where they deliver fatal bites with pinpoint accuracy to bees, butterflies, and other would-be pollinators.

Scorpions are nocturnal feeders that either lie in wait to ambush prey, or actively hunt. Their diet includes insects, centipedes, millipedes, snails, spiders, other scorpions and even small reptiles and mice. They detect them by air movement over the long, sensory hairs on the body that trigger a dash to capture the prey. The victim is caught by pincers and stung to subdue and kill it, before it is eaten head first. Scorpions do not eat every day and some can survive from 6–12 months without food. On any one night, therefore, only a small percentage may be seen feeding; the population may be much greater than a search might suggest.

### PLANTS TO ATTRACT SPIDERS

Blackthorn (*Prunus spinosa*)
Hawthorn (*Crataegus monogyna*)
Ivy (*Hedera helix*)
Lawson cypress (*Chamaecyparis lawsoniana*)

**Blackthorn**

**Hawthorn**

**Ivy**

**Lawson cypress**

### THREATS

**Habitat loss** Many spider species are restricted to particular habitats, such as wetlands, that are threatened by human development, resource extraction, and agricultural activities, with some species being very rare as a result.

**Persecution** Spiders have much more to fear from us than we do from them, and indeed the overblown fear of both spiders and scorpions has led to their being remorselessly persecuted in the home and garden.

**Pesticides** Spiders are extremely sensitive to the effects of pesticides in the environment, and often decline when they are used. The effects of pollution, acid rain, and climate change also pose a major threat.

**Predators** While scorpions and spiders are well equipped for survival, they are not without their natural enemies. Scorpions not only feed on each other but are prey to other animals, while spiders fall prey in large numbers to wasps and birds.

# BUTTERFLIES AND MOTHS

*Almost universally loved, butterflies are the epitome of insect activity on a warm summer afternoon. They are beautiful and graceful and, with their night-flying cousins, the moths, form an important group in many habitats. The larvae, or caterpillars as they are known, eat vegetation and, although we may regard them as pests for this, they form an important food item for larger animals in the garden.*

Above: *Moths differ from butterflies, with their ability to fold their wings horizontally and their short, feathery antennae.*

## ROLE IN GARDENS

Many gardeners claim to love butterflies, although they show considerably less concern for the larval stages. In fact, some gardeners develop an almost unnatural horror at the sight of a caterpillar, making open warfare that has led, in some cases, to an unprecedented decline in the numbers of certain species. With the additional loss of suitable breeding and feeding habitats, the picture for many butterfly and moth species looks bleak.

Both butterflies and moths are important elements of many habitats, as a source of food for many predators and as herbivores because their larvae often eat a considerable amount of plant material. From hatching to pupation a caterpillar increases its body size more than 30,000 times, and all this plant material that is converted into body tissue can be a rich source of protein for other animals. A few

Below: *Butterflies are almost always day-fliers, unlike most moths, and have brightly coloured wings and clubbed antennae.*

moths are infamous pests, such as the cabbage white, tortrix and tomato moth, but others actually eat weeds.

Moths, in particular, are extremely numerous and often form an extremely important part of the diet of many bat species. The bats locate the moths using high-pitched echolocation, although moths have sensitive "ears" and when some species hear the ultrasonic squeak of a bat, they close their wings, and drop like a stone out of harm's way. Other species even send out a jamming sound that effectively blinds the bat to their presence. In fact, it is widely believed that butterflies actually evolved from moths and became active by day to avoid night-flying predators.

Despite their basic similarities, butterflies and moths are quite easy to distinguish. The simplest way – if you can get close enough – is to look at the antennae. Butterfly antennae have a ball (or club) on the end of the antennae. Moths never have a club, and have either plain or feathery antennae. In addition, the majority of butterflies rest with their wings folded up above the body, whereas most moths rest with their wings folded along the body or outspread. Butterflies also have thinner bodies than moths and generally have a slower wing beat, tending to flutter; moths produce a whirring motion.

## HABITAT PREFERENCES

Most butterflies prefer a sunny feeding site by day, whereas moths need suitable species of night-scented flowers with nectar. Of equal importance to both, however, is a larval food plant in sufficient numbers to guarantee that enough caterpillars pupate and reach adulthood to maintain the population. Both adults and their young need your help, and plants should be chosen accordingly.

## PROFILE

**Climate change** The habitats of some butterflies have started to change and are now less suitable. Butterflies would normally migrate to combat this, but habitat fragmentation may make this impossible for some species.

**Collection** The wings of many butterflies and some moths are often sought by collectors, making some species scarce. Despite the legal protection of some species, the problem continues.

**Garden benefits** Both butterflies and moths are important elements of the food chain, and pollinate many plant species. Their grace and beauty also enhance the summer garden.

**Potential for nuisance** Despite their reputation, don't kill caterpillars because they may be doing no harm to ornamental plants. Bug screens across open windows will prevent moths from entering rooms on warm nights.

**Risk to people or pets** Some butterflies and moths variously hiss, mimic stinging insects or even have what look like eyes on their wings to ward off predators. They are harmless to us, but many caterpillars have irritant hairs that can cause rashes if touched.

**Supplementary diet** Butterfly-feeders contain a sponge chamber filled with honey or sugar water. Moths can be attracted using a solution of dark beer, molasses, brown sugar and a dash of rum, painted on to tree trunks.

## FEEDING STRATEGIES

Both butterflies and moths have a long, tube-like mouthpart kept in a tight coil. Once unfurled it's dipped into a flower for sucking out the nectar. Butterflies generally land on the flower or flower head to do this, whereas moths more commonly hover in front of the bloom when feeding, although all show a preference for scented flowers with long, tubular throats. Caterpillars, on the other hand, are simply eating machines

Right: *Some adult moths and butterflies have vivid eye spots on the wings. These are very effective in confusing or dissuading would-be predators.*

that consume vast amounts of plant material to convert it into body tissue, which they do with tremendous efficiency over quite a short period.

## A LIFE IN TWO HALVES

Both butterflies and moths have larvae that look nothing like the adults, and undergo a complete metamorphosis during the pupal stage. This cycle starts with the female butterfly laying eggs on or near a food plant. The young caterpillars hatch from the eggs after a few days or weeks, although eggs laid in autumn will not hatch until the following spring.

These young caterpillars are literally eating machines whose main purpose in life is to change plant matter into body tissue. Amazingly, they may eat 10 times their own eventual weight in food. As they grow, they fill their skins, shed them, and emerge with a new skin, four or five times, before turning into a chrysalis (the pupal stage). To do this, the fully grown caterpillar makes a button of silk that it uses to attach itself to a twig before shedding its skin, one last time. The new, exposed skin layer is hard and often golden (the word chrysalis means gold), although it usually darkens in time.

Right: Verbena bonariensis *is an absolutely wonderful butterfly attractor, even rivalling the well-known* Buddleja *in this respect.*

Inside the chrysalis, the body turns to a soupy liquid before, gradually, the wings, legs and other parts of the butterfly form. When the butterfly emerges from the chrysalis, its wings are initially wrinkled and gradually open. The butterfly hangs upside down and gently beats its wings, pumping air and liquid from the body into the wings before finally taking flight.

## LIFE CYCLE OF A BUTTERFLY

*The butterfly undergoes a complete change between the larval and adult stages. The caterpillars look like a different species, and need to eat large amounts of vegetation to grow. The adults live for a short time, mating and reproducing.*

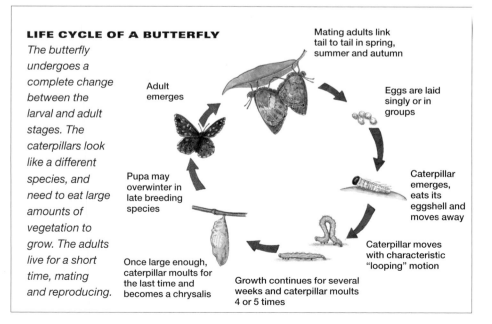

Adult emerges

Mating adults link tail to tail in spring, summer and autumn

Eggs are laid singly or in groups

Caterpillar emerges, eats its eggshell and moves away

Caterpillar moves with characteristic "looping" motion

Growth continues for several weeks and caterpillar moults 4 or 5 times

Once large enough, caterpillar moults for the last time and becomes a chrysalis

Pupa may overwinter in late breeding species

# BEETLES AND BUGS

*With about a quarter of a million species, beetles are by far the largest group of insects and probably the dominant group on the planet. They include a number of important garden predators among their ranks, as well as many strange and interesting species that fulfil a vast array of roles within almost every conceivable habitat in a garden. Bugs, on the other hand, while less diverse, include many familiar insects, comprising a number of both pests and predators.*

Above: *Ladybirds are a widespread and familiar group of beetles, well known to gardeners for their aphid-eating habits.*

### ROLE IN GARDENS

Beetles occur almost everywhere on the planet except for Antarctica, and are common in gardens. They can easily be recognized by the front wings that have hardened and modified into protective shells called elytra that usually cover the whole abdomen in most species. There are exceptions, of course, and they are very short in rove beetles and are completely absent from the female glow-worm, or firefly as it's sometimes known.

All species have biting mouthparts, although they can be extremely variable between different species. While most beetles can fly, some have no hind wings at all, and their elytra are fused together and immovable. As for those with the power of flight, most prefer to walk, scuttling away when disturbed, or simply dropping to the ground and "playing possum" (lying still and feigning death), with their legs held tight against the body.

The life cycle of many species is somewhat complex, and involves a metamorphosis with four or more larval stages and a pupa before the adult finally

Below: *Most beetles are easily recognized by their hardened front wings, modified into protective shells that cover the abdomen.*

emerges. The larvae are very diverse, sometimes legless, but nearly always with a well-developed head and biting jaws.

While bugs sometimes resemble beetles, their elytra always overlap. In addition, bugs have a piercing beak (or rostrum) that is never seen in beetles. Bugs also have a life cycle that involves an incomplete metamorphosis where the young (or nymphs) generally resemble small, wingless adults, although their colours and markings may be very different. Many species have young that exist with the adults and feed in the same way, whereas others, such as cicadas, have nymphs that are specialized for burrowing and appear quite different from the adults.

Both beetles and bugs fulfil a whole range of roles in the garden, acting as herbivores, predators and decomposers, at which some are highly specialized. Some beetles, such as the sexton or burying beetles, actually find and bury the carcasses of small rodents, using them as a food store for their young. Scarab beetles remove dung, and a whole host of beetles of all sizes chew their way through deadwood, helping to recycle and break it down. The sheer number of beetles and bugs (that, in turn, are taken by other predators) makes it possible only to generalize about their role in the garden, but they are possibly the most important creatures in any given habitat and, as such, a valuable part of the garden food chain.

### HABITAT PREFERENCES

Both bugs and beetles can be found almost anywhere, including aquatic habitats. Beetles are especially common in gardens because their tough elytra give them added protection, and allow them to occupy places that are denied to other winged insects. Many of them, for example, live in

the soil and under stones while others spend their lives groping their way through leaf litter and compost heaps. Water beetles use the spaces between their elytra and their bodies as rechargeable air cylinders that enable them to spend long periods under the water, whereas water bugs often breathe through a tail-like siphon that connects them to the air.

### PROFILE

**Diet** The diet of both bugs and insects is very eclectic because they live in virtually every type of ecosystem, both above and beneath the ground, as well as under water. They eat decomposing plant or animal material, living plants, or are predators.

**Life span** The life span of most adult beetles and bugs is short, although some wood-boring beetles live for more than 40 years, albeit mostly as larvae. Cicadas (a bug) also live for a long time, spending 3–17 years as nymphs.

**Risk of bite or sting** If roughly handled, many beetles discharge obnoxious fluids, and may squeak or buzz to alarm you. Large specimens can also inflict a sharp nip with their jaws, and some bugs, such as the aquatic backswimmer, can give very painful bites.

**The largest animal order** All beetles belong to the order *Coleoptera*, the largest order in the entire animal kingdom (there are more species of beetles than plant species). In total there are an estimated 350,000 named species, and many more still unnamed ones, constituting 30 per cent of all insects.

Above: *Leaf litter is home to many beetles, some of which feed upon it directly, whilst others hunt in its moist, shady shelter.*

### GARDEN BENEFITS OF BEETLES
Beetles can be very useful in the garden, consuming slugs, snails and caterpillars. In certain circumstances, however, they can compete for resources with other garden creatures, and attack and cause much damage to plants, furniture and buildings.

Beetles and their larvae are also an important source of food for many larger birds and mammals, and they are eaten by badgers, foxes, and toads as well as by many birds, such as thrushes, wrens, woodpeckers, crows and nuthatches. You will also often see crows, magpies and, occasionally, gulls, searching for chafer grubs in fields or, more annoyingly, in lawns, although this usually causes less long-term harm than the grubs might cause. Beetles also help in breaking down larger organic matter, such as carrion, dung and plant material, and some even aerate the soil and act as pollinators.

### PLANTS TO ATTRACT LADYBIRDS
Alpine cinquefoil (*Potentilla crantzii*)
Bugle (*Ajuga reptans*)
Fern-leaved yarrow (*Achillea filipendula*)
French marigold (*Tagetes patula*)
Penstemon (*Penstemon strictus*)
Prairie sunflower (*Helianthus maximiliani*)
Speedwell (*Veronica spicata*)
Tansy (*Tanacetum vulgare*)

Fern-leaved yarrow   French marigold

Speedwell   Tansy

### FEEDING STRATEGIES
Beetles eat a very wide range of foods, both animal and vegetable, living and dead. Most beetle larvae are rather stout and slow, but adults vary in size and shape, with some, such as longhorn beetles and impressive stag beetles, being very large indeed. Others, such as some of the pollen beetles, are merely tiny black specks to our eyes.

Of the predatory types, ground beetles and ladybirds are probably the best-known examples, both being excellent controllers of pests. Ground beetles are long-legged and fast, and while some have a beautiful metallic sheen, the majority are dark. They live in litter layers above the soil, and hunt slugs and other ground-living invertebrates. Ladybirds are also voracious predators that hunt on the plants themselves, feeding on aphids (greenfly), coccids (scale insects), mealybugs, whitefly and, occasionally, on other garden insect pests and crop plants, in both their larval and adult stages.

Bugs are similarly diverse, and have adapted to a wide range of habitats and lifestyles. Most bugs are herbivores and use their piercing "beaks" to suck plant sap directly from the cells or veins of leaves and stems. Possibly the best known is the aphid, that often plagues gardens in the summer, although many more plant-sucking bugs, such as leaf hoppers, capsid bugs and shield bugs, are also familiar garden species.

### THREATS
**Habitat loss** While many beetles in gardens are common and widespread, other species are very specific in their requirements. Many wood-boring beetles need deadwood for their larvae to eat and grow in.

**Human intervention** Beetles and bugs are often feared when encountered, and may be killed by people ignorant of their garden value. Some species are also taken by collectors, particularly if they are brightly coloured.

**Pesticides** Many beetles are predators, and they are extremely susceptible to even quite small residues of pesticide. This is most serious when prey species develop a resistance, and relatively large amounts of pesticide may accumulate in their body tissue.

**Predators** Beetles, like any other garden insect, have their enemies, and if they are large predators their protective armour will not be enough to save them. Foxes, badgers and even bats will take beetles if given the opportunity, or if other food is scarce.

### LIFE CYCLE OF A LADYBIRD
*The ladybird's larva is an even more voracious predator than the adult, and commences feeding as soon as it hatches. It often goes unnoticed because both it and the pupa resemble a bird dropping – an effective camouflage.*

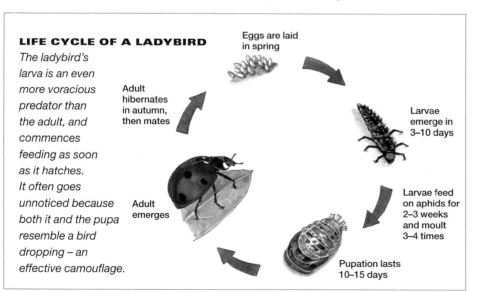

Eggs are laid in spring
Adult hibernates in autumn, then mates
Larvae emerge in 3–10 days
Larvae feed on aphids for 2–3 weeks and moult 3–4 times
Pupation lasts 10–15 days
Adult emerges

# BEES AND WASPS

*Both bees and wasps play a vital role in maintaining a balanced, healthy ecology in our gardens: bees are very effective pollinators, and wasps are good at controlling insect pests throughout the growing season. The latter especially may be hard to love, but without them, life outdoors would actually be more difficult. Wasps' hunting activities are extremely important in controlling numbers of potentially devastating garden pests, such as caterpillars, thus helping to reduce damage to plants.*

Above: *Bees are important natural pollinators of plants. Without them, many trees, such as this apple, would not be able to bear fruit.*

### ROLE IN GARDENS

Bees are immensely important in any habitat that contains flowering plants, and are the single most important insect pollinator in gardens. Around 80 per cent of the food we eat comes from crops that have been pollinated by bees and, without their efforts, many species would become rare and eventually die out in the wild. Ironically, bees originally evolved from solitary hunting wasps, becoming vegetarian in the process, and today there are about 19,000 known species of bee; while many remain numerous, some are rare or endangered.

Wasps differ from bees principally in the fact that they feed their young on meat – such as insect larvae and scraps of carrion – rather than nectar and pollen. Although there are some 75,000 different species of wasp, most of the attention is given to the larger, social wasps, so named because they live in colonies that can number thousands. They are also highly beneficial insects (eating their way through tens of thousands of garden pests each season), and are only annoying because some species have adapted to living in close proximity to us. Unlike the honeybee, social wasps have not developed methods of storing food for winter, which means their colonies last for only one season. In the autumn, new queen wasps leave the colony to search for a sheltered spot where they can spend the winter.

### HABITAT PREFERENCES

Most bees in the world are solitary with a short lifespan, living as adults for only about 6–8 weeks. A range of species has evolved to exploit particular environmental niches, and they emerge at different times of the year. Many have no sting because they do not store honey (and don't need a defensive weapon), and because their nest is only open for short intervals of time. Mated

female bees live alone in a hole or burrow in well-drained soil, in soft brick mortar, in wood (in the case of carpenter bees), or any other convenient hole that suits their needs.

Bumblebees and honeybees, on the other hand, live together in colonies (a hive) and store both honey and pollen to feed on in periods of food shortage or bad weather. Wasps are mostly solitary and, even in the case of the social wasps, the only individuals that survive a winter are the young fertilized queens.

### PROFILE

**Diet** Bees are exclusively vegetarian, and feed on a diet of sugary nectar and pollen. Wasps, on the other hand, are active hunters although many species have adults that are vegetarian, having a taste for sugar, while others feed on pollen or meat.

**Life span** In general, the life of an adult bee or wasp is relatively short, ranging from a few weeks to a few months. Few last longer than a season, and the only real exception is the queen honeybee that lives three or more years.

**Risk of bite or sting** For most people this is a mild, albeit painful annoyance, but a significant minority are allergic to stings and suffer extreme reactions.

**And if you are stung ...** The proper way to remove a bee sting is to scratch it out. Never pull one out because this forces venom from the sac into the skin, causing more swelling. Wasp stings are not left in the skin. Antihistamine cream will help reduce the swelling or other allergic reaction.

Above: *Social wasps, such as these yellow jackets, live in large colonies that they may fiercely defend using their stings if they are threatened.*

Left: *Wasps are excellent hunters, but only the larvae are carnivorous, with the adults depending upon sugary liquids instead.*

## DIFFERENCE BETWEEN POLLEN AND NECTAR

Nectar and pollen are produced by flowers, and both form an important part of the diet of bees. Nectar is a liquid that is extremely rich in sugars, and is produced in glands called nectaries, generally at the base of the flower cup. Pollinators are made to brush the flower's reproductive parts to reach it. Nectar that is produced outside the flower is generally produced to attract predatory insects, which eat both the nectar and plant-eating insects.

Pollen is produced by the male part of a flower, and its role is to fertilize the ovaries of the female part of a flower and promote diversity. As insects, or other pollinators, brush past the male parts of the flower when they gather nectar, they often become coated in it, and involuntarily transport it from flower to flower, thereby playing an important role in many plants' reproductive cycles. Bees actually eat the pollen and collect it by brushing it into pollen sacs, situated on their rear legs.

## PLANTS TO ATTRACT BEES

**Shrubby plants**
Blackberry (*Rubus fruticosus*)
Lavender (*Lavandula stoechas*)
Laurustinus (*Viburnum tinus*)

Lavender          Laurustinus

**Herbaceous and annuals**
Bee balm (*Monarda didyma*)
Catmint (*Nepeta racemosa*)
Giant yellow hyssop (*Agastache nepetoides*)

Bee balm          Catmint

## FEEDING STRATEGIES

Bees are characteristically busy because they must constantly forage across their range to gather enough nectar and pollen for their young to feed on.

Wasps are all carnivorous as larvae, although the adults often feed on high-energy food such as nectar and other sugary liquids. Of the 25,000-odd known species, about 16,000 are parasitic, feeding on the bodies or eggs of other insects or spiders. Other larger hunting wasps catch and kill insects that they chew into round food balls and carry home to the larvae. The larvae then secrete a sugary liquid that the adult social wasps feed on, and it is this that cements the bond in their hives.

Wasps vary greatly in size with some of the parasitic species being so small that several may develop in a small insect egg, while other species can reach a body length of about 5cm (2in). In gardens, you're most likely to see social wasps, especially in autumn when they're attracted to ripening fruit. As the adults begin to starve, with the number of grubs gradually decreasing from late summer, they desperately seek nutrition elsewhere, being attracted to sugary liquids. The combination of cooler weather and fermenting fruit often makes them highly irritable and more likely to sting.

Left: *Bees need plenty of flowering plants that bloom over a long period to provide them with enough food.*

## THREATS

**Habitat loss** Many bee species entered a decline during the twentieth century, and a number of species have already become extinct as a result. It is estimated that around 25 per cent of wild bees are currently either rare or threatened with extinction.

**Parasites** Almost all species of wasps and bees have parasites that attack them, particularly when they are larvae.

**Pesticides** Bees are very sensitive to many pesticides, especially insecticides that are absorbed by the plant. They can end up in the nectar and poison both the bees and their young. Wasps or their larvae often succumb to a build-up of insecticide residues from their prey.

**Predators** Both wasps and bees may be eaten by other insects or larger predators. Some birds, such as bee eaters and honey buzzards, specialize in eating bees or their young, and badgers often dig into wild bee nests to raid the honey and young grubs.

## LIFE CYCLE OF A BUMBLEBEE

*Bumblebees are social bees, meaning that they form cooperative colonies of very closely related individuals. Unlike honeybees, bumblebees don't survive the winter: a new colony is formed each spring, when the queen seeks a suitable nest site such as a rodent burrow.*

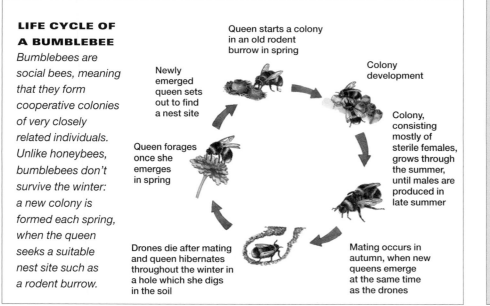

Queen starts a colony in an old rodent burrow in spring

Colony development

Newly emerged queen sets out to find a nest site

Colony, consisting mostly of sterile females, grows through the summer, until males are produced in late summer

Queen forages once she emerges in spring

Drones die after mating and queen hibernates throughout the winter in a hole which she digs in the soil

Mating occurs in autumn, when new queens emerge at the same time as the drones

# EARWIGS AND FLIES

*There are many species of earwig, easily recognized by their pincer-like appendages (or cerci) on the tail end that are straight-sided in females but curved and larger in males. They are omnivores, rarely causing serious damage to plants, but eating some garden pests. Flies, on the other hand, are extremely diverse, and aside from the familiar, irritating houseflies, count many useful predatory species in their ranks. Ultimately, both earwigs and flies form an important food source for other garden inhabitants.*

Above: *Earwigs are a common sight in many gardens, where they feed on decaying plant and animal matter and other insects.*

## ROLE IN GARDENS

The word earwig comes from the old English word *earwicga*, meaning ear beetle, following the old European superstition that these insects crawled into people's ears while they were asleep and bored into their brains.

Earwigs are unusual among insects because the females remain and care for both the eggs and young nymphs. In spring, the female, sometimes assisted by the male, builds a nest underground in which to lay her eggs. She then evicts the male and carefully attends to the eggs, turning them regularly and cleaning them until they hatch, after which she continues to tend and feed them until they can forage for themselves.

Flies belong to an immense order of insects known as *Diptera*, or the "true flies", with approximately 122,000 known species. It's an extremely diverse group, having evolved into a multitude of forms. Flies are generally recognized through their minute, pin-shaped hind wings, known as balancers, that act as gyroscopes and help maintain balance during flight.

Above: *Adult hoverflies feed mainly on nectar and pollen, but their larvae are often voracious predators of aphids.*

The fly life cycle is composed of four stages: egg, larva (or maggot), pupa and adult. The eggs are laid in, or near, the preferred habitat or food source of that particular species, which variously includes decaying flesh, animal manure, live prey, plants and pools of stagnant water.

Earwigs, particularly the European earwig, are often regarded as garden pests primarily due to their habit of chewing the flowers and young leaves of dahlias, clematis, chrysanthemums, lettuces and strawberries, etc. They can also be valuable predators of insect pests, such as aphids and mites. While most species are omnivorous, plant material almost always constitutes the bulk of the diet. Fortunately, earwig damage is not usually particularly severe, mostly restricted to a few species, and on the whole, their beneficial attributes of pest control and as a source of food for larger creatures outweigh this.

Left: *The late flowers of ivy (*Hedera*) offer a drink of nectar and some nutritious pollen to flies and other insects late in the season.*

Flies, on the other hand, are a much more mixed group and include some serious pests, such as the carrot and onion fly, as well as some of the most beneficial insects in the garden. The latter include the hoverflies and some midge species that are excellent controllers of aphids. The vast majority of the flies you see, however, act as scavengers and recyclers, feeding mostly

### PROFILE

**Diet** Earwigs are omnivorous, feeding on a wide variety of insects as well as live or decaying vegetation, and occasionally attacking garden plants. Flies have evolved to exploit just about every imaginable food source, and are ecologically very important.

**Garden benefits** Both earwigs and flies are important creatures in the garden, helping to recycle nutrients and maintain the balance of other animal populations, serving as both predators and prey within the garden ecosystem.

**Life span** Earwigs can live for as long as two years, although many perish before this as a result of predation. Flies, on the other hand, tend to be shorter lived, often living for just a few weeks, although some temperate species have a total life cycle covering a whole year.

**Risk of bite or sting** Earwigs cannot bite humans, and even their impressive pincers are capable of delivering only a puny nip. Most flies are also harmless, although some species (e.g. mosquitoes, horse and march flies) can bite humans.

## LIFE CYCLE OF A HOVERFLY

*The hoverfly is often visible in gardens, where it is sometimes mistaken for a bee or wasp. The larvae or maggots of certain species of hoverfly are predatory, and eat aphids during the summer months. The adults feed mainly on nectar and pollen.*

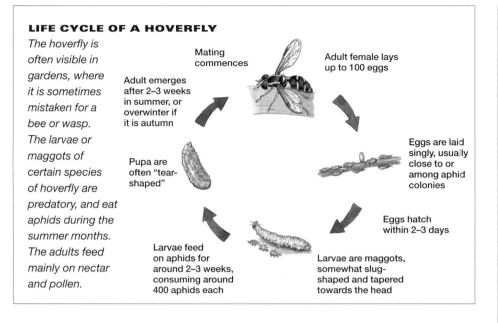

Mating commences

Adult emerges after 2–3 weeks in summer, or overwinter if it is autumn

Adult female lays up to 100 eggs

Eggs are laid singly, usually close to or among aphid colonies

Pupa are often "tear-shaped"

Eggs hatch within 2–3 days

Larvae feed on aphids for around 2–3 weeks, consuming around 400 aphids each

Larvae are maggots, somewhat slug-shaped and tapered towards the head

on decaying waste, such as dung and dead animals, and, ultimately, all become food for other insects and many birds. Flies are also extremely important pollinators, coming a close second to bees and wasps.

## HABITAT PREFERENCES

Earwigs live in a variety of habitats but many species spend part of their life below ground. They are mostly active at night, hiding in moist, shady places beneath stones, and among debris during the day. While many species do have wings, they rarely fly and are unable to crawl long distances. Despite this, they are often inadvertently transported long distances by humans, with some species – such as the European earwig – now being widely distributed as a result.

Flies, on the other hand, are masters of the air and disperse readily. Their larvae are less mobile, though, and many species have young with a particular diet; hoverfly maggots, for example, eat aphids. The parents are therefore restricted to areas that can provide such food, although in certain cases, such as the housefly, human activities have resulted in it becoming extremely widespread across the entire planet.

## FEEDING STRATEGIES

Earwigs are rapid runners that feed on a variety of foods that they consume with their biting and chewing mouthparts. While they fulfil a minor predatory role, feeding on aphids and other small invertebrates, they are primarily scavengers of dead plant material, although some do feed on live plants.

Adult flies feed almost exclusively on liquids, although a few hoverflies are able to crush pollen grains as part of their diet. Most use a variety of mouthparts to feed, ranging from the pad of the housefly that is used to regurgitate digestive juices on to the food before it and the food are sucked up, to piercing mouthparts that are used to suck the juices from plants or live prey. The larvae, on the other hand, have much simpler mouthparts that are used to swallow food or attack prey.

Tachinid flies, robber flies, bee flies and hoverflies are all carnivorous at some stage, and provide effective pest control in the garden. Other fly species, however, such as mosquitoes, horse and march flies, are bloodsuckers. While no adult flies ruin cultivated plants, the larvae of many species, including the carrot fly, leaf miner and leatherjacket, happily munch their way through garden plants and, if numerous, can become extremely damaging.

Flies will always be difficult to love in the garden, possibly because of their association with disease, death and decay, but also because they can be downright irritating when they buzz around you on a hot summer's day. Remember their importance as food for other animals, though, and that most species are actually on your side.

## PLANTS TO ATTRACT HOVERFLIES

Black-eyed Susan (*Rudbeckia fulgida*)
Carrot (*Daucus carota*)
Coriander (*Coriandrum sativum*)
Dill (*Anethum graveolens*)

Fennel (*Foeniculum vulgare*)
Lobelia (*Lobelia erinus*)
Wood betony (*Stachys officinalis*)
Yarrow (*Achillea millefolium*)

Black-eyed Susan

Coriander

Lobelia

Wood betony

# GRASSHOPPERS AND CRICKETS

*Forming a large and varied group of insects, grasshoppers and crickets are mostly big, easily recognized creatures that are commonly found in gardens and beyond. They can be an important source of food for many larger garden inhabitants. More often heard than seen, their distinctive noise provides a familiar soundtrack throughout the day and on into the night during the warmer months of the year.*

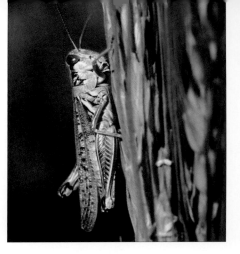

Above: *Grasshoppers are quite common in many areas, but need areas of long grass in which to hide and complete their life cycle.*

## ROLE IN GARDENS

Although some species of grasshopper can become garden pests, most are quite happy to live their lives in long grass and rarely venture into the more ornamental parts of the garden. A few, such as the locust, are capable of devastating crops and gardens, which means that in some parts of the world all grasshoppers are tarred with the same brush and are persecuted.

While most grasshoppers are vegetarian, many crickets are omnivores and never attack garden plants. In addition, both are an abundant and nutritious food source that is eaten by a number of predators, including spiders, centipedes, birds, reptiles, amphibians and small mammals.

Grasshoppers and crickets are closely related, and often bear quite a close resemblance at first sight. But closer inspection shows that grasshoppers have short antennae and are predominantly active during the day, whereas most crickets have antennae that reach their abdomens (and normally further), and are often nocturnal. Despite this, it can be difficult to tell them apart, and some of the insects that we call grasshoppers are actually more closely related to crickets than they are to other grasshoppers.

Although you often find both crickets and grasshoppers in a garden, most species are restricted to their favoured habitats. The most noticeable feature of grasshoppers and most crickets is their long, jumping hind legs that enable them to leap well over twenty times their body length. They are also noted for their ability to make a variety of sounds, many of which are intended to protect territory or attract mates. Only male grasshoppers make these noises as a rule, and in some species they use both sound and vision to impress potential partners. A few species may be

Left: *Although closely related, grasshoppers differ from crickets by their shorter antennae and by being active during the day.*

**PROFILE**

**Diet** Grasshoppers are mostly vegetarian but can become pests of certain crops. Crickets are much more eclectic in their tastes and, while the vast majority are omnivores, some have become almost entirely carnivorous.

**Garden benefits** Grasshoppers are vegetarian by nature, but are little threat to garden plants, while they are an important food source for various creatures. Many crickets are predatory.

**Life span** Most grasshoppers and crickets live for less than a year, and often have quite short adult lives. Eggs that are laid in late summer overwinter and hatch in the spring, and just occasionally nymphs or adults overwinter and lay eggs the following season.

**Risk of bite or sting** While the majority of grasshoppers cannot bite, some of the larger species of cricket are capable of delivering a bite that, in a few cases, can be quite painful. The sting-like ovipositor (or egg-layer) on the tail of some crickets is harmless.

**LIFE CYCLE OF A GRASSHOPPER**

*Most species have a yearly cycle that sees the young larval stage emerging in the spring and growing to maturity in late summer. Adults rarely overwinter and most will die by the late autumn, having mated and laid eggs that will overwinter and hatch next spring.*

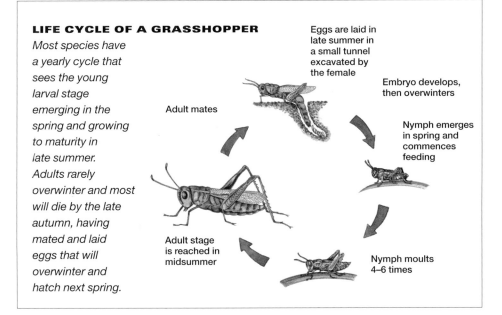

Adult mates

Eggs are laid in late summer in a small tunnel excavated by the female

Embryo develops, then overwinters

Nymph emerges in spring and commences feeding

Nymph moults 4–6 times

Adult stage is reached in midsummer

## "CHIRPING" AND "SINGING"

An attractive feature of many grasshoppers and crickets is their ability to "sing". Generally it's only the males that do this to attract a mate or warn off other males. Two different mechanisms are used to make this sound. Grasshoppers employ a comb-like structure with a row of teeth on the inside of the hind leg that they rub against a ridge on the wing. This produces a characteristic "chirping" sound. Crickets also have a comb-and-ridge mechanism, but the structures are on the left and right forewings, and their chirping is the result of rubbing these over each other.

Grasshoppers are mostly active during the day, and in warm, sunny weather their singing can be very loud. Crickets are mostly active at night, spending their days in shallow burrows, or beneath a stone or clod of dirt. Once the sun begins to set, the males begin their nightly serenade, attracting mates. These songs may vary according to the air temperature that often influences chirping rates. The warmer the night, the faster they chirp. There are separate songs for courtship, fighting, and sounding an alarm.

The loud buzzing heard in the day is often wrongly thought to be a type of grasshopper or cricket, but is actually made by cicadas. They sing loudly and well, but are not grasshoppers – they're a type of bug.

Above: *Long, flower-rich grassland provides the ideal habitat and food source for many grasshoppers and certain cricket species.*

seen in the summer taking short flights and flashing their brightly coloured wings while snapping them together, to produce a distinct sound. Such short-flight noises are called crepitation and are usually species specific. Males more commonly make a sound by scraping the hind leg against the hard outer wing casing (stridulation) to produce the characteristic rasping sound so commonly heard in summer. Crickets also stridulate, but they produce the noise by scraping one outer wing case over another, and are more generally known for doing this in the evening and at night.

## HABITAT PREFERENCES

Grasshoppers tend to inhabit grassland and are predominantly active during the day, especially during sunny weather. They can be quite choosy about which plants to eat, and many species are specialists, feeding on only a few particular grass types.

Crickets tend to be more general in their distribution, with some even living partially or entirely underground, or in caves. They are also more commonly active at night, and their dull colouration makes a very effective camouflage. Most crickets hide during the day and are hard to see, the only evidence of them being the sound they make at night.

## FEEDING STRATEGIES

Grasshoppers are mainly vegetarian, and often consume relatively large amounts of vegetation daily that they chew using their well-developed mandibles. They are mostly

Left: *The oak bush-cricket is a mostly carnivorous species, although it does eat some succulent plant material as well.*

specific in terms of their preferred food plants, but if numbers increase and food becomes short, they may switch their attention to other plants. This reaches its greatest extreme in the case of plagues of locusts that are capable of stripping all the vegetation from an area. Crickets, on the other hand, are mostly omnivores.

## THREATS

**Habitat loss** Many species of grasshopper and cricket rely on a particular food source, but changes in habitat can affect its availability. The behaviour of hunting crickets may also depend on particular habitats.

**Persecution** Being vegetarian, grasshoppers may be considered pests despite their being mostly harmless. Most species cause no real damage to garden plants. Crickets are often mistaken for cockroaches and killed.

**Pesticides** Pesticides aimed at one particular pest species often affect other species, particularly the carnivorous types of cricket, leading to a lethal build-up in their bodies.

**Predators** Both crickets and grasshoppers are an essential part of many food chains and, as such, many will be caught and eaten by larger predators, including mammals and even birds of prey.

## PLANTS TO ATTRACT GRASSHOPPERS

Cock's foot (*Dactylis glomerata*)    Crested dog's tail (*Cynosurus cristatus*)
Creeping bentgrass (*Agrostis stolonifera*)    Red fescue (*Festuca rubra*)

Cock's foot          Creeping bentgrass          Crested dog's tail          Red fescue

# DRAGONFLIES AND DAMSELFLIES

*Often considered to be the glittering jewels of the insect world, dragonflies and damselflies are a very successful group, with fossils dating back over 300 million years. Their colour and behaviour never fail to excite, but, far from being just beautiful, they are highly effective hunters, grabbing smaller prey in flight with their bristly legs. These rapacious insects have larvae that are some of the most effective hunters in freshwater ponds.*

Above: *Dragonflies are large and powerful hunters, whose body design has not changed in over 350 million years.*

### ROLE IN GARDENS

Dragonflies are some of the largest and perhaps most spectacular insects in the garden, often seen hovering and flitting over ponds. They even mate on the wing when a pair can be seen flying together, in tandem. Both dragonflies and damselflies have a high acceleration rate and speed, and they share the ability to hover or fly backwards and forwards. In fact, they are unmatched for speed and agility in the air, and hunt by sight, often ambushing prey with amazing accuracy.

There is often confusion between dragonflies and the smaller damselflies, but distinguishing between the two orders is easy when you see them resting. Dragonflies always sit with their wings open and flat, while the more diminutive damselflies close their wings and fold them tightly along the length of their body, often making them harder to spot when resting.

### HABITAT PREFERENCES

Some dragonflies insert their eggs into plant stems growing in the pond shallows, whereas others simply release them on to the water surface to sink or be trapped amongst the plants. Once hatched, the nymphs remain as nymphs from one to two years (sometimes three) and, during this time, they increase their size by periodically moulting their hard outer casing, swelling their body and bursting through this outer layer.

Eventually the nymphs climb out of the water, up the stem of a marginal plant, mostly under cover of night. After a short period, often as the first light of day returns, they moult one last time, splitting open the outer casing along the back. From this shell, the new adult emerges, and remains there while it pumps blood through the veins in its wings to fill them out to their full size. Once the wings have dried in the early morning sun, the adult may take to the air where it will spend much of its adult life.

All dragonfly species need a stable pond environment, and suitable surroundings with good feeding and roosting sites. Warmth is essential, and the best breeding ponds are those that are sunny and sheltered from the wind. Plenty of vegetation, both in and around the water, is another key ingredient.

### FEEDING STRATEGIES

While both the nymph and adult dragonfly are carnivores, they catch their prey in very different ways. The nymphs are entirely aquatic and hunt by stealth, catching their prey using an unusual mouthpart called a

### PROFILE

**Diet** Adults prey on other flying insects, particularly midges and mosquitoes, but they will take any prey that is small enough to catch. The larvae live in water and eat almost anything including small fish, tadpoles, bloodworms or other insect larvae.

**Garden benefits** Dragonflies are extremely effective hunters and eat large numbers of flying pests, given the right habitat. They also provide food for larger garden creatures, and their aerial antics are reason enough to want them.

**Life span** A dragonfly's minimum life cycle from egg to adult death is about six months, although it can be six to seven years with some of the larger dragonflies. Most of this time is spent in a pond in the larval form, with the adult stage only lasting a few months at best.

**Risk of bite or sting** While larger dragonflies may try to bite if held, their jaws are not powerful enough to break the skin. Despite stories to the contrary, no dragonfly can sting; they overcome their prey by strength.

Above: *Dragonflies are mostly larger than damselflies, and rest with their wings held out flat and away from the body.*

Above: *Damselflies are mostly smaller than dragonflies, and rest holding their wings upright above their body, like butterflies.*

## PLANTS TO ATTRACT DRAGONFLIES

**Oxygenating plants** These are a must to provide cover and oxygen for the larvae.

Curled pondweed (*Potamogeton crispus*)

Eurasian water milfoil (*Myriophyllum spicatum*)

Hornwort (*Ceratophyllum demersum*)

Water starwort (*Callitriche stagnalis*)

Curled pondweed    Hornwort

**Water lilies, deep-water aquatics and free-floating plants** Plants with floating leaves are useful for hiding larvae and providing basking sites for adults.

Floating pondweed (*Potamogeton natans*)

Frogbit (*Hydrocharis morsus-ranae*)

Water crowfoot (*Ranunculus aquatilis*)

Water lilies (*Nymphaea*)

Water smartweed (*Polygonum amphibium*)

Frogbit    Water lily

**Marginal plants** These are essential for the larvae as they climb out of the water, also providing perching, roosting and egg-laying sites for the adults.

Bogbean (*Menyanthes trifoliata*)

Flowering rush (*Butomus umbellatus*)

Water horsetail (*Equisetum fluviatile*)

Watermint (*Mentha aquatica*)

Yellow flag (*Iris pseudacorus*)

Brooklime (*Veronica beccabunga*)

Bulrush (*Typha minima*)

Burr reed (*Sparganium erectum*)

Pickerel weed (*Pontederia cordata*)

Water forget-me-not (*Myosotis scorpioides*)

Watermint    Yellow flag

mask. This appendage shoots out incredibly quickly to capture its victim in the sharp terminal pincers, and the prodigious speed of the mask makes it one of the fastest animal movements in nature. They detect prey mostly by sight, touch and vibrations, and devour everything from water fleas and other insects to larger prey, such as newts, small fish and even each other.

The adults, on the other hand, always catch their prey on the wing and this usually involves one of two strategies. Broadly speaking, dragonflies are either "darters" or "hawkers" because of the way they hunt. Darters perch on reeds or other vegetation, waiting for the prey to come past, and then dart out and catch it. Hawkers patrol up and down a territory, looking for prey to swoop on, grabbing smaller flying insects with their bristly legs before landing and consuming them. Whether a darter or hawker, all

Above: *An ideal dragonfly pond should have a mixture of plants to provide cover for the larvae and stems for them to climb out.*

## THREATS

**Collection** Dragonflies have long been admired, not only for their speed and agility in flight but also for the patterns and dazzling colours on their eyes, bodies and wings. Over-collection of some species has made them rare.

**Habitat loss** Many species of dragonfly and damselfly rely on water for their breeding cycle, and the loss of wetland is a serious threat. In addition, changes in the surrounding habitat might mean an absence of prey.

**Pesticides** Dragonflies are predatory in their larval stages and also when they are adults. If pesticides end up in tiny amounts in their prey, dragonflies can be poisoned through this.

**Predators** Despite their incredible aerial abilities, many adult dragonflies are caught by spiders, larger insects, mammals and even birds of prey.

dragonflies and damselflies share brilliant flying abilities, being both fast and agile, easily outmanoeuvring their prey.

They can actually make themselves invisible to airborne prey and territorial rivals. They do this by moving in such a way that they appear to be a stationary object blending into the background. This "motion camouflage" allows dragonflies to stalk their victims undetected.

## LIFE CYCLE OF A DRAGONFLY

*Dragonflies are instantly recognizable when they are seen flying during the summer months. However, this stage is only a short part of their life – they actually spend most of their life as nymphs underwater, feeding on a range of aquatic species. After emerging, the adults hunt on the wing, feeding on insects.*

Adults mate in tandem in summer

Once wings dry and harden, adult emerges and starts hunting for flying insects

Adult lays eggs in winter

Eggs hatch into nymphs

Nymphs spend 2 or more years underwater eating live prey

Skin splits below the head and the adult climbs out

Nymphs emerge in early summer and climb up an emergent (marginal) plant stem

# WORMS

*Familiar creatures to most gardeners, worms are elongated, soft-bodied creatures that lack both legs and backbone, and are usually found in the soil. Many worms are extremely useful in helping to break down dead and decaying plant material and aerating the soil. The best known worm is probably the earthworm, frequently encountered when digging. Worldwide, however, there are many thousands of species in almost every conceivable habitat, including a number of predatory species.*

Above: *Earthworms are a familiar sight in many gardens, where their feeding and tunnelling activities enrich and aerate soil.*

### WHAT ARE WORMS?

There are thousands of different kinds of worm – the largest measures several metres long, and the smallest cannot be seen without the aid of a microscope. Only a limited number actually live in our gardens, and the vast majority of these live in the soil or in rotting plant litter, while a few inhabit ponds. The majority of the larger species eat decaying plant material, but a few feed on animals, and some of the microscopic types live as parasites in animals and plants causing a number of diseases.

There are three main groups of worms that you would expect to live in a garden. The flatworms are mostly aquatic, and are usually carnivorous or parasitic. Many species are very small but some larger species, such as the New Zealand flatworm, are carnivores that capture and eat earthworms. Roundworms (or nematodes) are tiny, usually microscopic worms and are one of the most common groups of animals with over 20,000 known

Below: *Worms are very common in gardens, and tend to be eaten by a wide range of animals, such as this toad.*

Above: *Brandling worms live in decaying plant material, such as compost heaps, and are very useful in helping decomposition.*

species. They often outnumber other animals in a habitat, both individually and in the number of species. There are many parasitic forms, including some that cause disease to garden plants. However, nematodes can be beneficial because certain predatory ones kill garden pests, such as vine weevils and cutworms.

The segmented worms (or annelids) include the more familiar garden earthworms, but also include bloodsucking leeches. Earthworms are often highly abundant in gardens, and are especially numerous in soil that's rich in organic matter. They tunnel deeply into the ground, and bring soil from the lower layers closer to the surface, helping to mix the topsoil. In addition, the slime that they secrete to ease their passage through tunnels contains nitrogen, and helps bind together clusters of soil particles into aggregates.

Worms don't have true eyes, although they are able to sense light and quickly move away from a bright source. Indeed, if they are unable to escape this they can become paralyzed if the light exposure lasts

an hour or more. They can also be damaged and die if their skin dries out, as this is the prime way in which they breathe. For this reason, they often prefer a damp site, although they can easily drown if the ground becomes waterlogged. The likelihood of drowning makes them rush to the surface if they sense rain, and many birds exploit this by lightly pecking at the ground to simulate raindrops, catching the worms as they emerge.

### PROFILE

**Diet** The vast majority of larger worm species found in gardens eat decaying organic matter, and recycle nutrients. Many smaller worms are parasites or carnivores, and leeches are always carnivorous or blood-sucking.

**Garden benefits** Worms fulfil a huge variety of roles and functions, particularly in the soil, and are an essential part of this and many other food chains. Earthworms, in particular, are especially useful as decomposers of decaying matter.

**Life span** Worms vary in their lifespan according to species, but an earthworm may well live for up to eight years, and many other worms show a similarly long lifespan. However, few reach that age, being eaten by other creatures.

**Risk of bite or sting** Most garden worms are unable to bite (unlike some of their marine relatives), and are completely harmless. Some leeches, on the other hand, are bloodsuckers, even though few attack people.

## LEECHES

Chiefly because of their reputation as ruthless bloodsuckers, leeches are a much-maligned group of worms. While all leeches are carnivorous, most feed on a variety of invertebrates, such as worms, snails, insect larvae and crustaceans. Only a very few are parasitic bloodsuckers, and most of those limit this activity to amphibians, reptiles, waterfowl and fish, with only small numbers attacking mammals (including humans).

The best-known bloodsucker is probably the European medicinal leech that was once used to control diseases believed to be the result of an excess of blood. Though this now seems extraordinarily naïve, some surgeons are now using them following operations to reattach severed limbs or digits. Researchers have discovered that leeches are better at controlling and even reducing any swelling in the reattached limb during the healing process than conventional medicine, and additional research is being carried out into the anticoagulant secreted by leeches as they feed. This could also be medicinally useful.

Despite their predatory nature, leeches have many predators, including fish, aquatic insects, crayfish and even other leeches. They are to be found in most freshwater habitats and, although some are terrestrial, they mostly require warm, moist conditions.

Above: *The humid conditions and abundant plant material in a compost heap make it an ideal place for many worm species.*

## ROLE IN GARDENS

Worms play a diverse role in garden ecosystems, depending on the species concerned. Earthworms, for example, help maintain the fertility of the soil. Their tunnelling helps increase the amount of air and water that gets into the soil, and their feeding aids the breakdown of organic matter. Ultimately, their continued activity helps turn the soil.

Brandling worms (or redworms) are a special type of earthworm adapted to life among layers of decaying organic material, and are often found in compost and manure heaps. Their ability to speed up the conversion of green waste into compost means that they are used in worm composters. Finally, leeches are useful as they catch small prey.

## HABITAT PREFERENCES

While worms of all descriptions are widely distributed and differ in their habitat requirements, most prefer darkness and avoid light, emerging from cover only at night. This means that they are safe from many predators, although many nocturnal creatures actively hunt them, and creatures such as moles actually seek them out in their tunnels.

Earthworms form a burrow by entering the soil head first to a depth of several centimetres, before tunnelling back to the surface at a different point. They make this burrow partly by using the pointed head end to push soil particles aside, but also by taking in soil that passes through the body, being left as castings at the entrance to the burrow. In the winter or periods of drought, earthworms retreat deep into the soil.

## FEEDING STRATEGIES

Worms that spend some of their time above ground, such as earthworms, tend to be nocturnal feeders, and spend the daylight hours with the head just below the soil surface of the exit. They often hide this exit with a pebble or piece of leaf drawn over the opening, and at night they come part way out of the ground, leaving the tail end in the burrow to make a hasty retreat if necessary. In this position they feed on decaying plant and other organic matter, before retreating back at the first sign of dawn.

Leeches rarely eat, often surviving for months on a single meal. Some are bloodsucking but the majority eat smaller prey, such as snails and other worms, that they mostly capture under cover of darkness.

Below: *Despite its name, the pond-dwelling horse leech does not suck horse blood, but feeds on worms and decaying flesh.*

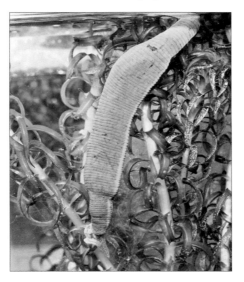

## THREATS

**Habitat change** Increased cultivation and reliance on synthetic chemical fertilizers often results in a decrease in soil organic matter (especially at the surface), which is a worm's prime food. This layer also helps keep soil cool and moist in summer, and warm in winter.

**Pesticides** Carelessly applied pesticides frequently reach the soil, and decaying plant matter often has residues. Even if the worms are not killed by this toxicity, they can accumulate pesticides in their bodies that, in turn, lethally affect the wildlife that feeds on them.

**Pollution** Synthetic chemical fertilizers can have a disastrous effect on earthworm populations, many tending to create acid conditions that are often fatal to worms. Pollutants can also accumulate in their bodies to levels around twenty times higher than in the soil they inhabit.

**Predators** Earthworms have many predators, but introduced predators can wreak havoc. In the UK they are threatened by the accidentally introduced New Zealand flatworm that feeds on the earthworm, but lacks any natural predators. Worms are a vital food source for many larger creatures, and their loss may in turn cause food shortages for these animals.

# OTHER INVERTEBRATES

*There are too many types of invertebrates to mention in this book. Many are commonly encountered in gardens, and it is often tempting to assume that they are pests if they seem unfamiliar. Most, if not all, creatures play a significant (albeit small) role in the garden, and it is only when their numbers are out of balance or when species are introduced to areas where they formerly never occurred that they are likely to become a problem.*

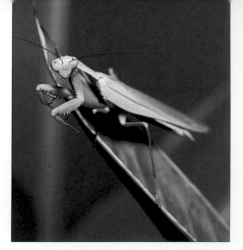

Above: *The praying mantis feeds primarily on other insects, although larger species can consume small reptiles, mammals or birds.*

## COCKROACHES

These are an ancient group of insects, whose basic body design of a flattened body, bristly legs and long antennae has remained unchanged for hundreds of millions of years. They can eat almost anything, giving them the edge when competing with other species for food. Only a few species ever venture into our homes, with most being the outdoor, nocturnal kind. By day they hide in crevices, or under rocks, logs or in burrows, and are often important elements in the food chain, being eaten by larger predators.

## MANTISES

The mantises, or "mantids" as they are sometimes called, are a distinctive group of insects, being related to cockroaches and crickets. They're widely distributed throughout warmer areas of the world. They prefer areas rich in plants and other insects, and are carnivores feeding primarily on other invertebrates, although it is not

Below: *Termites are extremely common in warmer regions. They are tremendously important recyclers of plant matter.*

Above: *Cockroaches often invoke revulsion when encountered, but most are outdoor-living and few species ever enter our homes.*

uncommon for larger mantises to consume small reptiles such as geckos, and even small mammals or birds. Mantises are often extremely well camouflaged, moving slowly and blending in with their surroundings while they wait for their prey to come within striking distance. They use their front legs to snatch their victim quickly, which is immediately devoured. In turn, mantises are devoured by bats, the larger birds, spiders, and even bigger mantises.

## TERMITES

Termites are very simple insects in their design, but have an astonishingly complex social behaviour, often involving several different "castes" of adults that undertake specific roles in the colony. They play an essential role in the decomposition and recycling of plant material, being especially abundant in drier or tropical environments. They feed on wood, grass and other plant matter, according to species, and also eat fungus that some species cultivate in dark, humid parts of their nest or find growing on moist wood. Termites are often mistakenly called white ants because of their social

habits, but are actually most similar to cockroaches, with which they are thought to share a common ancestry.

## STICK INSECTS AND LEAF INSECTS

These are plant-eating insects (most being closely related to cockroaches, grasshoppers, crickets and mantises) that are mainly restricted to tropical regions, with only a few species in temperate places. As their name suggests, they are usually long and slender, and bear an uncanny resemblance to the structure and colour of twigs and leaves of the woody plants on which they live and eat. They move very slowly – if at all – during daylight hours, and most species tend to restrict their movements and other activities, including feeding, to the hours of darkness.

## ANTS

Living in large, highly cooperative colonies, ants often function as if they were one large organism. They are most closely related to

Below: *Ants are extremely common in gardens everywhere, and in many cases they are important predators and recyclers.*

Above: *Millipedes have long cylindrical bodies with many tiny pairs of legs, and if disturbed often form a defensive coil.*

wasps and, in many ways, an ant resembles a wasp without its wings, and indeed the flying forms of ants (the new queens and males) greatly resemble and are often mistaken for wasps.

Ants are extremely important elements of many habitats, and are important predators of some insects that they capture and kill for their young. Like social wasps, the adults have a sweet tooth and their search for sugary substances, as well as their wide-ranging search for food, often brings them into conflict with home owners.

## CENTIPEDES AND MILLIPEDES

With their long, segmented, elongated bodies, centipedes have one pair of legs per segment. They range in size from 2cm (¾in) to giant specimens in warmer regions that can reach 15–20cm (6–8in) long. All are fast-moving predators that feed on any small creatures, with smaller species preying mostly on insects. The larger centipedes often sport bright colours to warn that they can inflict a painful bite. All species lack a waxy layer on their outer shell and are prone to desiccation. They consequently shun the sun, being mostly nocturnal, or spend their lives underground.

While they resemble centipedes, millipedes have long, cylindrical bodies with two pairs of legs on each segment. They are found worldwide (except in polar regions), being most abundant in tropical climates, and all species feed on decaying organic material. Like centipedes they are nocturnal and prefer a humid environment, and often spend most of their time underground. If disturbed, millipedes roll into a defensive coil and some species exude foul-tasting chemicals so that they aren't eaten. They don't bite.

Above: *Woodlice are unusual in being land-living crustaceans that breathe with gills, so they prefer living in damp or humid places.*

## WOODLICE

Also known as pillbugs, woodlice are easily recognized by their flattened or round-backed profile, seven pairs of legs, and sharply angled antennae. While they look a little like insects, they are in fact crustaceans, being closely related to lobsters, crabs or shrimps, and are the ones from this group to have successfully colonized land. They breathe by means of gills and, for this reason, prefer damp, humid places, such as leafy compost heaps, where they feed on dead vegetation. All species are nocturnal and only venture into the open at night. Some species roll into a ball when disturbed – hence the name "pillbug".

## SLUGS AND SNAILS

These are molluscs, and belong to the same group as shellfish (e.g. oysters and clams). They are legless creatures that glide along on a path of mucus and are invariably regarded as pests, with herbivorous species feeding during the night. The shiny mucus trail left behind is the only clue as to where

Below: *Slugs are molluscs that lack a protective shell. Whilst some species are pests, most eat carrion or decaying material.*

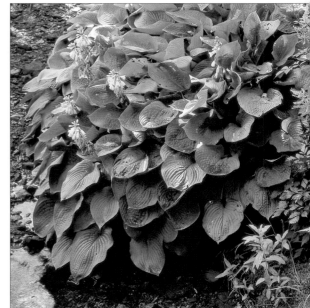

Above: *Areas of dense vegetation, particularly if they are near water, often harbour a rich diversity of invertebrates.*

they have been. Their damage to plants can be very significant, generally being worse in damp conditions when they emerge en masse from their hiding places. They are an important part of many habitats, and many species of slug and a few snails eat only decaying matter and cause precious little damage to garden plants, with a few species being carnivorous.

While slugs and snails are a severe irritation to any gardener, they are a vital and rich source of food for many other garden predators, so you should never attempt to poison them with chemicals – such chemicals may end up being ingested by one of the predators. Instead of focusing on killing slugs and snails, try encouraging the predators instead.

Below: *Snails are frequently a problem when they attack garden plants, but are preyed upon by many other garden animals.*

# PLANTS TO ATTRACT GARDEN WILDLIFE

Choosing plants is one of the most exciting aspects of landscape or garden design. For all species in this directory, the particular types of wildlife that they attract are clearly outlined, so that you can select the best plants for the creatures that live in your area. The plants are grouped into standard categories – annuals and biennials, bulbs, perennials, herbs, shrubs, hedges, trees, climbers, pond and bog plants, and fungi and decomposers – with tips on how they are cultivated, wildlife benefits and suggestions for closely related species.

Left: *Insects are a vital part of the food chain. Careful plant selection will ensure that food and shelter are provided for them.*

Above: *Huge quantities of nectar produced by lupin flowers attract several species of bee. The blooms brighten up garden borders.*

Above: *Heleniums are good in herbaceous borders or naturalistic plantings. Their bright daisy flowers attract many insects.*

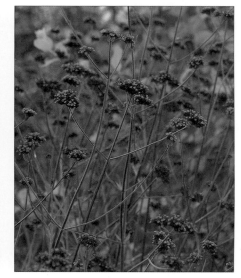

Above: *Verbena bonariensis is probably the best plant to attract garden butterflies. It flowers for a long period in the summer.*

# HOW PLANTS ARE NAMED

*All living things are classified according to a system based on principles that were devised by the 18th-century Swedish botanist, Carl Linnaeus. This system states that a particular plant genus (plural: genera) is a group of plants containing similar species. Beyond that there may be plants that are simply a slight variation of a species, or are a hybrid (cross) of different species or variations.*

Above: *All plants in the directory are divided into groups. This yellow flag iris can be found in the Pond and Bog Plants section.*

### SCIENTIFIC NAMES

Under this system, plants have botanical names – often Latin but also derived from other languages – that consist of the genus name (for example, *Verbena*), followed by the name that denotes the particular species (for example, *hastata*). Some genera contain a huge number of species that may include annuals, perennials, shrubs and trees, while others contain just one species. Although all members of a genus are assumed to be related to each other, this is not always visually obvious.

It is useful to keep in mind that a species is defined scientifically as consisting of individuals that are alike and tend naturally to breed with each other.

Despite this system, botanists and taxonomists (the experts who classify living things) often disagree about the basis on which a plant has been named. This is why it is useful for a plant to retain its synonym (abbreviated to syn. in the text), or alternative name. Incorrect names often gain widespread usage, and in some cases, two plants thought to have separate identities, and with two different names, are found to be the same plant.

A well-known example of naming confusion is the genus *Pelargonium*. Until the 19th century, pelargonium plants were included in the genus *Geranium*, and despite being classified separately for over a century, they are still popularly known as geraniums.

### VARIATIONS ON A THEME

Genetically, many plants are able to evolve over time to adapt to a changing environment. In the wild, individuals within a species that are not well adapted will not survive, so all survivors will look the same. The average garden is a more controlled environment, so gardeners can choose to encourage and grow on variations within a species that have small but pleasing differences such as variegated leaves and double flowers. The terms for these variations are subspecies (abbreviated to subsp.), variety (var.), form (f., similar to variety and often used interchangeably) and cultivar (cv.). A cultivar is a variation that would not occur in the wild but has been produced and maintained solely by cultivation. Variations are given names in single quotes, for example *Papaver orientale* 'Allegro'.

### HYBRIDS

When plant species breed with each other, the result is a hybrid. Rare in the wild, crossing is very common among plant-breeders, and is done specially in order to produce plants with desirable qualities such as larger or double blooms, variegated foliage and greater frost resistance. A multiplication sign (x) is used to indicate a hybrid, and the name often gives a clear idea of the hybrid's origins.

### GROUPS

A Group of plants is a group of very similar variations. Their names do not have quotation marks around them – for example *Tradescantia* Andersoniana Group.

### HOW THE DIRECTORY IS ARRANGED

Within the plant directory, plants are arranged alphabetically, by genus. Each main entry features a general introduction to that genus, plus specific information such as tips on propagation and which hardiness zone the genus belongs to. This is followed by a selection of plants from that genus, also arranged alphabetically according to their most widely accepted names. One of these entries might be a species, a hybrid (or group of hybrids), a variety, form or cultivar. Each is given a description that may include height and spread.

Left: *The Japanese rose is classified as a shrub but can also be found in the Single-Species Hedges section because it forms an excellent barrier.*

# HOW TO USE THE PLANT DIRECTORY

Within the plant directory, the plants are arranged principally according to their habit of growth and life cycle. The plants are split into sections such as Annuals and Biennials, Bulbs, Perennials etc, which makes it easier to use. Each main entry features the common and botanical names, the plant's family and where it is originally a native. This is followed by a general introduction to that genus, including a description of the plant, including the leaves, flowers and height. There are also brief cultivation notes and propagation tips, as well as information relating to its hardiness zone.

Notes on each plant's uses show how it can be used in the garden, and the section on wildlife benefits describes the range and types of creatures it might normally attract. Lastly, the directory suggests a selection of closely related species that may fulfil a similar role in the garden.

**Photograph**
Each entry features a full-colour photograph that makes identification easy.

**Caption**
The full botanical name of the plant in question is given with each photograph.

**Genus and species name**
This is the internationally accepted botanical name for a group of related plant species. This starts with the current botanical name of the plant in bold, and this can refer to a species, subspecies, hybrid, variant or cultivar. If a synonym (syn.) is given, this provides the synonym, or synonyms (alternative names) for a plant. A common name may be given after the botanical name.

**Common name**
This popular, non-scientific name applies to the whole of the plant genus.

**Family**
This shows the larger grouping to which the plant belongs and can reveal which plants are related to each other.

**Native**
The nativity of a species refers to its original home range although it often occurs outside this range now as a result of cultivation.

**Cultivation**
This section gives the level of sun or shade that the plant either requires or tolerates, with advice on the best type of soil in which they should be grown. Methods of propagation are listed, as well as any other helpful tips that might be appropriate.

**Uses**
This section advises on how to get the best from a plant, for example using it in borders or containers or to brighten up dark corners. In some cases, suggestions are also given for plants that complement each other well.

**Wildlife benefits**
The plant is intended to be useful for wildlife and so the principal species they normally attract are listed here. The list is not always exhaustive and most plants will attract many others as well.

**Closely related species**
This section provides information about common types that are available and other recommended plants to look out for. Both wild plant species and cultivars are listed. In several cases, plants that are not beneficial to wildlife are also listed. This will help you to decide which plants to avoid when planning a wildlife garden.

*Ceanothus thyrsiflorus*

*Ceanothus thyrsiflorus*
## CALIFORNIAN LILAC
Family: Rhamnaceae
Native: California and S Oregon

The Californian lilac is one of the best shrubs to attract huge numbers of bees. It is a large, vigorous, evergreen shrub growing to 6m (20ft) high.

**Cultivation**  Grow in full sun in a sheltered location, protected from cold winter winds. The roots favour fertile, well-drained soil. Propagate by semi-ripe cuttings in mid–late summer. ❄ ❄ ❄ Zone 8.

**Uses**  Ideal for planting in a large shrub border, or train against a sunny wall where it provides a valuable source of food for insects. Also, several species of birds are likely to nest in the network of branches.

**Wildlife benefits**  A huge favourite with bees and bumblebees seeking mainly pollen and, occasionally, nectar. The leaves are eaten by caterpillars of several common butterflies and moths. Songbirds feast on the numerous visiting insects that take refuge in the dense foliage.

**Closely related species**  Research has shown that *C.* 'Ray Hartman' is a fantastic plant to attract bees. *C. impressus* is another real favourite, attracting several species of insect. It is an evergreen shrub with dark blue flowers in mid- to late spring.

**Genus description**
This provides a general introduction to the genus and may state the number of species within that genus. Other information featured here may include general advice on usage, preferred conditions, and plant care, as well as subspecies, hybrids (indicated by an "x" in the name), varieties and cultivars (featuring names in single quotes) that are available.

**Size information**
The average expected height and spread of a genus or individual plant is frequently given, although growth rates may vary depending on location and conditions. Metric measurements always precede imperial ones. Average heights and spreads are given (as H and S) wherever possible and appropriate, and more consistently for perennials and bulbs, although it must be noted that dimensions can vary a great deal.

**Plant hardiness and zone**
A plant's hardiness and zone are given at the end of this section. Hardiness is indicated by the number of snowflake symbols. Zones give a general indication of the average annual minimum temperature for a particular geographical area. The smaller number indicates the coolest zone it can survive in and the higher number the warmest zone that the plant will tolerate. In most cases, only one zone is given. (See page 128 for details of hardiness symbols, zone entries and zone maps.)

## PLANT SELECTION
The plants in this directory can be used internationally in ornamental gardens, and have been chosen for their ability to benefit wildlife. Unfortunately, only a limited number could be included, but additional information can be found in each section on closely related species.

# ANNUALS AND BIENNIALS

*Agrostemma githago*
**CORN COCKLE**
Family: Caryophyllaceae
Native: S Europe and W Asia
A delightful summer-flowering hardy annual that was formerly a common weed in cereal crops but is becoming rare due to modern farming practices, such as increased use of herbicide and good seed-cleaning techniques. It reaches a height of 60–90cm (2–3ft), has lance-shaped green leaves and is graced with pretty, open, trumpet-shaped pink flowers, 8cm (3in) wide. The seed is poisonous.
**Cultivation** Grows best in full sun, in well-drained soil with low fertility. Fully hardy, surviving temperatures down to -15ºC (5ºF). Sow direct in the ground in spring or early autumn; after germination, thin out and transplant when the seedlings are small. Protect overwintering seedlings with pea sticks that will then support the willowy growth. Deadhead to promote new flowers. ❀ ❀ ❀ Zone 4.
**Uses** A popular garden plant that is widely used in annual or mixed borders, and is often used in cottage gardens. It is also commonly found in annual meadow mixes, along with annual poppies, corn marigolds and annual cornflowers.
**Wildlife benefits** The flowers are a great source of nectar for bees and the occasional butterfly.
**Closely related species** The following *A. githago* cultivars are excellent nectar producers: try 'Milas' with plum-pink flowers, 'Milas Cerise' bearing deep red flowers and 'Milas Rosea' with pale lilac-pink flowers.

*Alcea rosea*

*Alcea rosea*
**HOLLYHOCK**
Family: Malvaceae
Native: Unknown – probably Turkey or Asia
A tall, majestic biennial that can often survive three or more years. The erect stems can grow to 3m (6–7ft) or more, and bear spikes of rosette-like flowers 5–10cm (2–4in) across in a range of colours, from white to pink or purple, and sometimes pale yellow. The green leaves are rounded, lobed and have a rough texture.
**Cultivation** Although fully hardy, it needs a sunny location with well-drained soil. Propagate in late summer for flowering the following year. ❀ ❀ ❀ Zone 5.
**Uses** Gives height to herbaceous borders, also terrific in mixed borders when planted sporadically throughout the border. Very effective in cottage gardens.
**Wildlife benefits** The large flowers are popular with bees looking for nectar. Avoid double-flowering cultivars of hollyhock, such as *A. rosea* 'Charters Double Hybrids', as

they have little wildlife benefit.
**Closely related species** Single-flowering cultivars, such as *A. r.* 'Indian Spring' and *A. r.* 'Nigra', are ideal for visiting bees. *A. rugosa* is a tall, elegant species that bears pale yellow flowers and is also a good nectar producer.

*Amaranthus caudatus*
**LOVE-LIES-BLEEDING**
Family: Amaranthaceae
Native: Peru, Africa and India
An exotic, late-summer hardy annual, growing to 1.5m (5ft) tall. Used for its plume-like tassel flower heads that reach 45cm (18in) long, and contain hundreds of tiny, crimson flowers. The pale green leaves turn beautiful bronze in autumn.
**Cultivation** Although it can tolerate poor ground, it thrives in any fertile, well-drained soil in full sun. Sow direct outside in mid-spring or, for an earlier show, sow indoors in early spring and then plant out, after hardening off in late spring. ❀ Zone 5.
**Uses** Excellent in a tropical bedding scheme with the likes of *Canna* 'Orange Perfection', *Dahlia* 'Bishop of Llandaff' and *Salvia uliginosa*. A real talking point if grown in pots in prominent places.
**Wildlife benefits** The seed is a popular choice with many birds, including collared doves, reed buntings, dunnocks, sparrows and finches.
**Closely related species** *A. tricolor* is also a favourite with birds. Gardeners particularly like the cultivars *A. t.* 'Joseph's Coat' with scarlet, green and yellow oval leaves and *A. t.* 'Molten Fire' with crimson, bronze and purple leaves.

*Agrostemma githago*

*Amaranthus caudatus*

*Antirrhinum majus*

### *Antirrhinum majus*
### SNAPDRAGON
Family: Scrophulariaceae
Native: SW Europe and
Mediterranean

Grown in cottage gardens for centuries, it's still a big favourite. Although it is classed as a short-lived perennial, it is best grown as a half-hardy annual. The lance-shaped leaves are borne on stems that can reach 90cm (3ft) high; flowers are normally pink or purple.

**Cultivation** Grows best in full sun in fertile, well-drained soil. Add organic matter to the soil before planting if necessary. If grown as a half-hardy annual, sow indoors in early spring and plant out after the risk of frost has passed, usually in late spring or early summer. Deadhead to promote new flowers. ❊ Zone 7.

**Uses** Most commonly used in annual bedding schemes because of the range of colours and sizes. With other tall varieties, like the Rocket Series, it can be used for cut flowers, while dwarf varieties ('Tom Thumb') are ideal for window boxes and tubs.

**Wildlife benefits** The fragrant flower spikes are full of nectar, and are a great temptation to bumblebees that either snap off the flower heads or eat the corolla tube to obtain the nectar if the entrance to the flower is too small.

**Closely related species** *A. molle* is a small hardy perennial, shrubby species

which has pale pink, white or yellow flowers, and is ideal for the rock garden or for naturalizing in walls. *A. sempervirens* is another dwarf, shrubby species that suits a free-draining area and has nectar-rich cream-white or yellow flowers.

### *Borago officinalis*
### BORAGE
Family: Boraginaceae
Native: Europe

A beautiful annual herb that grows to 60cm (2ft) high, with hairy stems, simple leaves and flowers that are sky blue with tinges of white and pink. The edible flowers can be picked for salads, or frozen in ice cubes and served in summer drinks.

**Cultivation** Thrives in a sunny location in free-draining, fertile soil. Sow seed outdoors *in situ* about late spring; it will self-seed, coming up year after year. ❊ ❊ ❊ Zone 7.

**Uses** Can be used in annual borders, mixed borders and dotted around vegetable gardens to encourage pollinators. The leaves taste of a salty cucumber, and can be used in salads.

**Wildlife benefits** Excellent at attracting many different bee species. It is pollinated by honeybees and bumblebees attracted by the abundance of nectar.

**Closely related species** *Borago officinalis* 'Alba' has white flowers and 'Variegata' has variegated leaves; both good at encouraging bees. *B. pygmaea* is a short-lived perennial for woodland edges, preferring moister soil.

*Borago officinalis*

*Calendula officinalis*

### *Calendula officinalis*
### ENGLISH MARIGOLD
Family: Asteraceae
Native: Origin unknown

A brightly coloured hardy annual that is a big hit with many different wildlife species. A spring- or summer-flowering bushy plant, it can often grow to 60cm (2ft) high, with lance-shaped, strongly aromatic, pale green leaves. The stunning disc of flowers ranges from yellow and brown to orange.

**Cultivation** Thrives in full sun in well-drained soil. Sow *in situ* in autumn for early spring flowering, or in mid-spring for summer flowering. Deadhead at regular intervals to prolong flowering. ❊ ❊ ❊ Zone 6.

**Uses** The brightly coloured flowers liven up a vegetable patch and encourage beneficial insects, providing natural pest control. Can also be used in hardy annual borders, as fillers for mixed borders, and in window boxes and hanging baskets.

**Wildlife benefits** A favourite with pest-controlling hoverflies, it also attracts pollinating honeybees and bumblebees and the occasional butterfly. Always plant single-flowering cultivars or the species to encourage wildlife. Avoid the double-flowering *C.* 'Art Shades' and Calendula Fiesta Series.

**Closely related species** The field marigold (*Calendula arvensis*) is an annual, 30cm (1ft) high. The colour ranges from yellow to brown, and is excellent for bees.

*Cerinthe major*
HONEYWORT
Family: Boraginaceae
Native: S Europe

An eye-catching hardy annual that produces stunning bright blue bracts and nectar-rich yellow and purple flowers with smooth, hairless, lance-shaped foliage. The stems, which may need supporting with pea sticks, can quickly reach 60cm (2ft) high.

**Cultivation** An undemanding species that will grow in most free-draining garden soils, in full sun or partial shade. The fleshy roots can rot in prolonged wet weather. Propagate by seed *in situ* in autumn or spring, or start off in the greenhouse and harden off before planting in its final position. ❀ ❀ ❀ Zone 5.

**Uses** Looks great in a mixed border, especially amongst grasses and with purple-leaved plants, such as *Physocarpus opulifolius* 'Diabolo' or *Sambucus nigra* 'Black Beauty'. Can also be used in annual borders, although it does tend to self-seed freely around the garden.

**Wildlife benefits** It attracts so many honeybees you can hear them clearly humming on the plant as you walk past. One of the best bee plants for a large or small garden.

**Closely related species** Without doubt the best cultivar of *Cerinthe major* is 'Purpurascens'; the deep purple colour of the bracts is absolutely amazing, and it's just as attractive to bees. *C. minor* is an annual or short-lived perennial for the shady flower border. It reaches 60cm (2ft) high and has nectar-rich yellow, violet or purple flowers.

*Cerinthe major*

*Daucus carota*

*Daucus carota*
WILD CARROT
Family: Apiaceae
Native: Europe to India

We always think of the carrot as a big, orange, edible root, but its not-so-well-known flowers that appear in the second year of growth are both simple and elegant. This 1m (3ft) high biennial produces dense umbels of white flowers that are often tinged purple in the centre in late summer, and have finely cut foliage.

**Cultivation** Grows best in free-draining, slightly acidic soil in full sun, although it will grow well in most soils. Sow *in situ* in spring or autumn, and it will flower the following year. ❀ ❀ ❀ Zone 5.

**Uses** Carrots can be used in all sorts of situations. Try planting in tubs, plant randomly in mixed borders or use as fillers in herbaceous borders. Another good tip is to allow a certain percentage of carrots from the vegetable garden to overwinter and flower next year, attracting many species of beneficial insects into the garden, helping to control pests. Wild carrot is commonly used in wildflower meadow mixes, but tends to die out as the meadow matures.

**Wildlife benefits** The leaves are a food plant for the caterpillars of the swallowtail butterfly, and the flowers are an excellent source of nectar and pollen for bees and various species of hoverfly.

**Closely related species** *D. carota* subsp. *sativus* is the garden carrot with an orange, fleshy taproot; it's equally beneficial to wildlife.

*Dianthus barbatus*
SWEET WILLIAM
Family: Caryophyllaceae
Native: S Europe

A gorgeous, short-lived perennial that is normally grown as a biennial, growing to 60cm (2ft) high. Sweet William produces beautifully fragrant flowers in large, dense heads that are white, pink or red in late spring and early summer, with lance-shaped leaves.

**Cultivation** Grows well in an open, sunny situation in free-draining, fertile soil. Sow seed in late spring to plant out in early autumn, and it'll flower the following spring. Deadhead to promote new flower heads. ❀ ❀ ❀ Zone 4.

**Uses** A cottage garden favourite that can be used in spring bedding displays with wallflowers (*Erysimum cheiri*) and pansies (*Viola* x *wittrockiana*), and a selection of spring-flowering bulbs. Dwarf cultivars, such as *Dianthus barbatus* Roundabout Series, are ideal for tubs and window boxes.

**Wildlife benefits** Nectar-hunting butterflies and bumblebees are attracted to the fragrant flowers. Avoid the many double-flowered cultivars because they are unproductive for visiting insects; only single-flowering species should be selected.

**Closely related species** Another good wildlife-attracting species is *D.* 'Brympton Red', which is an old-fashioned pink with bright crimson single flowers with deeper shading. *D. deltoides*, a maiden pink, is another single-flowering species that is ideal for the rockery or stone wall.

*Dianthus barbatus*

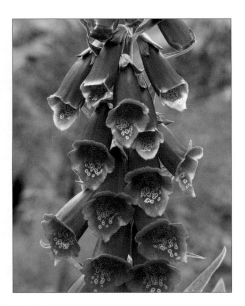

*Digitalis purpurea*

## *Digitalis purpurea*
### FOXGLOVE
Family: Scrophulariaceae
Native: Europe

A fantastic plant with tall spikes of tubular white, pink or purple flowers, with spotted markings inside, that blooms from late spring to early summer. Its nectar-rich flower spikes can reach heights of 90cm–1.5m (3–5ft), and the rough-textured, deep green leaves are found in a basal rosette. It is usually grown as a biennial, but is often a short-lived perennial; every part of the plant is poisonous.

**Cultivation** Grow in moist but well-drained soil that is rich in humus. Foxgloves are a natural woodland plant that can grow in full sun but thrive in semi-shade. Sow seed *in situ* from late summer to autumn for flowering the following year. ❁ ❁ ❁ Zone 4.

**Uses** An excellent plant to brighten up a shady border, especially if using the naturally occurring white form, *D. alba*. It is also a winner if planted randomly throughout a mixed or herbaceous border, and can be an inexpensive way of providing colour in large drifts under trees.

**Wildlife benefits** Excellent for bumblebees seeking nectar. Fallen seed will be eaten by birds foraging in the border. Don't cut back the old flower stems because many insects spend winter inside them in the tubular flowers.

**Closely related species** All *Digitalis* species are particularly good nectar-producing species, although some flowers are smaller than others, hampering bee visitation. Bees will then drill into the side of the flower to obtain the nectar. *D. ferruginea* has rust red flowers. *D. grandiflora*, the large yellow foxglove, has pale yellow flowers netted with brown veins.

## *Dipsacus fullonum*
### COMMON TEASEL
Family: Dipsacaceae
Native: Europe, Asia and N Africa

A majestic architectural biennial that produces nectar-rich, egg-like flower heads on erect stems that can reach 2m (6½ft) high. The pale lilac flowers are borne from midsummer on, and open a few at a time, prolonging the flowering period. Water collects at the base of the stem leaves, providing drinking pockets for small insects.

**Cultivation** Prefers full sun or dappled shade in good, fertile soil, including heavy clay. Sow seed *in situ* in autumn or spring. ❁ ❁ ❁ Zone 3.

**Uses** Best used in a wild garden where the plant can seed freely, or use in a wildflower meadow mix. Teasel can be used in cultivated mixed borders but self-seeding can be a big problem.

**Wildlife benefits** The flowers are visited by bees and butterflies seeking nectar. The seed is loved by birds, such as goldfinches and crossbills, because they have bills long and narrow enough to reach them. The larvae of the marsh fritillary butterfly feed on the leaves.

**Closely related species** Fuller's teasel (*Dipsacus sativus*) is similar in height but has extremely stiff seed heads and, like common teasel, has fleshy seed with an oily coating.

*Dipsacus fullonum*

*Erysimum cheiri*

## *Erysimum cheiri*
### WALLFLOWER
Family: Brassicaceae
Native: S Europe

A sweet-scented, short-lived perennial that is cultivated as a biennial predominantly for spring bedding displays. It is variable in height, ranging from 25–80cm (10–32in); the stems are sturdy, bearing lance-like leaves, and the flower heads range from purple-green to bright yellow, orange and striped red-purple.

**Cultivation** Prefers full sun but will grow in dappled shade in any well-drained soil, especially in alkaline conditions. ❁ ❁ ❁ Zone 7.

**Uses** One of the main ingredients in spring bedding displays. This is mainly because it flowers reliably, but also due to the great range of height and colours that many of the cultivars provide. It is one of the better species for planting into old walls, and can then be allowed to naturalize.

**Wildlife benefits** The sweetly scented flowers attract bees to the pollen and nectar, and butterflies can be seen sitting on the flattened flower parts drinking nectar in spring.

**Closely related species** The cultivar *E.* 'Bowles Mauve' is a bushy, short-lived perennial that has nectar-rich, purple-mauve flowers from late winter to early spring, providing a welcome early source of nectar. The short-lived perennial species are also good for wildlife. *E.* x *allionii* is a pretty, bright orange flowering cross that grows to 60cm (2ft). *E.* x *kewensis* flowers from winter through to summer and sports orange-yellow flowers that will turn purple.

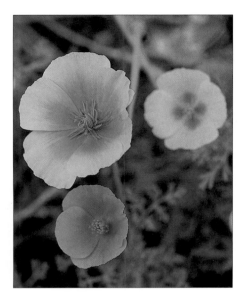

*Eschscholzia californica*

## *Eschscholzia californica*
## CALIFORNIA POPPY
Family: Papaveraceae
Native: NW America

A really pretty hardy annual that provides an inexpensive splash of colour during the spring and summer months. Variable in height and colour, often reaching 60cm (2ft), with flowers ranging from pale yellow to bright orange. The divided foliage has a blue tinge that nicely complements the flower colours.

**Cultivation** Like many annuals, it requires full sun for optimum germination and will grow well in any light, well-drained soil. Sow *in situ* in spring or autumn. ❀ ❀ ❀ Zone 6.

**Uses** California poppies can be used to fill gaps in mixed borders. They are also ideal to use in traditional hardy annual borders, and can even be sown as a filler in a rocky dry garden. They will look good planted next to the purple-flowering *Salvia nemerosa* and the silver-leaved small shrub, *Artemisia* 'Powis Castle'. A very versatile plant that is both heat- and drought-tolerant. Once it has been sown, it will self-seed and come back year after year.

**Wildlife benefits** The bright orange flowers are great at tempting beneficial insects, such as hoverflies, into the garden for nectar. The flowers are also a favourite of bees and bumblebees searching for food.

**Closely related species** The tufted *Eschscholzia caespitose* is smaller than *E. californica*, and is ideal in a rock garden. It has bright yellow flowers and reaches 25cm (10in) high.

## *Helianthus annuus*
## SUNFLOWER
Family: Asteraceae
Native: N and S America

Sunflowers are a great favourite with children, and it's easy to see why when they bear huge, yellow, daisy-like flowers from summer to autumn on stems that can grow up to 5m (17ft) high. The leaves are pale green. Modern cultivars offer a range of tall, medium and dwarf sizes, and a range of colours to suit all tastes.

**Cultivation** To obtain the best growth from a sunflower, grow it in well-drained, fertile soil in full sun. Stake the taller varieties as they grow. Can be sown direct outside in mid-spring, or start off indoors in early spring, hardening off before planting out in late spring. ❀ ❀ ❀ Zone 4.

**Uses** Excellent in a children's garden, and also looks great if planted in large groups in annual borders or dotted around mixed or herbaceous borders. Dwarf varieties, such as *H*. 'Teddy Bear', can be used in tubs and window boxes, intermediate varieties (*H*. 'Taiyo') are ideal for bedding, and the tall *H*. 'Russian Giant' gives height in herbaceous or mixed borders.

**Wildlife benefits** Honeybees and bumblebees love its nectar and pollen, and the flowers are visited by the occasional butterfly. When the flowers fade, the oily seed attracts many birds, including collared doves, greenfinches, nuthatches, long-tailed tits, crossbills and bramblings, as well as other seed-eaters.

**Closely related species** *Helianthus* x *laetiflorus*, reaching 2m (6½ft) high, and *H. salicifolius*, 3m (10ft), are both perennials that can be used effectively in a wild garden or at the back of herbaceous borders.

*Helianthus annuus*

*Heliotropium arborescens*

## *Heliotropium arborescens*
## HELIOTROPE
Family: Boraginaceae
Native: Peru

Heliotrope is a half-hardy shrub that is treated as a half-hardy annual because it doesn't withstand the frost. It bears heads of small, tubular, white, or purple to pink flowers with oblong, rough-textured leaves. It can grow up to 45–60cm (1½–2ft) when grown as an annual. The smell is like sweetly scented marshmallows, which will attract many night-flying insects.

**Cultivation** Prefers full sun but will also grow in dappled shade, in fertile, well-drained soil. Sow seeds in spring, or alternatively take semi-ripe cuttings in autumn before frost damage occurs. ❀ Zone 10.

**Uses** Heliotrope has been used for many years in traditional summer bedding schemes, but it can also be used to fill gaps in mixed borders. When positioning heliotrope, try to plant it around doors and paths to gain maximum benefit from the strongly scented flowers. It's also a big success when used in containers.

**Wildlife benefits** Bees and bumblebees seek out the nectar-rich flowers. The tubular flowers make the nectar accessible to many species of butterfly, such as the comma, painted lady and the colourful peacock. Day-flying moths, for example the hummingbird hawk moth, find the nectar irresistible.

**Closely related species** One of the most popular cultivars is *H. a.* 'Marine', with compact, bushy growth, purple flowers and a height of 45cm (18in).

## *Hesperis matronalis*
### SWEET ROCKET
Family: Brassicaceae
Native: S Europe to Siberia

A gorgeous, scented, summer-flowering biennial or short-lived perennial. The flowers are strongly scented in the evening and are violet to white; their stems grow to 75cm (2½ft) high, and the leaves are smooth and narrowly oval.

**Cultivation** Sweet rocket requires free-draining, neutral to alkaline soil, in a sunny position. Sow seed *in situ* in autumn or spring. ✿ ✿ ✿ Zone 3.

**Uses** Great for planting in mixed borders or as a gap-filler in herbaceous borders. Violet-flowering strains look striking when planted next to the dark foliage of the smoke bush (*Cotinus coggygria* 'Royal Purple') and *Iris* 'Matinata'. Also useful in a wild garden.

**Wildlife benefits** The leaves are a food source for the caterpillars of the orange tip butterfly, and a nectar source for many species of butterfly.

**Closely related species** *Hesperis bicuspidata* is a small, violet-flowered perennial growing to 30cm (1ft) high, and is suitable for growing in rock gardens. *H. tristis* is ideal in the wild garden and for planting in old walls. It is a biennial or short-lived perennial that produces white or cream flowers with the occasional purple.

## *Iberis amara*
### CANDYTUFT
Family: Brassicaceae
Native: W Europe

A lovely, summer-flowering hardy annual with masses of fragrant, white- and pink-domed flower heads with fine, lance-

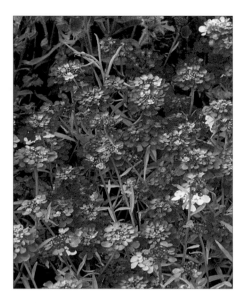

*Iberis amara*

shaped leaves. Fast growing, it quickly reaches 30cm (1ft) high.

**Cultivation** Likes well-drained, chalky soil in a sunny situation. Candytuft will even tolerate poor, dry soils, and also ones with low levels of acidity. Sow *in situ* in spring. ✿ ✿ ✿ Zone 7.

**Uses** A great addition to an annual border, or sow in bare spots to fill up herbaceous beds, a mixed border or a special butterfly border.

**Wildlife benefits** The fragrant, nectar-rich flowers attract bees seeking pollen and nectar. Also a great butterfly plant for nectar-hungry adults, such as the small gatekeeper.

**Closely related species** *Iberis umbellata* Fairy Series is a popular choice. Its heads of small, four-petalled flowers in shades of purple, pink, red or white appear from summer to early autumn and are really

popular with butterflies. *I. saxatilis* is a dwarf evergreen sub-shrub which produces numerous small white flowers in late spring and early summer. Excellent in the rock garden, or as an edging plant in a mixed border.

## *Limnanthes douglasii*
### POACHED EGG PLANT
Family: Limnanthaceae
Native: California and S Oregon

A stunning, fast-growing hardy annual reaching just 15cm (6in) high. The prolific white flowers with yellow centres are cup-shaped, and appear from early to late summer; the feathery leaves are light green.

**Cultivation** Easily grown in moderately fertile soil with added organic matter to aid moisture retention. Position in full sun for the best growth. Sow direct into the soil in autumn or spring. ✿ ✿ ✿ Zone 8.

**Uses** Ideal for a hardy annual border, or as edging for mixed or herbaceous borders. To create an informal look to a pavement or patio, sow the seed between the cracks; the young growth will soften the look of the hard landscape and add colour. If you have a hedge that's bare at the bottom and facing a sunny location, benefit the wildlife by sowing seed here. It'll create a fantastic display of flowers in summer, that's also a haven for several species of insects.

**Wildlife benefits** The brightly coloured, lightly scented flowers are an excellent nectar source for bees. They also attract an abundance of hoverflies that are great predators of garden pests, such as aphids.

**Closely related species** *Limnanthes douglasii* var. *sulphurea* has stunning yellow flowers that are just as attractive to visiting insects.

*Hesperis matronalis*

*Limnanthes douglasii*

*Lobelia erinus*
**EDGING LOBELIA**
Family: Campanulaceae
Native: S Africa

This small perennial is normally grown as a short annual, 7.5–15cm (3–6in) high, in summer bedding schemes. The slender stems support small, ovate leaves, and the flowers are white to blue and violet.

**Cultivation** Sow seed indoors in early spring. Harden off before planting outside in late spring in rich, moist soil. Grow in full sun or light shade for best results. ❁ Zone 9.

**Uses** Choose between the upright edging and trailing kind. Upright cultivars, such as *L.* 'Cambridge Blue', are ideal plants for edging summer bedding schemes and lining pathways. Trailing cultivars, such as *L.* 'Colour Cascade', are one of the best pendulous plants for window boxes, hanging baskets and tubs.

**Wildlife benefits** The flowers are a favourite with bees, daytime moths and butterflies seeking nectar. At night, as the light fades, take a torch outside and you will marvel at the number of night-flying moths visiting the flowers for their sugary drink. One plant can often be covered in many different species of moth.

**Closely related species** *Lobelia cardinalis* is a short-lived perennial that flowers profusely in late summer, growing to 90cm (3ft) high. The spikes of stunning, scarlet, tubular flowers attract day-flying moths and butterflies. Best planted in drifts in a bog garden or by a stream edge.

*Lobelia erinus*

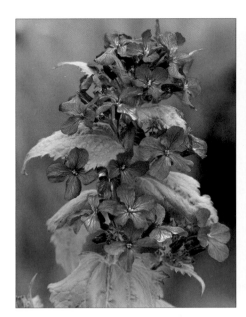

*Lunaria annua*

*Lunaria annua*
**HONESTY**
Family: Brassicaceae
Native: C and S Europe

A biennial, growing 90cm (3ft) high, with lanceolate to cordate leaves that are coarsely toothed. Honesty produces beautiful, purple-red flowers in late spring and summer. The seed heads are flat and rounded and, as they mature, turn attractive silvery grey, making them more frequently used in floral arrangements than the flowers.

**Cultivation** Grow in well-drained soil in full sun or dappled shade. To attract the greatest number of insects, place in full sun. Sow seed *in situ* in late summer to have flowering plants the following year. ❁ ❁ ❁ Zone 8.

**Uses** If you have a shady corner of the garden, honesty is the ideal candidate to brighten up the area. Can also be used to provide a rich nectar source around a woodland edge, and is excellent when naturalized in a wild garden.

**Wildlife benefits** The scented flowers attract butterflies and moths, and bees and birds are often observed feeding on insects on the plant. The leaves of honesty are the larvae food plant of the orange tip butterfly. When the plant sets seed, it's quickly eaten by bullfinches.

**Closely related species** Perennial honesty (*Lunaria redivia*) is similar to *L. annua*, except the leaves are finely toothed and the plant lives for three years or more. The flowers are also scented and attract visiting insects.

*Myosotis arvensis*

*Myosotis arvensis*
**FIELD FORGET-ME-NOT**
Family: Boraginaceae
Native: Europe, NE Africa and Asia

A pretty annual (or sometimes biennial) that will grow to 50cm (20in) high. It has lance-shaped leaves, and the spring to autumn flowers are bright blue to dark purple, being followed by a healthy production of seed.

**Cultivation** Will grow in sun or semi-shade, and likes fertile, well-drained soil. Propagate by seed in autumn. ❁ ❁ ❁ Zone 6.

**Uses** Good for naturalizing in the wild garden. The closely related *Myosotis sylvatica* and its hybrids are used in spring bedding to provide a splash of colour after the dull winter months. Plant with wallflowers (*Erysimum cheiri*), tulips and pansies (*Viola* x *wittrockiana*) for a stunning spring display.

**Wildlife benefits** Bees and bumblebees seek out the flowers in spring for pollen and nectar. Occasionally butterflies drink the nectar. In autumn, birds such as chaffinches, linnets and a number of finches feast on the seeds.

**Closely related species** The water forget-me-not (*M. scorpioides*) is an excellent perennial that's a spring-flowering marginal plant. Unlike *M. arvensis*, which prefers well-drained soil, the roots of this species flourish at the edge of a pond in moist soil or shallow water. Colourful cultivars of *M. sylvatica* include 'Blue Ball' (a small, compact plant with rich indigo flowers), 'Blue Bird' (tall with deep blue flowers), and 'Rosea' (tall with pink flowers).

## *Nicotiana sylvestris*
## TOBACCO PLANT
Family: Solanaceae
Native: Argentina

A perennial (grown as a half-hardy annual) that's best described as graceful, elegant and simple. The large, elliptic leaves are a terrific feature, as are the 1.5m (5ft) stems with long, white, tubular flowers that are sweetly fragrant on summer evenings. All *Nicotiana* species are poisonous.

**Cultivation** Thrives in well-drained garden soil in sun or shade. Can be grown as a biennial if late spring flowering is required, in which case sow in late summer under glass, and plant out in early to mid-autumn after hardening off. ❁ Zone 8.

**Uses** Good for height in summer bedding schemes. It also looks extremely lush if used in tropical bedding schemes, especially if planted with sunflowers (*Helianthus annuus*), cannas and busy lizzies (*Impatiens*). One of the great assets of the tobacco plant is that it grows extremely well in sun or shade, making it one of the most versatile annuals.

**Wildlife benefits** The fragrant evening flowers are a big attraction to moths and, as the food chain progresses, bats. Day-flying moths are also drawn to the long, white, tubular flowers for a satisfying drink of nectar.

**Closely related species** All nicotianas are great for attracting moths. *N. alata*, often called jasmine tobacco, is a perennial (grown as an annual) that is often used in summer bedding schemes and pots. The

*Nicotiana sylvestris*

*Oenothera biennis*

cultivars are uniform in growth reaching 75cm (30in) high. *Nicotiana* 'Domino Series' are cultivars that are relatively slow-growing bushy annuals in a range of colours from white to pink and red; ideal for window boxes.

## *Oenothera biennis*
## EVENING PRIMROSE
Family: Onagraceae
Native: E North America

A true biennial with tall spikes of yellow scented flowers reaching up to 90cm (3ft) tall in summer. The leaves have a bluish tinge, with the basal rosette leaves being 10–30cm (4–12in) long and the stem leaves 8–15cm (3–6in) long.

**Cultivation** Needs full sun on sandy, well-drained soil. Sow seed in late spring and early summer for next year's flowers. ❁ ❁ ❁ Zone 4.

**Uses** Can be used in a mixed border or to fill gaps in herbaceous borders. Excellent for naturalizing in wild areas where birds can forage about in the undergrowth for its seed.

**Wildlife benefits** The evening-scented flowers attract late flying bees to collect pollen and night-flying insects, such as moths, for a nightcap of nectar. Other insects drawn to the plant are hunted by hungry warblers. Evening primrose is a prolific seeder, and attracts birds such as finches, crossbills, chaffinches and siskins seeking an easy meal.

**Closely related species** *Oenothera speciosa*, the white evening primrose, is a short-lived summer-flowering perennial that grows to 45cm (18in) high. *O. caespitosa* is

*Papaver rhoeas*

only 12cm (5in) high and ideal for the rock garden. Its white, fragrant flowers open at sunset in summer. Both are excellent nectar and pollen producers.

## *Papaver rhoeas*
## CORN POPPY
Family: Papaveraceae
Native: Temperate Old World

This tall annual, up to 90cm (3ft) high, bears big, bright red flowers from late spring to summer. They are commonly seen on waste ground and in gardens. After flowering, the plant has heads full of nutritious seed.

**Cultivation** Grow in full sun in any well-drained soil. Sow seed direct in the soil in early spring. ❁ ❁ ❁ Zone 5.

**Uses** A welcome addition to an annual border, providing a big splash of colour. Also commonly included in an annual cornfield wildflower mix.

**Wildlife benefits** A popular insect plant, with the flowers attracting bees and bumblebees, hoverflies and the occasional butterfly. The seed is eaten by sparrows, siskins, linnets, dunnocks and a number of finches.

**Closely related species** The Oriental poppy (*Papaver orientale*) and opium poppy (*P. somniferum*) are excellent in gardens. The former is a bold plant, loved by bees, and can be used in herbaceous or mixed borders. It comes in many colours, from white, red and purple to pink. The latter can be used similarly to *P. rhoeas,* and the flower colour ranges from white to purple.

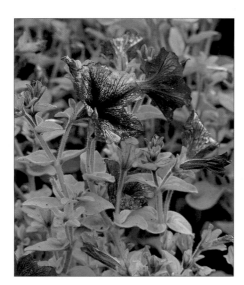

*Petunia* x *hybrida*

## *Petunia* x *hybrida*
### PETUNIA
Family: Solanaceae
Native: Garden origin

An excellent, versatile half-hardy annual that can be used in many situations. Grow as an upright bedding plant or as a trailing plant for hanging baskets and tubs. It produces large trumpet flowers, that vary in colour from white, pink and purple to reds and yellows, throughout summer until the first frosts. The leaves are green and lance-shaped.

**Cultivation** Petunias thrive in hot, dry summers but languish in wet, cool weather when root rot can occur. Requires a sunny situation that is sheltered from the wind. Remove deadheads to encourage new flowering. Can be prone to cucumber mosaic virus and tomato spotted wilt. ❀ Zone 7.

**Uses** The trailing cultivars are ideal for hanging baskets. Cultivars found in the Cascade Series are excellent for wildlife because they have single flowers, making the nectar more accessible. The Recoverer Series includes a number of upright cultivars that are ideal for incorporating in summer bedding displays. Do not grow double cultivars such as the Bonanza Series.

**Wildlife benefits** Bees are keen daytime visitors to the trumpet flowers, whereas moths are drawn to the sweet-smelling flowers in early evening.

**Closely related species** *Petunia axillaris* offers simplicity and has large white flowers, while the relatively prostrate *P. integrefolia* bears violet to rose red flowers. Petunia cultivars 'Resisto' and 'Plum Crazy' perform better in wet and windy conditions.

## *Silybum marianum*
### MILK THISTLE
Family: Asteraceae
Native: Mediterranean,
SW Europe to Afghanistan

A fantastic biennial that looks just as spectacular in the wild as it does in the garden. It grows to 1.5m (5ft) high, and produces tall, purple-pink thistle flowers in summer that are slightly scented. The leaves have unusual white veins and sharp spines around the edges.

**Cultivation** Grow in full sun in well-drained soil. Sow in autumn for flowers the following summer. The young growth is prone to snail damage. ❀ ❀ ❀ Zone 7.

**Uses** A brilliant plant, ideally suited to the wild garden, or cultivate and control in a mixed border. Remove any unwanted plants or it'll take over.

**Wildlife benefits** Bees and bumblebees are frequent visitors. When the seed matures it is a real favourite with goldfinches.

**Closely related species** *Silybum eburneum* is very similar to *S. marianum* except the stems are white to pale green, and the leaves have yellow-brown spines and are at least twice as big.

## *Tagetes patula*
### FRENCH MARIGOLD
Family: Asteraceae
Native: Mexico and Guatemala

The subtle orange flowers are a real winner for many insects. This is a half-hardy annual which grows to 20–50cm (8–20in) high and flowers all summer until the first

*Silybum marianum*

*Tagetes patula*

frosts. The deeply divided leaves are attractive and add a tropical look to a border.

**Cultivation** Prefers full sun in fertile, well-drained garden scil. Sow indoors in early spring and plant out in late spring after hardening off. Deadhead to prolong the flowering period. ❀ Zone 9.

**Uses** An excellent edging plant for a summer bedding scheme. A mix of just African marigolds (*Tagetes erecta*) and French marigolds with a simple dot plant in the middle to provide height is absolutely stunning. Both can also be used as companion plants in vegetable gardens to attract beneficial insects to prey on pests, or act as pest deterrents.

**Wildlife benefits** Select species or single-flowered cultivars, as they are popular with many species of hoverfly and several butterflies. The hoverflies (and their larvae) will feed on 40–50 aphids daily. Avoid the many double-flowered cultivars, such as 'Honeycomb', because they are of little use to wildlife due to the many petals produced.

**Closely related species** All single-flowering *Tagetes* are excellent for wildlife, and many are also used in companion planting. *T. minuta* has been effective in helping to prevent the spread of garden weeds, such as celandine (*Ranunculus ficaria*) and ground elder (*Aegopodium podagraria*). *T. minuta* can also be used for planting between potato rows to provide a deterrent against the destructive keeled slugs. However, *T. patula* doesn't reliably protect brassicas against the cabbage butterfly.

*Tropaeolum majus*
## NASTURTIUM
Family: Tropaeolaceae
Native: Columbia to Bolivia

This strong-growing annual climber is a great asset to any wildlife garden. It produces trumpet-shaped flowers in reds, oranges and yellows from early summer to the first frosts. The trailing stems grow to around 60cm (2ft) long, and are clothed with bluish-green leaves.

**Cultivation** Nasturtiums thrive in poor, well-drained soil in a sunny site or partial shade. If grown in fertile soil, too much leafy growth will be made at the expense of flowers. Sow *in situ* in late spring. ❀ Zone 8.

**Uses** Adds colour in herb containers, vegetable hanging baskets and window boxes. Often grown in the vegetable garden to lure aphids away from other more valuable crops. The cabbage white butterflies tend to lay their eggs on the nasturtiums' leaves instead of on brassicas, such as cabbages.

**Wildlife benefits** The nectar-rich flowers are visited by butterflies and bees. Ladybirds, parasitic wasps and hoverflies, all voracious aphid-eating insects, are also drawn to the plant.

**Closely related species** Cultivars come as trailing plants and dwarf, bushy types. Choose cultivars with single flowers, such as Tom Thumb Series, with flowers in a range of colours and about 25cm (10in) high. The herbaceous climber, Canary creeper (*Tropaeolum peregrinum*), grown as an annual, hits 2m (6½ft) high with bright yellow flowers set off by grey-green leaves.

*Tropaeolum majus*

*Verbena bonariensis*

*Verbena bonariensis*
## TALL VERBENA
Family: Verbenaceae
Native: S America

The abundance of butterflies, bees and moths that visit the clusters of nectar-rich flowers of this annual (or short-lived perennial) is astounding. It grows to 1.8m (6ft) high and bears blue, violet and purple flowers. The leaves are toothed and lance-shaped.

**Cultivation** Grows best in a sunny site in any well-drained soil. Because it seeds freely around the garden, it will need to be thinned to stop it becoming invasive. Best to sow indoors and plant out where required. ❀ ❀ Zone 8.

**Uses** Ideal for an annual bedding scheme, especially if height is needed. It also looks great if used to add colour in mixed borders. A good wildlife idea is to plant it as the sole plant along the sunny side of a path for about 6m (20ft). When in flower there should be dozens of butterflies nectaring on the flowers, clearly visible from the path.

**Wildlife benefits** It attracts more butterflies than the butterfly bush (*Buddleja davidii*) because it flowers for longer. It also flowers when many other nectar plants have finished, and it therefore gives butterflies an essential energy boost, especially if they are to survive the winter months. The hummingbird hawk moth, a day-time flying species, loves the flowers, as do many night-flying species that visit the flowers at dusk.

**Closely related species** *Verbena* x *hybrida* and *V. rigida* are half-hardy annuals which are used frequently in hanging baskets and window boxes. They are both popular with wildlife, especially moths.

*Zinnia elegans*
## ZINNIA
Family: Asteraceae
Native: Mexico

A half-hardy annual with pretty, daisy-like florets from summer to the first frosts. The tiny petals range in colour from red, white, yellow and orange to pink, scarlet, lilac and purple. The stems can reach from 60–90cm (2–3ft) in height, and are graced with simple, lance-shaped green leaves.

**Cultivation** Zinnias grow extremely well in full sun, in free-draining soil. Warm, dry summers are best; they'll perform poorly in cold, wet seasons. Deadhead regularly to promote new flowers. ❀ Zone 9.

**Uses** A colourful addition to any summer bedding scheme, window box or container. Also use in tropical bedding schemes or summer bedding displays. The cultivars' flowers can be any colour except blue, making them ideal for any colour scheme.

**Wildlife benefits** The flowers are visited frequently by bees seeking nectar and pollen. They also attract the occasional butterfly.

**Closely related species** Cultivars of *Zinnia elegans* are available in many different flower shapes. The dahlia-flower kind, such as the pom-pom types (as in the Marvel Series, or cultivars resembling the cactus-flowered dahlia, for example *Z*. 'Burpees Zenith') are very pretty, but by far the best for wildlife are the simple daisy blooms of the old-fashioned *Z. haageana* 'Old Mexico'. The annual *Z. angustifolia* is ideal for the rock garden. It grows 40cm (16in) high and bears orange, yellow-brown flowers with black or deep purple centres.

*Zinnia elegans*

# BULBS

*Allium giganteum*
## ORNAMENTAL ONION
Family: Alliaceae
Native: C Asia

This spring-flowering ornamental onion has large, round flower heads that can reach 10cm (4in) across, on stems 90cm–1.8m (3–6ft) tall. The scores of tiny individual flowers are star-shaped and purple or, occasionally, white. The grey-green foliage contrasts well with the flower colour. A wonderful genus, excellent at providing nectar for bees and many other insects.

**Cultivation** Alliums like well-drained soil in a sunny location. Plant bulbs 15cm (6in) deep, and leave the flower heads on the plant after flowering to provide a habitat for insects and because they look very attractive, especially adorned with frost. ❀ ❀ ❀ Zone 8.

**Uses** For maximum visual impact, plant bulbs throughout herbaceous or mixed borders, from the middle ranks to the back (with the tallest plants). *Allium giganteum* is thrilling next to plants with silver, blue or purple foliage or flowers, for example sea holly (*Eryngium giganteum*), the smoke bush (*Cotinus coggygria* 'Royal Purple') and honeywort (*Cerinthe major* 'Purpurascens').

**Wildlife benefits** Good at attracting bees, white butterflies and many other insects seeking a rich source of nectar. Choose carefully to have several allium species in flower over a long period, ensuring a steady supply of nectar.

**Closely related species** All alliums are an excellent source of nectar for wildlife. *A. christophii*, the star of Persia, reaches

*Allium giganteum*

*Chionodoxa luciliae*

20–50cm (8–20 in) in height, and supports purple-violet flower heads. *A. cernum*, the wild onion, has flowers ranging from white through pale and deep pink, to maroon.

*Chionodoxa luciliae*
## GLORY OF THE SNOW
Family: Hyacinthaceae
Native: W Turkey

A pretty bulb with soft violet-blue flowers and a small white centre; the leaves can be 20cm (8in) long, and the flowers open on stalks 30cm (12in) high. It's closely related to *Scilla* and the two species, both spring flowering, are sometimes difficult to distinguish.

**Cultivation** Glory of the snow is easy to grow, thriving in any good, well-drained soil in full sun or light shade. Plant the extremely small bulbs in autumn. ❀ ❀ ❀ Zone 4.

**Uses** Ideal in the wild garden, or for planting beneath shrubs and taller plants in the mixed border. It can also be planted in large drifts in grassed areas that are cut down in summer. This looks really eye-catching, and provides a nectar-rich restaurant for spring-flying insects.

**Wildlife benefits** Many species of insect, especially bees, visit the nectar- and pollen-rich flowers. Cultivars of *Chionodoxa luciliae* include 'Alba' with white flowers and 'Rosea' with pink flowers, both good insect attractors.

**Closely related species** *C. forbesii* bears deep blue flowers and a white centre, is as beneficial as *C. luciliae*, and grows up to 30cm (12in) high. *C.* 'Tmoli' is a dwarf cultivar with bright blue flowers reaching 10cm (4in).

*Crocus chrysanthus*

*Crocus chrysanthus*
## CROCUS
Family: Iridaceae
Native: Balkans and Turkey

A spring-flowering bulb that is an important early source of pollen and nectar for bees. The colour ranges from creamy yellow to golden, with the petals arranged in a tube that can be up to 10cm (4in) long. The narrow leaves are dull green and contrast well with the flowers.

**Cultivation** Provide well-drained, moderately fertile soil in sun or partial shade, sheltered from the wind. Plant in autumn, possibly encasing the bulbs in wire mesh when there's a danger that burrowing mice, rabbits and other pests may eat them. ❀ ❀ ❀ Zone 4.

**Uses** It is ideal for naturalizing in grassland or creating colourful pockets in shrub or mixed borders. The cultivars range from blue, violet, purple and white to many different shades of yellow, making it easy to select one for a particular colour theme.

**Wildlife benefits** Bees visit the tubular flowers for nectar and pollen. Cultivars can also be used in the wildlife garden, including 'Blue Peter' with rich, deep purple petals on the outside and soft blue inside. 'Zenith' is a lovely violet-blue on the outside and silver-blue inside.

**Closely related species** Many species of crocus will not tolerate large amounts of summer rain, and care is therefore needed when selecting those for the garden. *Crocus tommasinianus* and *C. vernus* are more robust than most species, and suit a range of conditions.

## *Eranthis hyemalis*
### WINTER ACONITE
Family: Ranunculaceae
Native: S Europe

One of the first flowers of the year to emerge, starting in late winter and ending in early spring. It provides a display of bright yellow, buttercup-like flowers, and reaches 10cm (4in) high. Many tubers need to be planted to make an effective carpet of flowers.

**Cultivation** Winter aconites naturally occur in damp woodland and shady places, and in gardens thrive in deep, humus-rich, preferably heavy soil in full sun or partial shade. Like the snowdrop (*Galanthus*), it is difficult to establish from dry tubers. Divide clusters and replant when still in leaf ("in the green"). ❀ ❀ ❀ Zone 5.

**Uses** It tolerates partial shade and is therefore ideal for planting under deciduous trees, brightening up parts of the garden that would otherwise be devoid of foliage and colour in late winter. Also plant the tubers under winter-flowering shrubs, such as honeysuckle (*Lonicera fragrantissima*) or Persian ironwood (*Parrotia persica*). Plant in large groups for the best effect.

**Wildlife benefits** An early source of pollen for bees and the first of the emerging insects. The cultivar 'Aurantiaca' sports orange flowers and is equally good for wildlife. Birds may peck at the open flowers.

**Closely related species** *Eranthis cilicica* and *E.* x *tubergenii* are ideal for growing in pots and displaying in a cold conservatory or alpine house. *E. cilicica* flowers later than *E. hyemalis* and has leaves that are tinged bronze when first opening. It is a good pollen producer whereas *E.* x *tubergenii* is a sterile hybrid with abortive anthers; no pollen is produced, and it has little value to wildlife.

*Eranthis hyemalis*

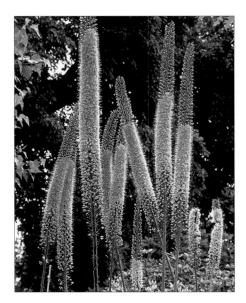

*Eremurus stenophyllus*

## *Eremurus stenophyllus*
### FOXTAIL LILY
Family: Asphodelaceae
Native: C Asia to W Pakistan

An excellent, eye-catching architectural plant for any garden. This species and its cultivars have flower colours ranging from beautiful rich golden colours and coppery yellows to orange, red and pink. The tall flower stems can reach up to 1.5m (5ft) and are complemented well by the linear, sometimes hairy, dark green leaves.

**Cultivation** As the foxtail lily naturally occurs in rocky, semi-desert areas, it requires fertile, well-drained soil and full sun. Winter is a crucial time – if the ground is too wet the rhizome may rot and die, but without a cold spell it won't flower well. Taller cultivars and species require staking, especially in a windy site. Mulch with bracken in winter to prevent frost damage. ❀ ❀ ❀ Zone 5.

**Uses** Very effective when planted in large numbers. The most economical way to create new plants is by dividing clumps after flowering. Looks magnificent when used among old-fashioned roses, poking up through the bushes, and in mixed borders. Place amongst hot colours, such as *Sambucus racemosa* 'Plumosa Aurea' whose leaves turn from bronze to flashy yellow.

**Wildlife benefits** The striking hot colours of the flower spikes are great attractants for nectar-hunting bees and bumblebees.

**Closely related species** All *Eremurus* species are good at attracting summer bees to the garden. A white species,

*E. himalaicus*, produces gorgeous flowers 2–2.5m (6–8ft) tall, and *E. robustus* sports pink blooms at much the same height. A small species, *E. spectabilis*, reaches 1.2m (4ft) high and bears pale yellow flowers with red anthers in early summer.

## *Fritillaria imperialis*
### CROWN IMPERIAL
Family: Liliaceae
Native: S Turkey to Kashmir

An exotic bulb with a tall stem reaching up to 1.5m (5ft) high, adorned with bright green, glossy leaves. The stem culminates in an impressive flower head of bright orange flowers in spring. The individual flowers are bell-shaped and nodding.

**Cultivation** The crown imperial prefers well-drained, fertile soil in semi-shade or full sun. The bulbs need to be planted at a depth of 20cm (8in) in autumn. ❀ ❀ ❀ Zone 4.

**Uses** Plant in the peripheral areas of a woodland garden, to brighten up a border or mixed scheme. The flower heads are best displayed against a solid green background, for example an evergreen shrub such as laurel (*Prunus lusitanica* or *P. laurocerasus*), or a yew (*Taxus baccata*) hedge.

**Wildlife benefits** A fantastic source of nectar for several species of birds, including blue tits and black caps. Bees and bumblebees frequently visit the large orange flowers.

**Closely related species** Nectar-rich cultivars are available in red and yellow forms. *Fritillaria imperialis* 'Rubra Maxima' is very sturdy, bearing red flowers, whereas *F. i.* 'Lutea' has lovely yellow flowers. The species, *F. persica*, flowers in spring after reaching 1.5m (5ft) tall. The flowers are brown, with 10–20 on any one head.

*Fritillaria imperialis*

*Fritillaria meleagris*

*Hyacinthoides non-scripta*

## *Fritillaria meleagris*
## SNAKE'S HEAD FRITILLARY
Family: Liliaceae
Native: Europe

The beautiful, solitary flowers appear in spring. They are found in different shades of purple and white, in a checkerboard pattern, reaching to 30cm (12in) high on slender stems. The narrow leaves are grey-green.

**Cultivation** The snake's head fritillary's natural habitat is a damp water meadow, meaning it needs damp garden soil when the bulb is in full leaf. Site in full sun or semi-shade. Propagate by seed when ripe. ❀ ❀ ❀ Zone 4.

**Uses** Best planted in areas of grass that can be left long, not being mown until the bulb's leaves have died down in summer. Plant numerous bulbs together for maximum impact. They can also be used in mixed borders, but avoid soil that might dry out.

**Wildlife benefits** The chequered flowers produce an important, early source of nectar for many insects, especially bees and butterflies. The white 'Alba' is also favoured by bees.

**Closely related species** *F. pyrenaica* is a spring-flowering species with lance-shaped, grey-green leaves and nodding, solitary, deep brown or blackish flowers. It grows 15–30cm (6–12in) tall and is ideal for the herbaceous border. *F. verticillata*, to 90cm (3ft) high, is another good spring-flowering species.

## *Hyacinthoides non-scripta*
## ENGLISH BLUEBELL
Family: Hyacinthaceae
Native: W Europe

It has drooping heads packed with blue-violet (or occasionally pink or white) tubular flowers. The leaves are narrow and curved, and both leaves and flowers can reach 40cm (16in) high.

**Cultivation** Its natural habitat is oak or beech woodlands. It therefore flourishes in gardens where the soil is rich in humus, and there's partial shade. If planted in a sunny area, the intense light will bleach the flowers. Propagate by division of established colonies. ❀ ❀ ❀ Zone 5.

**Uses** Plant in large groups under deciduous trees, in woodland gardens or in flower beds. Excellent if used in a shady area where it is allowed to naturalize. Do not plant beside the Spanish bluebell (*H. hispanica*) because the two species will hybridize, and *H. hispanica* will eventually take over.

**Wildlife benefits** Bluebells are loved by bees seeking pollen and nectar in spring, and by the occasional butterfly. The white *H. h.* 'Alba' and pink 'Rose' also attract insects.

**Closely related species** *Hyacinthus orientalis* can be grown outside, reaches 25cm (10in) high, and is packed with scores of tiny flowers. The different cultivars provide a wide range of colours, and attract bees seeking pollen and nectar.

## *Muscari armeniacum*
## GRAPE HYACINTH
Family: Hyacinthaceae
Native: SE Europe to Caucasus

A colourful spring-flowering bulb reaching 20cm (8in) tall. The bright blue, fragrant flowers are bell-shaped and produce good quantities of rich nectar. The green leaves are long and narrow, often being paler on the upper surface. The grape hyacinth is a real favourite with wildlife gardeners.

**Cultivation** The bulb prefers full sun to dappled shade. Plant in autumn to a depth of 7.5cm (3in), in large groups to give a strong, bold effect. Divide occasionally to improve the show. ❀ ❀ ❀ Zone 4.

**Uses** Excellent for a mixed border, woodland edge or for lining a path. The grape hyacinth is not an ideal species for growing in grass because it can't cope with the competition. It can also be used in hanging baskets in spring for extra colour, alongside cowslips, polyanthus and forget-me-nots, as well as other bulbs, such as dwarf daffodils and tulips.

**Wildlife benefits** Grape hyacinth is an early source of nectar for insects, particularly for bees and butterflies such as the brimstone and small tortoiseshell. Do not use 'Saphir' because the flowers are sterile and of little value to wildlife.

**Closely related species** The tassel grape hyacinth (*M. comosum*), a late spring-flowering bulb with brownish-yellow flowers, is good at attracting wildlife. The cultivar, *M. c.* 'Plumosum' is sterile and of limited use to wildlife. *M. azureum* bears bright blue flowers.

*Muscari armeniacum*

*Narcissus pseudonarcissus*

## *Narcissus pseudonarcissus*
## WILD DAFFODIL
Family: Amaryllidaceae
Native: W Europe to N England

There are scores of different daffodil cultivars, vastly ranging in size and strengths of yellow, orange and white. *N. pseudonarcissus*, sometimes called the lent lily, will grow to 30cm (12in) tall and bears yellow trumpet-shaped flowers in spring and long, linear leaves with a blue tinge.

**Cultivation** Daffodils grow in any good garden soil, in full sun or semi-shade. Plant in autumn to a depth of 7.5cm (3in). When the bulbs stop flowering in abundance, lift, divide and replant. This will allow them to flower profusely again. ❀ ❀ ❀ Zone 4.

**Uses** A versatile plant that can be used in numerous situations. Daffodils can be naturalized in grass in large numbers for the best effect. Use under deciduous trees or in groups in mixed borders. Dwarf cultivars can be used in rock gardens, hanging baskets, window boxes and tubs. The taller cultivars can also be used in spring bedding schemes.

**Wildlife benefits** The trumpet-shaped flowers provide a welcome early nectar source for bees and bumblebees. Do not use double flowering varieties, such as 'Texas', because they have no wildlife value.

**Closely related species** Several small species are excellent for wildlife. The hoop-petticoat daffodil (*N. bulbocodium* subsp. *bulbocodium*) is a vigorous species reaching 8–15cm (3–6in) tall, which successfully naturalizes in grass. *N. cyclamineus*, which grows to 15cm (6in) high and flowers from late winter to early spring, produces delicate, nodding flowers with reflexed petals. *N.* 'February Gold', an early spring flowering cultivar, is 30cm (12in) tall.

## *Sternbergia lutea*
## AUTUMN DAFFODIL
Family: Amaryllidaceae
Native: Spain to Afghanistan

An autumn-flowering bulb with sweetly scented, crocus-like flowers. The flowers are deep yellow and grow to 2.5–20cm (1–8in) tall. The bright green leaves are slender and narrow, appearing with or just after the flowers.

**Cultivation** It prefers a hot, sunny site with free-draining soil that dries out in summer. The bulbs are naked at this time of year, and it is essential that they are dry or they will rot. Although the plant is frost hardy, it needs the protection of a sunny wall in colder areas. Propagate by division of offsets when dormant. ❀ ❀ Zone 7.

**Uses** Plant out in a sunny herbaceous or mixed border; rock gardens are also ideal. The autumn-flowering daffodil can also be used in borders against a conservatory or greenhouse, which will offer extra warmth and protection during the winter months, when frost damage can kill the plants.

**Wildlife benefits** This nectar-rich plant is a real autumn bonus for insects, especially bees and bumblebees, because many of their abundant nectar suppliers have finished flowering.

**Closely related species** One of the most robust species for the garden is *S. sicula*, which has funnel-shaped yellow flowers that grow from 2.5–7cm (1–2¾in) in autumn. Another reliable species is *S. clusiana*, which produces yellow or greenish-yellow autumn flowers which are 4–8cm (1½–3in) with grey-green leaves.

*Sternbergia lutea*

*Tulipa biflora*

## *Tulipa biflora*
## TULIP
Family: Liliaceae
Native: S Yugoslavia and SE Russia

A real winner with wildlife, *T. biflora* sports yellow-centred white flowers in early spring with a lovely, sweet smell. It is a small species, just 5–10cm (2–4in) high with narrow, oval, green-grey petals and thin leaves with a bluish edge and red tip.

**Cultivation** Tulips thrive in full sun. Plant the bulbs 15cm (6 in) deep in well-drained, fertile soil. Avoid using fertilizer that's high in nitrogen or fresh manure because they encourage soft growth that is susceptible to disease. Propagate by seed in autumn. ❀ ❀ ❀ Zone 7.

**Uses** Ideal for planting permanently at the front section of a mixed border, or in a rock garden. Alternatively, grow the bulbs in pots and stand them around the garden to provide spring colour. When the bulbs have finished flowering, replace the pots in late spring with summer bedding plants. This is an excellent way to keep changing the look of your garden.

**Wildlife benefits** Recent observations at a tulip trail with many different species and cultivars showed that *T. biflora* was the most frequently visited plant. It was a magnet mainly for bees, though bumblebees also sought out the nectar and pollen.

**Closely related species**
*T. kaufmanniana*, an early flowering species that has red and cream striped flowers, reaching 20cm (8in) high, is a great attraction for bees and bumblebees seeking pollen and nectar. *T. sprengeri*, with bright red flowers, and *T. sylvestris*, bearing golden blooms that are sometimes tinged pink, are the best species for naturalizing in grass.

# PERENNIALS

*Achillea filipendula*
**FERN-LEAVED YARROW**
Family: Asteraceae
Native: Caucasus, Iran,
Afghanistan and C Asia
A graceful, upright plant, culminating in large, flat, yellow flower heads during summer. The flat heads provide an ideal landing platform for many visiting insects seeking nectar. The stems grow up to 1.2m (4ft) high, and bear fern-like foliage that is extremely attractive.
**Cultivation** Prefers a site in full sun in any good, well-drained soil. Propagate by division in autumn or early spring. ❀ ❀ ❀ Zone 3.
**Uses** An excellent structural plant for the herbaceous border, the flat flower heads providing an unusual shape. Plant next to species with red or orange flowers, such as crocosmia and rudbeckia, to create a focal point.
**Wildlife benefits** Hoverflies swarm to the nectar, while bees, bumblebees and numerous other species of insects are also frequent visitors. Favoured by insect- and seed-eating birds, especially house sparrows, tits and chaffinches.
**Closely related species** All achilleas are great insect attractors. *A. millefolium* is one of the best, being a firm favourite with hoverflies, wasps and bees. Birds feed on the insects and mature seeds.

*Achillea filipendula*

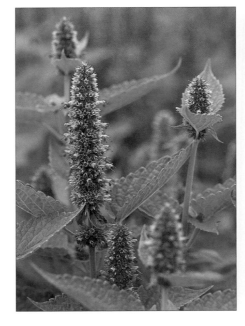

*Agastache foeniculum*

*Agastache foeniculum*
**ANISE HYSSOP**
Family: Lamiaceae
Native: N America
A great perennial for attracting wildlife, it grows to 60cm (2ft) high and bears small leaves, shiny green above and bluish below. The flowers are lilac but occasionally white. Although *A. foeniculum* is one of the hardier species, it will not survive severe frosts.
**Cultivation** Anise hyssop thrives in a sheltered location in full sun. Plant in any free-draining soil. Propagate by seed or division in early spring. ❀ ❀ Zone 8.
**Uses** An excellent plant for the front of the herbaceous or mixed border. It is also an ideal plant for rock gardens, or can be grown as an annual, especially in colder regions.
**Wildlife benefits** The upright flower heads are a real magnet for bees and bumblebees. Garden butterflies, for example red admiral and painted lady, are also frequent visitors. Seed-eating birds, such as goldfinches, eat the mature seeds during winter.
**Closely related species** *A. rugosa* and *A. urticifolia* are both as hardy as *A. foeniculum*. *A. rugosa* grows to 1.2m (4ft) high and bears rose or violet flowers, whereas *A. urticifolia* reaches 1.8m (6ft) high and produces violet to rose flowers.

*Ajuga reptans*

*Ajuga reptans*
**BUGLE**
Family: Lamiaceae
Native: Europe, Iran and Caucasus
A versatile plant that can be used in many situations. Bugle is a ground-cover plant that reaches only 20cm (8in) high. Popping up from the matt of green foliage are spikes of nectar-rich, blue-purple flowers during summer. Over 20 different cultivars are available, many from North America.
**Cultivation** Bugle prefers partial shade, in humus-rich, moist soil with some added leaf mould. Propagate by division in autumn or early spring. ❀ ❀ ❀ Zone 6.
**Uses** One of the best ground-hugging plants, it's ideal in a woodland garden or under shrubs to create ground cover. It is also very effective in hanging baskets or tubs where it will trail over the sides.
**Wildlife benefits** The flowers are frequently visited by bees and bumblebees seeking nectar. Butterflies, ladybirds and hoverflies also visit large patches of flowering bugle, especially if conditions are calm and sunny.
**Closely related species** The pyramid bugle (*A. pyramidalis*) is an evergreen perennial with blue, nectar-rich flowers. *A. genevensis* is taller, bearing blue flowers and reaching 40cm (16in). The latter prefers full sun.

*Anthemis tinctoria*

## *Anthemis tinctoria*
### YELLOW CHAMOMILE
Family: Asteraceae
Native: Europe, Caucasus and Iran

An extremely good-value garden plant, producing masses of yellow to pale cream daisy flowers from spring through until autumn. It is a clump-forming perennial that bears evergreen, fern-like, crinkled, mid-green leaves which are slightly hairy. The stems easily reach 60–90cm (2–3ft) high in one season.

**Cultivation**  Yellow chamomile thrives in an open site in full sun and needs well-drained soil. Propagate by basal cuttings in spring or semi-ripe cuttings in late summer. ❀ ❀ ❀ Zone 6.

**Uses**  A great plant for herbaceous and mixed borders, providing a burst of bright colour. It is also ideal for adding height to summer-bedding containers. For good colour combinations, plant with blue-purple trailing lobelia, petunias and fuchsias.

**Wildlife benefits**  Numerous beneficial insects feed on the pollen and nectar, particularly hoverflies, lacewings, parasitic wasps, ladybirds and tachinid flies. Leave the old foliage until spring before cutting back to provide good hibernating sites for insects.

**Closely related species**  'E. C. Buxton' is often said to be the prettiest cultivar of *A. tinctoria*, sporting beautiful lemon-coloured flowers. *A. punctata* subsp. *cupaniana* bears aromatic silver foliage, adorned by sharp white flowers in summer.

## *Aquilegia vulgaris*
### COLUMBINE
Family: Ranunculaceae
Native: W, C and S Europe

A typical cottage-garden plant that produces unusual, pretty flowers which have nectar-rich spurs. The flowers are borne in late spring and early summer, their colour ranging from blue to purple, red or white. Columbines can grow up to 60–90cm (2–3ft) high, and bear deeply divided leaves that are dark green with a flush of blue.

**Cultivation**  Plant in organic-rich soil to retain moisture over summer in full sun or semi-shade. Propagate by seed in late summer. ❀ ❀ ❀ Zone 4.

**Uses**  Fantastic for a woodland garden because it can withstand shade and provide a real splash of colour in the under-storey. Plant in drifts along pathways for the best impact. Allow the columbines to self-seed in a wild or naturalistic garden.

**Wildlife benefits**  The nectar-rich spurs found at the back of the flower head attract mainly insects able to reach far into the flower, particularly long-tongued bumblebees, butterflies and moths. Leave seed heads uncut for foraging birds in autumn.

**Closely related species**  All species of aquilegias are good nectar producers and an asset to wildlife, especially *A. canadensis*, a native of north-eastern North America with yellow to red flowers in spring and summer. *A. skinneri* has green-orange and bright red flowers in summer.

*Aquilegia vulgaris*

## *Asclepias tuberosa*
### BUTTERFLY WEED
Family: Asclepiadaceae
Native: E and S North America

A brightly coloured border plant that's a winner in drought-tolerant gardens. It can easily grow up to 90cm (3ft) high and produces red, yellow or orange flowers in summer that are fantastic nectar producers. The stems bear mid-green leaves that are long and lance-shaped.

**Cultivation**  It prefers dry, free-draining soil and should be located in full sun. Propagate by tip cuttings or seed throughout spring. ❀ ❀ ❀ Zone 3.

**Uses**  An extremely good herbaceous border plant that will provide a real focal point, especially if planted beside red or yellow flowering plants. *A. tuberosa* is often selected when short-listing plants for a specialist butterfly border.

**Wildlife benefits**  The nectar-rich flowers attract the monarch butterflies, and its caterpillars feed on the leaves of the plant. A chemical substance within the leaves makes the grubs unpalatable to birds. Bees and other butterflies also frequent the flowers in large numbers.

**Closely related species**  *A. syriaca*, with pink to mauve flowers, is best suited to the wild garden and naturalistic plantings, and is particularly good at providing nectar for bees. Swamp milkweed (*A. incarnata*) prefers damp habitats and grows to 2m (6½ft) tall, bearing white to pink flowers.

*Asclepias tuberosa*

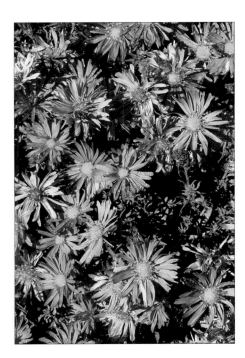

*Aster novi-belgii*

## Aster novi-belgii
### MICHAELMAS DAISY
Family: Asteraceae
Native: N America

A classic autumn perennial that provides a welcome boost of nectar in gardens as winter approaches. The flower heads can reach 90cm–1.2m (3–4ft) and contain many violet-blue flowers with yellow centres. The leaves are lance-shaped and prone to powdery mildew in dry summers.

**Cultivation** Michaelmas daisies thrive in full sun and prefer the soil to be slightly moist. Propagate by division in spring or autumn. ❀ ❀ ❀ Zone 2.

**Uses** A brilliant plant for herbaceous or mixed borders. Many different cultivars are available, enabling small or very tall cultivars of *A. novi-belgii* to be selected for the front or back of the border, and with most colour schemes.

**Wildlife benefits** The flowers are a real favourite with butterflies, especially species preparing to overwinter. The rich nectar helps to build up their body weight to help them through hibernation. Seeds provide food for various birds, such as crossbills and finches.

**Closely related species** *A. novae-angliae* grows to 1.5m (5ft) high and bears purple flowers with a yellow centre. *A. lateriflorus* produces white flowers with a dark centre, and *A.* 'Coombe Fishacre' is one of the best single-flowering cultivars with pink-tinged flowers.

## Aubrieta deltoidea
### AUBRETIA
Family: Brassicaceae
Native: Aegean

During the spring months when aubretia is in flower, the leaves are hardly noticeable because the lilac-red flowers are so numerous. Though only 10cm (4in) high, it is a prolific spreader, either on a slope or down a wall. It is also fairly drought-tolerant, which is an excellent quality if used in dry gardens, walls and containers.

**Cultivation** Grows well in full sun in any good, free-draining garden soil. Propagate by softwood cuttings in summer. Cut back hard after flowering to maintain a good shape. ❀ ❀ ❀ Zone 7.

**Uses** Aubretia looks delightful when planted in dry banks and cracks in walls, where it hangs down, softens the hard surface and offers a vibrant splash of colour when in flower. It is also useful for planting in a rock garden or in spring-flowering hanging baskets and containers, where it is used as a trailing plant.

**Wildlife benefits** It attracts early flying butterflies, bees and bumblebees in spring. Birds are then drawn to the area to feed on the visiting insects. The flowers are often taken by garden birds for use in nesting.

**Closely related species** Take care to avoid double-flowering cultivars, for example *A. d.* 'Doctor Mules'. A better bet for insects is the single-flowered *A. d.* 'Gurgedyke' with purple flowers in spring.

*Aubrieta deltoidea*

*Aurinia saxatilis*

## Aurinia saxatilis
### YELLOW ALYSSUM
Family: Brassicaeae
Native: C and SE Europe

This traditional rock-garden plant, formerly known as *A. saxatile*, originates from rocky and mountainous habitats. It grows 20cm (8in) high and produces numerous rich chrome-yellow flowers from late spring to early summer. The stems bear leaves that are linear, grey and slightly hairy.

**Cultivation** Yellow alyssum grows in any garden soil, but will perform well even in poor ground. Site in full sun. Propagate by soft cuttings in early summer. ❀ ❀ ❀ Zone 3.

**Uses** Although ideal for rock and gravel gardens, the plant, especially the flowering heads, can become unruly and invasive, therefore care needs to be taken when positioning it. Yellow alyssum can also be used when planting in containers, particularly for spring bedding ones.

**Wildlife benefits** Produces an early source of pollen for bees to take back to their hives and feed the larvae. Emerging butterflies drink from the nectaries to build up their strength before breeding begins.

**Closely related species** *A. s.* 'Citrinum' is good for wildlife, bearing bright lemon flowers. *A. petraea,* with yellow flowers, is very similar to *A. saxatilis*, but is more compact and less hardy. *A. rupestris* is a low-growing species bearing white flowers with attractive silver-grey leaves, and again is less hardy.

## *Baptisia australis*
### FALSE INDIGO
Family: Papilionoideae
Native: E North America

A graceful, upright perennial reaching up to 75cm (2½ft) tall. The delicate, pea-like violet flowers are borne on flower spikes throughout the summer months. The stem bears attractive bright green leaves that are divided into ovate leaflets. Ornate, dark grey seedpods form after flowering, and often persist on the plant over winter.

**Cultivation** False indigo thrives in full sun, in free-draining soil that is neutral or acid. Propagate by division in early spring or by seed in autumn. ❀ ❀ ❀ Zone 5.

**Uses** Owing to its upright habit, false indigo is ideal in herbaceous or mixed borders. It is also often grown with old-fashioned roses and other beauties, especially polemoniums, aquilegias and lupins.

**Wildlife benefits** False indigo is a real winner with bumblebees and the occasional butterfly. Avoid cutting back in autumn because seed-eating birds are readily drawn to the mature seedpods from autumn to winter.

**Closely related species** Both *B. alba*, which grows to 1.8m (6ft) tall with creamy white flowers, and *B. bracteata* var. *leucophaea*, bearing white to yellow-orange flowers and stems up to 60cm (2ft) high, are particularly suited to dry, sunny banks. Most *Baptisia* species naturalize in wild areas if sown or planted.

*Baptisia australis*

*Campanula latifolia*

## *Campanula latifolia*
### BELLFLOWER
Family: Campanulaceae
Native: Europe to Kashmir

This is one of the showiest herbaceous perennials for the back of a border. The tall stems, 1.2m (4ft) high, bear pale blue or light lavender bell-shaped flowers in summer. The foliage is long and ovate at the base, becoming distinctly rounder and more ovate near the top of the plant.

**Cultivation** Although the greater bellflower can be grown in full sun, it prefers light shade. It will grow in most soils but thrives in damp, fertile ground. Propagate by division in spring. ❀ ❀ ❀ Zone 3.

**Uses** An extremely useful plant for placing at the back of the herbaceous border, providing height and a showy display. For a bigger impact, plant with other perennial species such as *Phlox*, *Delphinium* and *Monarda*.

**Wildlife benefits** Bees are attracted to the flowers' pollen and nectar, and insect-eating birds are often found feeding on aphids around the flower head. Do not cut back the old stems until spring because the dense foliage offers protection through winter to hibernating insects.

**Closely related species** Harebell (*C. rotundifolia*) grows in grasslands. It has fine leaves and nodding blue flowers, and can be grown in meadows or rock gardens. *C. punctata* has large pale blue to white flowers in summer and grows to 1.5m (5ft) tall.

## *Cardamine pratensis*
### CUCKOO FLOWER
Family: Brassicaceae
Native: Europe

A delicate perennial, often associated with meadows and natural areas, the cuckoo flower sports beautiful white flowers flushed with lilac, and distinctive yellow stamens. It grows up to 30cm (1ft) high, with the stems producing deeply cut, glossy dark green foliage.

**Cultivation** The cuckoo flower is great for growing in full sun or light shade. Grow in damp soil with low fertility. Propagate by seed or division in autumn. ❀ ❀ ❀ Zone 4.

**Uses** An ideal plant for incorporating into a meadow mix for sites where the soil remains damp for prolonged periods. The cuckoo flower is also well suited to wild gardens, where it can easily naturalize and self-seed around an area.

**Wildlife benefits** The leaves of the cuckoo flower are the caterpillar food plant for the orange-tipped, green-veined, various brown and white butterflies. Bees are often observed visiting the flowers seeking nectar.

**Closely related species** *C. trifolia* is a creeping perennial suitable for rock gardens, bearing pure white flowers in late spring. *C. bulbifera* is useful for wild or naturalistic plantings. Do not select double-flowering cultivars of *C. pratensis*, such as 'Edith' and 'Flore Pleno', for example, as they are of little benefit to wildlife.

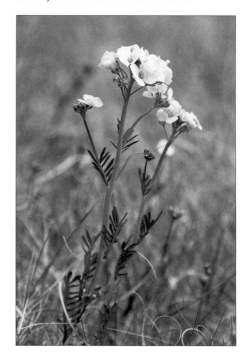

*Cardamine pratensis*

## *Centaurea montana*
### PERENNIAL CORNFLOWER
Family: Asteraceae
Native: Mountains of Europe

A wonderful, spreading perennial that produces an abundance of lance-shaped leaves with flower heads popping through, reaching 50cm (20in) high. The early summer thistle-like flowers are surrounded by a ray of slender petals which are purple, pink, blue or white.

**Cultivation** Prefers full sun in any well-drained soil, even if it is infertile, dry or chalky. Propagate by division in spring or autumn. Alternatively, take root cuttings in spring and place in an open propagating case in a sandy compost. ❀ ❀ ❀ Zone 3.

**Uses** A great plant for the front of the herbaceous border or for a large rock garden. The pale blue foliage of *Cerinthe major* 'Purpurascens' and the dark blue-purple flowers of *Centaurea montana* complement each other well.

**Wildlife benefits** The gorgeous blue flowers are irresistible to bees and bumblebees seeking nectar in summer. The seeds mature in autumn and are often eaten by greenfinches, goldfinches, crossbills, linnets and blue tits.

**Closely related species** Cornflower (*Centaurea cyanus*) is an annual reaching up to 90cm (3ft) high with violet to blue flowers. It is ideal for using in wildflower mixes or wild areas. *C. dealbata*, to 90cm (3ft) high, bears deeply cut silver foliage with lilac-purple flowers.

*Centaurea montana*

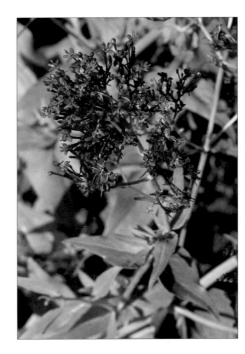

*Centranthus ruber*

## *Centranthus ruber*
### RED VALERIAN
Family: Valerianaceae
Native: Europe, N Africa and Asia Minor

The beautiful flowers, which range from crimson to pale red, are commonly seen in gardens in summer and autumn. The stems reach up to 60cm (2ft) high, and bear succulent, pale green foliage that allows the plant a degree of drought tolerance.

**Cultivation** Grow in full sun to obtain maximum flowering. They enjoy poor, dry soil, making them ideal candidates for growing in walls and rockeries. Propagate by seed in spring or autumn. ❀ ❀ ❀ Zone 3.

**Uses** A fantastic plant for rock gardens, and for growing in planting pockets in walls. The surface will be softened by the flower heads that cascade down the brickwork. Also very effective in herbaceous and mixed borders.

**Wildlife benefits** A renowned nectar provider for bees and several species of butterfly, including red admirals and small tortoiseshells. Moths, particularly hawk moths, are attracted by the fragrant flowers and seek nectar in the evening.

**Closely related species** Common valerian (*Valeriana officinalis*) is one of the best perennials for attracting many species of insects, especially beneficial ones. It is closely related to *C. ruber*, and bears spikes of white to deep pink flowers throughout summer.

## *Cichorium intybus*
### CHICORY
Family: Asteraceae
Native: Europe, W Asia and N Africa

The electric blue flowers are stunningly beautiful and eye-catching, especially on a sunny day. The flowering period is long, and ranges from late spring to early autumn. Growing out of a basal rosette of leaves are stems that can reach up to 1.2m (4ft) high.

**Cultivation** Site in full sun in any moderately fertile, well-drained soil. Take care when using chicory because it can freely seed in the garden. Propagate by seed in spring or autumn. ❀ ❀ ❀ Zone 3.

**Uses** Chicory will look amazing if used in meadows, especially when planted with colourful perennials such as milky bellflower (*Campanula lactiflora*), *Knautia macedonica* and campion (*Lychnis calcedonica*). Also use in the wild garden and allow it to self-seed freely around an area.

**Wildlife benefits** The flowers are visited by bees and bumblebees seeking nectar and pollen. The nectar production will peak in the morning because each individual flower will only last for one day. Leave the stems uncut over winter to aid overwintering insects.

**Closely related species** *C. spinosum* is a dwarf perennial that grows to 20cm (8in) high and produces blue, occasionally white or pink flowers in summer. Endive (*C. endivia*) is very like *C. intybus*, but is normally an annual or biennial.

*Cichorium intybus*

*Cirsium rivulare*

*Coreopsis verticillata*

### *Cirsium rivulare*
### PLUME THISTLE
Family: Asteraceae
Native: SW Europe

Often thistles are thought of as weeds, but this species is particularly ornamental though still invasive if left to self-seed. The tall, erect stems reach up to 1.2m (4ft) high and produce round, button-like, purple flower heads with 2–5 in a cluster. Leaves are narrow, oval and deeply cut.

**Cultivation** Plume thistle prefers sun or semi-shade in any type of soil except one that is constantly wet. Best propagated by seed in autumn. ❀ ❀ ❀ Zone 5.

**Uses** *C. rivulare* is ideal for growing in the wild garden where it's free to self-seed and spread. It is better here than in the herbaceous border where it tends to die out on a frequent basis and constantly needs replacing.

**Wildlife benefits** The pincushion blooms attract many species of insect, particularly bees and bumblebees seeking nectar. Do not cut down the seed heads after flowering because they attract dunnocks, linnets, finches and crossbills.

**Closely related species** The closely related musk thistle (*Carduus nutan*) has the same cultivation requirements as *C. rivulare*. It's a big attraction for bees and butterflies seeking nectar from the semi-nodding, crimson flowers.

### *Coreopsis verticillata*
### TICKSEED
Family: Asteraceae
Native: Maryland and W Virginia to S Carolina

A brightly coloured perennial, native to the east coast of North America. The stems grow to 60cm (2ft) high and produce deeply divided, dark green leaves, and culminate in branched stems bearing numerous golden-yellow daisy-like flowers in summer.

**Cultivation** Tickseed thrives in full sun in fertile, well-drained soil. *C. verticillata* is fairly tolerant of dry soils. Propagate by seed or by division in spring. ❀ ❀ ❀ Zone 6.

**Uses** Excellent in the herbaceous or mixed border. The brightly coloured flowers look stunning if planted next to other perennials, such as *Salvia nemorosa* 'May Night' with almost purple-black flowers, and the purple *Cirsium rivulare* 'Atropurpureum'.

**Wildlife benefits** Honeybees seek out the bright yellow flowers that are rich in pollen and nectar. It is also excellent for encouraging butterflies, hoverflies and ladybirds. Do not cut back after flowering because birds, especially finches, devour the mature seeds in autumn.

**Closely related species**
*C. pubescens,* to 1.2m (4ft) high, can be naturalized in wild gardens, and it flowers in several flushes from spring to late autumn. *C. tripteris,* to 3m (10ft) high, is a back-of-the-border plant but can also be planted in the wild garden and in partial shade.

### *Dahlia* Collerette Group
### DAHLIA
Family: Asteraceae
Native: Garden origin

The Collerette Group of dahlias was raised in France at the beginning of the twentieth century. The blooms have an open centre, and are surrounded by an inner circle of short florets (the collar). There are one, sometimes two, rows of normally flat outer ray florets. The cultivars grow to 1.2m (4ft) high, and are found in a range of colours.

**Cultivation** Dahlias grow well in a sheltered, sunny site, with high light levels and rich, well-drained soil. Propagate by division of the tubers or cuttings in spring. ❀ Zone 9.

**Uses** Dahlias can be used for seasonal interest in summer-bedding schemes, tropical borders, tubs and containers. They are also very effective at filling gaps in herbaceous borders, especially if used in large groups making plenty of impact.

**Wildlife benefits** The open flowers of species dahlias or Collerettes are excellent for providing nectar to butterflies and bees. Dahlias in other Groups, for example the Pompon and Cactus, have too many petals covering the sexual parts to be of any benefit.

**Closely related species** The Collerettes include several excellent cultivars, including *D*. 'Clair de Lune' with yellow ray petals and an inner circle of paler yellow petals. *D*. 'La Cierva' has purple-tipped white outer petals with a white collar.

*Dahlia* Collerette Group

*Deschampsia flexuosa*

### *Deschampsia flexuosa*
### WAVY HAIR GRASS
Family: Poaceae
Native: Europe, Asia, NE North America and S America

This produces one of the most attractive inflorescences, with panicles of golden seed-heads tinged purple in late summer. The leaves are thread-like and will reach up to 20cm (8in) high, but the seed-heads grow to 90cm (3ft) tall.

**Cultivation** Although wavy hair grass will grow in most soils, it will thrive in acid ground in full sun or semi-shade. Propagate by division in spring. ❀ ❀ ❀ Zone 5.

**Uses** A wonderful plant to use in naturalistic plantings with perennials including rudbeckias, eryngiums and fennel. Wavy hair grass can also be used to create movement in winter borders, and can be sited on the edge of woodland gardens because it tolerates partial shade.

**Wildlife benefits** Many different insects shelter and hibernate amongst the thick foliage over winter. It is also the food plant for the caterpillars of the ringlet butterfly.

**Closely related species** All grasses should be left uncut over winter to offer a home to many species. Tufted hair grass (*D. cespitosa*) is an evergreen perennial grass reaching up to 1m (3ft) high. It produces panicles of minute, pale brown spikelets in summer.

*Echinacea purpurea*

### *Echinacea purpurea*
### CONEFLOWER
Family: Asteraceae
Native: E North America

Produces a beautiful, erect daisy-like flower that is both eye-catching and a fantastic plant for attracting numerous species of wildlife. The deep crimson-pink flower heads, with conical brown-pink centres, are borne singly in late summer, and the lance-shaped leaves are dark green with a rough texture.

**Cultivation** The coneflower prefers full sun but will tolerate partial shade. Plant in humus-rich soil that is well drained. Propagate by division in spring. ❀ ❀ ❀ Zone 3.

**Uses** A versatile plant that can be used in many different situations. It looks superb in naturalistic plantings when planted in large drifts with rudbeckias, verbenas, grasses and campanulas. Also very effective in herbaceous or mixed borders.

**Wildlife benefits** The coneflower is very popular with bees and bumblebees taking nectar from the conical brown centres that produce petal-less flowers. Butterflies and hoverflies are occasional visitors seeking nectar.

**Closely related species** *E. pallida*, to 90cm (3ft) high, is very similar to *E. purpurea* and produces purple flower heads in late summer. *E. angustifolia*, which grows to 1.5m (5ft) high, has decidedly smaller light purple to rose-pink flowers.

### *Echinops ritro*
### GLOBE THISTLE
Family: Asteraceae
Native: C and E Europe

A striking architectural plant grown for its globe-like, spiky flower heads that appear in summer. The purple-blue flower heads can reach up to 1.2m (4ft) high. The attractive, large foliage is striking, silver-grey and deeply divided.

**Cultivation** Plant out in full sun in well-drained soil. It will grow adequately in poor ground, though the tall stems may need staking. Propagate by division or seed in autumn. ❀ ❀ ❀ Zone 3.

**Uses** Very popular for the back of the herbaceous or mixed border, giving height and structure. Globe thistles are stunning when sited next to plants with purple foliage, for example the smoke bush (*Cotinus coggygria* 'Royal Purple').

**Wildlife benefits** Extremely attractive to bees and bumblebees. Butterflies are also frequent visitors to the round blue flower heads. The autumn seed is eaten by the likes of goldfinches.

**Closely related species** Other excellent insect attractors are the 1.2–1.5m (4–5ft) high *E. bannaticus* with pale to mid-blue flower heads. *E. sphaerocephalus* is an extremely large perennial growing to 2m (6½ft) high with greyish-white flower heads.

*Echinops ritro*

*Eryngium alpinum*

## *Eryngium alpinum*
### SEA HOLLY
Family: Apiaceae
Native: Europe

A superb eye-catcher and structural plant for any border. Sea holly produces basal rosettes of heart-shaped, deeply toothed, glossy foliage. The stems bear purple-blue flower heads surrounded by metallic blue bracts with large, soft spines throughout the summer months. This unusual plant will reach 75cm–1m (2½–3ft) high.

**Cultivation** Sea holly thrives in full sun in moderately fertile, free-draining soil, although it will tolerate a range of soil conditions. Propagate by seed in autumn. ❀ ❀ ❀ Zone 5.

**Uses** A versatile plant at home in a dry or seaside garden, sea holly can also be used in a herbaceous or mixed border. The beautiful purple-blue colours contrast well with silvers, pinks and purples, making it ideal in an old-fashioned rose garden.

**Wildlife benefits** It attracts bees and bumblebees that congregate in large numbers, seeking the nectar-rich, thistle-type flowers. The occasional butterfly and a rare beetle visiting the flower head have also been recorded.

**Closely related species** All the eryngiums are excellent nectar producers and benefit many insects. *E. giganteum* is another attractive species that is equally beneficial to wildlife. It is a biennial or short-lived perennial bearing blue flowers with silver bracts. *E.* x *oliverianum* has lavender-blue flowers and grows to 1m (3ft).

## *Festuca glauca*
### BLUE FESCUE
Family: Poaceae
Native: Europe

A wonderful plant that is frequently used in modern planting schemes. It is an evergreen tuft-forming grass growing up to 10cm (4in) high and produces narrow, blue-silvery white foliage. The foliage is definitely the most attractive part of the plant because the flower spikes are small and insignificant.

**Cultivation** Fescues are easily grown in poor, dry conditions, in full sun. Constantly remove the dead leaves to promote good leaf colour. Divide every 3–4 years in spring. ❀ ❀ ❀ Zone 5.

**Uses** The colour of the fine leaves is one of the loveliest shades of blue in the garden. The grass is also ideal in containers and winter hanging baskets because it gives a good colour boost in the dull, dormant months. Blue fescue can also be used effectively in a dry garden, or in herbaceous or mixed borders.

**Wildlife benefits** The thick tufts offer shelter to overwintering insects and small mammals. Larvae of several different species of butterfly will use the fine leaves as their food plant. Small insects will use the dense foliage to shelter in during summer and winter.

**Closely related species** Sheep's fescue (*F. ovina*) is excellent for wildlife. Similar to *F. glauca*, it is an important caterpillar food plant for garden butterflies, and is ideal in wildflower meadow mixes.

*Festuca glauca*

## *Foeniculum vulgare*
### FENNEL
Family: Apiaceae
Native: Mediterranean

A wonderful plant that provides good structure in borders. The soft, fern-like foliage adorns the rigid zigzag pattern of the green stems. The foliage is aromatic, especially if crushed or brushed past. The large, flat flower heads are full of small yellow flowers borne from summer to autumn.

**Cultivation** Fennel thrives in full sun in any well-drained garden soil. It will set seed freely and can become a problem in a small garden, so frequent weeding is needed to remove the seedlings before they take over the border. Propagate by seed or division in spring. ❀ ❀ ❀ Zone 5.

**Uses** Excellent in the herbaceous border or wild garden where it's allowed to self-seed and naturalize freely. Grow amongst echinaceas and verbenas.

**Wildlife benefits** The nectar-rich flowers attract many species of insects including lacewings, ladybirds, parasitic wasps, wasps and bees. The caterpillar of the swallowtail butterfly will eat the leaves of fennel. Many species hibernate n the uncut, hollow stems.

**Closely related species** Giant fennel (*Ferula communis*), a close relative, also attracts insects, and reaches 1–3.7m (3–12ft) high. A summer-flowering perennial, it's grown for its bold architectural form and yellow flower heads.

*Foeniculum vulgare*

*Geranium maculatum*
## GERANIUM
Family: Geraniaceae
Native: NE North America
Geraniums create excellent ground cover and provide lovely drifts of colour if planted in large groups. The saucer-shaped, upward-facing flowers are light to deep pink and appear from spring to summer. They are borne above deeply cut, mid-green leaves.

**Cultivation**  Plant in full sun or partial shade in any well-drained soil. Cut back after flowering to promote a second flush. Propagate by division in autumn or spring. ❀ ❀ ❀ Zone 4.

**Uses**  All geraniums are excellent as ground cover. They can be planted under shrubs and trees, can be used at the front of herbaceous borders or naturalized in meadows.

**Wildlife benefits**  The dense leaf cover provides protection for a host of species that will hide and forage in the foliage. Being long-flowering, it is an essential plant for the wildlife garden, especially for bees seeking nectar.

**Closely related species**  Most geraniums provide good ground cover and are attractive to bees. *G. sylvaticum* and *G. pratense* can be naturalized in meadows and wild areas. *G. psilostemon*, a taller geranium, has flashy magenta flowers with a deep purple centre.

*Helenium autumnale*
## SNEEZEWEED
Family: Asteraceae
Native: N America
It is grown for its daisy-like flowers that appear in late summer and autumn. Each flower head has a round central disc and a nectar-rich, bright yellow ray floret. Thin, lance-shaped leaves adorn the stems that grow to 1.5m (5ft) high.

**Cultivation**  Sneezeweed will grow in any fertile soil, except when it's very dry, in full sun. Propagate by division in spring or autumn, or by seed in spring. ❀ ❀ ❀ Zone 3.

**Uses**  An ideal plant for using in herbaceous or mixed borders to add height and colour. Plant beside tall grasses, such as cultivars of *Miscanthus sinensis*, *Panicum virgatum* and other late-flowering species for a graceful autumnal effect.

**Wildlife benefits**  The yellow flowers of sneezeweed are a beacon for bees and bumblebees; the colour sends out a message that nectar is available. Butterflies, especially sulphurs, are also drawn to the flower heads when seeking late-season nectar.

**Closely related species**  *Hymenoxys hoopesii,* to 90cm (3ft) high, occurs naturally around woodland edges and is a welcome addition to any dappled, shady area. *H. bigelovii* grows to 90cm (3ft) high and is a moist, meadowland plant that is suitable for naturalizing in meadows and wild gardens.

*Holcus lanatus*
## YORKSHIRE FOG
Family: Poaceae
Native: Europe
*Holcus lanatus* is a perennial grass that can grow up to 90cm (3ft) high. It bears ornamental seed heads in a dense panicle up to 15cm (6in) long, and they appear above the slender, grey-green leaves, which are slightly hairy. It produces strong, rhizomatous creeping roots that can become invasive when planted next to less vigorous species.

**Cultivation**  Grow in full sun in well-drained soil that is also moisture retentive.

*Holcus lanatus*

Propagate by division in autumn or spring, or by seed when ripe. ❀ ❀ ❀ Zone 5.

**Uses**  Ideal for growing in meadows or the wild garden. One drawback is that this species can overwhelm finer grasses that have essential benefits to wildlife, making creeping soft grass (*H. mollis*) a better all-round choice for a wildflower mix.

**Wildlife benefits**  The leaves of Yorkshire fog are eaten by the caterpillars of the speckled wood and small skipper butterflies. The dense foliage is ideal for small mammals and invertebrates that hide and forage around in it.

**Closely related species**  *H. mollis* is best suited to acid soil in slightly shady areas or hedge banks. It is slightly smaller than *H. lanatus*, growing up to 60cm (2ft) high, and produces wider foliage that is soft and velvety.

*Geranium maculatum*

*Helenium autumnale*

*Knautia macedonia*

## *Knautia macedonia*
### KNAUTIA
Family: Dipsacaeae
Native: C Europe

A beautiful, graceful perennial that is ideal in the ornamental garden and wildflower meadow. The slender stems reach up to 90cm (3ft) high and, in summer, bear deep purple to crimson flowers in round, pincushion flower heads. The stems bear many narrow, deeply divided, oval-shaped leaves.

**Cultivation**  Site in full sun and in any free-draining soil. Propagate by seed in autumn or by basal cuttings in spring. ❀ ❀ ❀ Zone 6.

**Uses**  A lovely plant to use in naturalistic plantings. It works extremely well with *Miscanthus,* rudbeckias and verbenas. *Knautia* is a firm favourite in herbaceous and mixed borders, providing a good splash of colour over several weeks.

**Wildlife benefits**  The flowers are visited by bees and butterflies, particularly the red admiral and painted lady. They are drawn to the nectaries by nectar guides that are invisible to the naked eye, but not to insects. Birds will eat the seed in autumn if the old flower heads are left uncut.

**Closely related species**  Field scabious (*K. arvensis*) can be grown in lightly shaded areas or full sun, preferably on calcareous soil. It grows up to 1.5m (5ft) high, and bears pale purple-blue flower heads. Use in a wildflower meadow mix or in a wild garden.

## *Lamium album*
### WHITE DEAD NETTLE
Family: Lamiaceae
Native: Europe to W Asia

*Lamiums* are well known for their nectar, and draw large numbers of bee species to the white, tubular summer flowers. The erect, square stems reach up to 90cm (3ft) tall, and bear green, kidney-shaped leaves with toothed margins.

**Cultivation**  *L. album* is at home in sun or semi-shade, and grows best in humus-rich soil. Propagate by potting up rooted running stems, or by seed in autumn. ❀ ❀ ❀ Zone 4.

**Uses**  White dead nettle is a natural woodland plant and is therefore best suited to light shade. Grow under trees, in woodland edges and in drifts in a woodland garden, although it can be invasive. Excellent as ground cover in a wild garden.

**Wildlife benefits**  Adored by bees and bumblebees that visit the flower to drink from the generous nectaries. White dead nettle also produces an abundance of foliage, which provides valuable cover for many species at ground level, including insects and spiders. The nutlets are eaten by birds such as finches.

**Closely related species**  Other excellent nectar-producing species include the herbaceous perennial *L. orvala* that grows to 60cm (2ft) high, and bears red to purple, tubular flowers. *L. maculatum*, to 60cm (2ft) high, is a fantastic plant for ground cover, producing red to purple flowers.

*Lamium album*

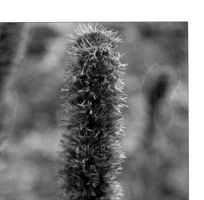

*Liatris spicata*

## *Liatris spicata*
### GAYFEATHER
Family: Asteraceae
Native: E North America

Valued for its late summer, rose-purple flowers borne in spikes to 60cm (2ft) high. The flower heads are unusual because they start to flower from the top downwards, and are set off beautifully by the grass-like, mid-green leaves. The rootstocks are thickened, corm-like structures.

**Cultivation**  *L. spicata* prefers fertile, free-draining soil, which also retains moisture, and flourishes if planted in full sun. Propagate by division in spring, or seed sown in autumn. ❀ ❀ ❀ Zone 3.

**Uses**  Excellent when used in large clumps and planted in drifts to create a real impact. Gayfeather is also ideal in herbaceous and mixed borders. It is often used in partial shade, but in dry conditions can be prone to powdery mildew, which will affect its growth and flowering.

**Wildlife benefit**  The nectar-rich flowers are a real magnet for bees, moths and butterflies. Dry, blackened seed heads are visited in late autumn and winter by birds, particularly finches seeking a protein-rich meal.

**Closely related species**  Cultivars worth growing of *L. spicata* include 'Alba' with white flowers, and 'Floristan Violett' with deep violet flowers. Another species native to North America is *L. squarrosa* that grows to 60cm (2ft) high. It produces red-purple flowers in late summer–autumn.

*Linaria vulgaris*

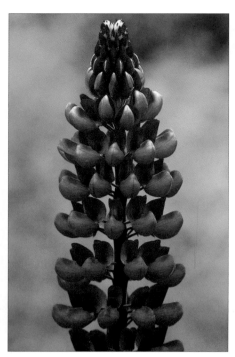

*Lupinus nootkatensis*

## *Linaria vulgaris*
### TOADFLAX
Family: Scrophulariaceae
Native: Europe

Toadflax is often seen flowering in roadside verges and on dry banks, being especially noticeable in drier years when more flowers are produced. The flowers are pale to bright yellow with a coppery spur, and appear from spring to autumn. The stems grow to 30–90cm (1–3ft) high and bear delicate, linear, mid-green leaves.

**Cultivation** Easily grown in dry, sandy soil in full sun. Propagate by division in spring or by seed in spring or autumn. ❀ ❀ ❀ Zone 4.

**Uses** It is best grown in a hedge bank, wildflower meadow or wild garden because of its fantastic ability to self-seed. Ideal for using on free-draining soil that dries out easily.

**Wildlife benefits** Bees and bumblebees almost fight at the flower base to land and collect pollen and nectar. Beneficial insects, including hoverflies and parasitic wasps, are also attracted to the nectar.

**Closely related species** Purple toadflax (*Linaria purpurea*) carries beautiful spikes of purple-blue flowers, and is ideal for the herbaceous border. *L. alpina* is a tuft-forming, short-lived perennial with yellow-centred purple flowers, and is suitable for a rock garden.

## *Lupinus nootkatensis*
### LUPIN
Family: Papilionaceae
Native: NW North America

A highly attractive plant grown for its beautiful foliage and large violet, pink, white or multi-coloured flower spikes. The individual flowers are pea-like in appearance, and the deeply divided mid-green leaves are borne on stems reaching up to 60cm (2ft) high.

**Cultivation** Prefers moist soils with good drainage, in full sun. Raise from fresh seed in autumn, or by cuttings from basal shoots in spring. ❀ ❀ ❀ Zone 4.

**Uses** Although short-lived, lupins are one of the very best plants for the herbaceous border because their magnificent flower heads provide a great splash of colour. Also widely used in wildflower meadows and the wild garden.

**Wildlife benefits** The brightly coloured flowers and sweet-smelling secretions are a great draw for bees and bumblebees seeking pollen. The plant is prone to attack from aphids that, in turn, attract birds, ladybirds and lacewings.

**Closely related species**
*L. polyphyllus* and *L. arboreus* were the main breeding species used to create the ornamental lupin cultivars grown today. *L. polyphyllus* grows to 1.5m (5ft) high with blue, purple, pink or white flowers. Excellent in a wildflower meadow.

## *Monarda didyma*
### BERGAMOT
Family: Lamiaceae
Native: Canada

Also called bee balm, it attracts various species of bee seeking the flowers' nectar. The flower heads are rounded discs with sterile, bright crimson, tubular flowers sited around the peripheral area of the head.

**Cultivation** Plant in full sun in fertile, free-draining soil that stays moist. Propagate by division of clumps or by seed, both in spring. ❀ ❀ ❀ Zone 4.

**Uses** A classic herbaceous perennial that is as popular today as it was 30 years ago. Great for the middle to the back of the herbaceous bed, or in a mixed border to create drifts of colour. Grow beside *Achillea* 'Goldplate' for a good colour combination.

**Wildlife benefits** The flowers produce high yields of nectar that are a magnet for bees, bumblebees and parasitic wasps. Leave the stems on over winter, and all the small crevices and hollows will provide a site for small insects, including ladybirds.

**Closely related species**
*M. russeliana* bears pink flowers with purple spots and *M. bartlettii* produces magenta flowers. *M. citriodora* is an annual with white or pink flowers that is another good bee attractor.

*Monarda didyma*

## *Nepeta* x *faasenii*
### CATMINT
Family: Lamiaceae
Native: Garden origin

This lovely, ornamental, herbaceous perennial has lilac-blue flowers from early summer to late autumn, and is adored by cats, which rub themselves against the grey-green foliage, releasing the scent. It is a rampant spreader and reaches 45cm (18in).

**Cultivation** It thrives in sunny locations in free-draining soil (avoid any other kind or the growth might be severely affected). Propagate by division in spring or autumn. ❊ ❊ ❊ Zone 3.

**Uses** It looks delightful when used as an edging plant amongst old-fashioned roses. Also use at the front of herbaceous borders or mixed borders where it is best placed next to plants with silver, purple or pink foliage or flowers.

**Wildlife benefits** Bees and bumblebees visit the small purple flowers seeking nectar. There are also occasional visit from butterflies and parasitic wasps. The dense foliage provides excellent cover for insects and small mammals that hide and forage here.

**Closely related species** *N. grandiflora* is a taller species with attractive, rich blue flowers. Catnip (*N. cataria*) is believed to repel rats, but the essential oils that are released when it is crushed are irresistible to cats. Both attract masses of bees.

## *Papaver orientale*
### ORIENTAL POPPY
Family: Papaveraceae
Native: SW Asia

Ornamental poppies are big, blowsy and great fun. The solitary flowers are red, orange or pale pink with a purple blotch at the base. The stems reach up to 90cm

*Nepeta* x *faasenii*

*Papaver orientale*

(3ft) high and bear deeply divided, large, hairy leaves that are light green-blue. Many cultivars are now available.

**Cultivation** Poppies thrive in a sunny location in free-draining, fertile soil. Propagate by division in early autumn or spring, or by seed in spring. ❊ ❊ ❊ Zone 3.

**Uses** The huge flowers and beautiful seed heads are a must for any mixed or herbaceous border. Do not plant at the front of a border because they die back early in the season, and leave a big, obvious gap. Grow beside *Limonium* or *Gypsophila* to help fill the gaps.

**Wildlife benefits** The flowers have easily accessible nectaries, making it a popular site for bees and hoverflies. The seed head is like a "pepper pot" filled with small seeds that get shaken out unless eaten by birds such as dunnocks, sparrows, linnets and finches.

**Closely related species** Other poppies useful to wildlife are the corn poppy (*P. rhoeas*), a tall annual herb that bears large scarlet flowers. The Icelandic poppy (*P. nudicaule*) is best grown as a biennial and bears pretty yellow, orange, peach, white or pale red flowers in summer.

## *Penstemon barbatus*
### PENSTEMON
Family: Scrophulariaceae
Native: New Mexico to Utah, Arizona and N Mexico

Penstemons are one of the best value garden plants because they flower for weeks and are really easy to grow. *P. barbatus* grows to 90cm (3ft) high or more, and produces beautiful tubular flowers that are red with a tinge of pink to carmine throughout summer. The thin, mid-green leaves are lance-shaped.

**Cultivation** Penstemons are best grown in well-drained soil in full sun, although they tolerate light, partial shade. Propagate by semi-ripe cuttings in late summer. ❊ ❊ ❊ Zone 3.

**Uses** Without a doubt penstemons offer huge bursts of radiant colour in herbaceous or mixed borders. Plant in large groups to create the best colour effect, and site at the front of a border.

**Wildlife benefits** The flowers are very popular with bees and bumblebees. If the flower parts are too small to enter, the bees will puncture a hole at the base of the petals with their mouthparts to access the nectaries. Hoverflies and ladybirds are occasional visitors.

**Closely related species** Bees also favour rock penstemon (*P. rupicola*), which has deep rose-coloured flowers and is just 10cm (4in) tall. It is ideal for a rock garden.

*Penstemon barbatus*

## *Phlox paniculata*
### SUMMER PHLOX
Family: Polemoniaceae
Native: N America

A majestic herbaceous perennial, it is great for providing late summer colour in the garden. The tall flower heads reach up to 1.2m (4ft) high, and produce tubular, scented, white, purple or pink flowers that are ideal for attracting butterflies and moths. Long, mid-green leaves are carried right up the stem; they are lance-shaped with toothed margins.

**Cultivation** Summer phlox will grow in almost any soil but prefers rich, moist but free-draining ground in full sun or semi-shade. Propagate by division in early spring. ❀ ❀ ❀ Zone 4.

**Uses** Often used in herbaceous beds, mixed borders or in a specialist butterfly border. Plant beside other butterfly-attracting species, such as *Scabiosa*, *Sedum* and *Verbena*, to create a nectar-rich haven for butterflies and other insects.

**Wildlife benefits** Butterflies, in particular swallowtails, fritillaries and skippers, are daytime visitors lured by the sweetly scented flowers for nectar. Hawkmoths may hover around the flowers from late afternoon until dusk, and several species of night-flying moths are also attracted.

**Closely related species** Other species popular with butterflies and moths include annual phlox (*P. drummondii*) that grows up to 30cm (1ft) high and produces purple-pink flowers. Prairie phlox (*P. pilosa*) grows to 60cm (2ft) high with lilac-purple flowers.

*Phlox paniculata*

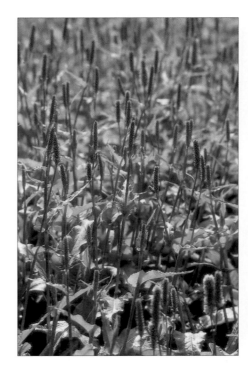

*Polygonum bistorta*

## *Polygonum bistorta*
### COMMON BISTORT
Family: Polygonaceae
Native: Russia and Turkey

*P. bistorta* is an extremely showy plant when in flower, and can grow up to 60cm (2ft) high. It grows in meadows and at the bottom of hedgerows. The stems produce triangular leaves and culminate in dense, cylindrical spikes of pink, occasionally white, flowers that appear in summer.

**Cultivation** Plant common bistort in full sun or semi-shade in moisture-retentive soil that is not too fertile. Propagate by division in autumn or spring. ❀ ❀ ❀ Zone 4.

**Uses** Fantastic in herbaceous borders or for providing colour in a woodland garden. Plant in large drifts at the edge of a woodland garden to provide colour in the under-storey, and use with species such as *Astilbe* and *Doronicum*.

**Wildlife benefits** During summer the pink flowers attract bees and bumblebees in large numbers. After flowering the plant produces red-brown fruits that, when ripe, attract many bird species, particularly dunnocks, finches and sparrows.

**Closely related species** *P. affine* is an evergreen, ground-hugging perennial producing dense spikes of rose-red flowers in autumn. *P. amplexicaule* is a taller perennial which grows up to 1.2m (4ft) high and produces delicate, rich red flowers from summer to autumn.

*Primula veris*

## *Primula veris*
### COWSLIP
Family: Primulaceae
Native: Europe and W Asia

When this beautiful grassland plant flowers, it's a sign that spring has arrived. The yellow flowers, with an orange mark, are slightly nodding and sweetly scented. Due to the ground-hugging habit of the green, crinkled leaves it is able to withstand periodic mowing or grazing.

**Cultivation** Plant in the garden in full sun or semi-shade in any good garden soil. Propagate by seed when fresh. The seed will need a cold spell before germination occurs. ❀ ❀ ❀ Zone 5.

**Uses** It is extremely well suited to meadows, and will also thrive if planted in borders. As it withstands semi-shade, it is ideal for planting around the base of deciduous shrubs and trees to provide an early source of nectar.

**Wildlife benefits** The cowslip is an excellent nectar source for overwintering butterflies and bees. It is also eaten by the caterpillars of the Duke of Burgundy butterfly. The seeds are eaten by chaffinches, and sparrows occasionally attack the flowers.

**Closely related species** With similar benefits to wildlife, the primrose (*P. vulgaris*) is also an early flowering species and is found in hedgerows and woodlands. The seeds of the plant are eaten by chaffinches.

## *Pulmonaria officinalis*
## LUNGWORT
Family: Boraginaceae
Native: Europe

A very effective ground-cover plant, no more than 30cm (1ft) tall, for shady borders. It has green hairy leaves that bear white to silver blotches, and spring flowers that are pink when shut, but are violet-blue when open.

**Cultivation** Prefers moist soil rich in humus, and full or semi-shade. Divide in autumn after flowering. ❁ ❁ ❁ Zone 6.

**Uses** Produces excellent ground cover in borders or woodland gardens. As lungwort will thrive in full shade, it can be planted in a woodland or dark, shady border. *Dicentra* and *Primula denticulata* are ideal woodland garden companions.

**Wildlife benefits** The flowers are a firm favourite with early flying bees seeking nectar. Solitary bees, such as the spring (hairy footed) flower bee, have been seen with their long tongues still out between taking nectar from one flower and the next. Plant in large groups to provide a valuable source of early nectar.

**Closely related species** Although there are many cultivars of *P. officinalis*, the species is the best provider of nectar for visiting wildlife. *P. angustifolia* has narrow, lance-like leaves, produces heads of pink-tinged, deep blue flowers, and may be naturalized in a meadow.

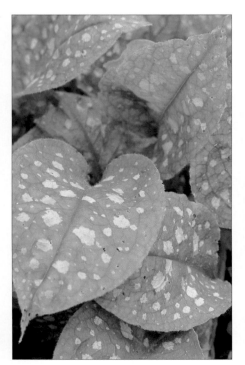

*Pulmonaria officinalis*

## *Rudbeckia fulgida*
## CONEFLOWER
Family: Asteraceae
Native: SE North America

The coneflower adds vibrant colour from late summer to autumn. The plant produces flower heads with long, bright yellow petals with dark, almost black centres. The stems are 60–90cm (2–3ft) tall, and the lance-shaped leaves are rough and hairy.

**Cultivation** Although it will grow in almost any soil, it does require full sun or part-day shade. Propagate by division in spring. ❁ ❁ ❁ Zone 4.

**Uses** Great for using in drifts in naturalistic planting and in herbaceous and mixed borders. Also ideal next to other late summer-flowering plants, such as crocosmias, dahlias and various grass species.

**Wildlife benefits** The flowers are visited by bees and bumblebees for nectar. Late flying butterflies, such as painted ladies and small tortoiseshells, have been noted in large numbers taking nectar in early autumn.

**Closely related species** Popular cultivars of *R. fulgida* are var. *sullivanii* 'Goldsturm', which has narrow golden petals and is a real gardener's favourite, and var. *deamii*, which is extremely drought-tolerant. Many other species, including *R. hirta*, *R. nitida* and *R. californica*, are also excellent insect attractors.

*Rudbeckia fulgida*

*Salvia nemerosa*

## *Salvia nemerosa*
## WOOD SAGE
Family: Lamiaceae
Native: Europe to C Asia

Definitely one of the best plants to attract different bee species into the garden. In summer, wood sage produces nectar-rich flowers that are violet to purple but occasionally white or pink. The stems reach up to 90cm (3ft) high, and bear narrow, oval, mid-green leaves with a rough texture.

**Cultivation** An easy-to-grow perennial that will grow in almost any soil in full sun. Propagate by softwood cuttings at any time of the growing season. ❁ ❁ ❁ Zone 5.

**Uses** An attractive species that belongs to the front of the herbaceous or mixed border, but note it can self-seed and spread prolifically. The better option might be to use it in a meadow mix or the wild garden.

**Wildlife benefits** One of the best plants for attracting bees and bumblebees into the garden. At times the flower spikes will bend due to the sheer number of insects taking nectar. Plant in large groups to attract butterflies because they are less likely to visit single specimens.

**Closely related species**
*S.* x *sylvestris* bears dark violet flower spikes, *S.* x *superba* produces bright violet to purple flowers, and meadow clary (*S. pratensis*) has violet flower heads. All are herbaceous perennials, superb for herbaceous borders or wild areas.

*Scabiosa caucasica*

## *Scabiosa caucasica*
### SCABIOUS
Family: Dipsacaceae
Native: Caucasus

A wonderful showy plant that produces large, lilac-blue flower heads with pincushion-like centres from summer to late autumn. It has light green lance-shaped basal leaves and deeply cut, grey-green stem leaves, and will easily reach 60cm (2ft) high.

**Cultivation**   Site in full sun in neutral to alkaline free-draining soil. Propagate by seed or basal cuttings in spring. ❀ ❀ ❀ Zone 4.

**Uses**   Ideally place to the front of the herbaceous or mixed border, with *Knautia macedonica* and *Polygonum bistorta* to provide a strong focal point. Can also be used in specialist butterfly borders. Plant in large drifts to create the best visual effect.

**Wildlife benefits**   *S. caucasica* is popular with several different species of butterflies, and is also a winner with bees. This is due to the large amount of nectar produced and because of its long flowering period, offering insects food for many weeks.

**Closely related species**   *S. lucida* has rose-lilac flowers and *S. columbaria* red-purple or lilac-blue flowers. Both are suited to a sunny area in a wild garden, and are an invaluable source of pollen and nectar to many insects, particularly bees and butterflies.

## Syn. *Sedum spectabile*
## (*Hylotelephium spectabile*)
### ICE PLANT
Family: Crassulaceae
Native: China and Korea

A lovely structural plant for the garden. The succulent foliage and stems are light green and bear large, flat heads of small, pink-red flowers from late summer to the first frosts. It remains rigid in the dormant season and, if left uncut, will add structure to the border.

**Cultivation**   It is essential that the ice plant is given full sun and free-draining soil. Propagate by division in autumn or spring. ❀ ❀ ❀ Zone 6.

**Uses**   One of the best plants for a naturalistic planting alongside coneflowers (*Rudbeckia*), grasses (e.g. *Deschampsia*) and fennel (*Foeniculum*). It is also an ideal plant for the front of the herbaceous or mixed border.

**Wildlife benefits**   Overwintering butterflies, particularly small tortoiseshells, peacocks and red admirals, drink large amounts of nectar to survive hibernation. The flowers are also a popular choice with bees and other insects.

**Closely related species**
*Hylotelephium telephium* is equally loved by insects and is ideal for a flower border, growing to 60cm (2ft) high. It bears purple flowers with purple-tinged foliage.

Syn. *Sedum spectabile*

*Silene dioica*

## *Silene dioica*
### RED CAMPION
Family: Caryophyllaceae
Native: Europe

A pretty wild flower of woodland edges and hedgerows. It produces attractive rose-pink flowers from spring to early summer on leafy stems reaching up to 45cm (18in) high. The leaves, found all the way up the stem, are ovate and decrease in number as they reach the flower head.

**Cultivation**   Red campion prefers light, well-drained soil in full sun, and will also thrive in semi-shady conditions. Propagate by seed when fresh. ❀ ❀ ❀ Zone 6.

**Uses**   Best suited for growing in meadows, but it will also grow extremely well in herbaceous borders and woodland edges. Light blue bluebells make good planting companions, mixing well with the light pink.

**Wildlife benefits**   The flowers are a good early source of nectar for butterflies and moths. The leaves are eaten by the caterpillars of several moths. Leave the old stems uncut to allow the seed to drop freely for birds and small mammals, and to create hibernation sites.

**Closely related species**   *S. latifolia*, which grows to 90cm (3ft), bears white, scented flowers in summer. Bladder campion (*S. vulgaris*) is best suited to grasslands in a sunny location. All species attract butterflies and moths to their nectar.

*Solidago virgaurea*
## GOLDEN ROD
Family: Asteraceae
Native: Arctic and W Europe

A fantastic insect attractor that produces tall spikes of golden flowers with lance-shaped green leaves, and reaches up to 90cm (3ft) high. The flowering period is long, from summer to autumn, when golden rod produces large amounts of nectar, making it invaluable to any wildlife garden.

**Cultivation** It prefers full sun with its roots in any type of well-drained soil. Propagate by division in autumn or spring. ❀ ❀ ❀ Zone 5.

**Uses** *S. virgaurea* is best suited to the wild garden where it can run rampant. Garden cultivars are a better choice for more managed gardens where they can be grown in herbaceous or mixed borders.

**Wildlife benefits** The nectar-rich flowers are very attractive to bees, butterflies and moths. Ladybirds and parasitic wasps are also frequent visitors, with soldier beetles hiding in the dense foliage. Seeds are eaten by birds, particularly finches and linnets.

**Closely related species** *S. virgaurea* and *S. canadensis* have been crossed to produce garden-worthy hybrids such as *S.* 'Cloth of Gold' and *S.* 'Golden Mosa'.

*Stachys officinalis*
## BETONY
Family: Lamiaceae
Native: Europe and Asia

A wonderful woodland plant that produces large, showy flower heads that contain numerous lilac-purple, very occasionally pink or white, flowers. They are borne throughout summer on stems that grow to 90cm (3ft) high, and bear oblong leaves with a heart-shaped base.

**Cultivation** Plant around the garden in full sun or partial shade. It will grow in any soil, ideally one enriched with humus. Propagate by seed or division. ❀ ❀ ❀ Zone 5.

**Uses** The attractive flowers are a welcome sight when used in large drifts along a woodland edge. Plant with other shade-tolerant plants, in particular heucheras and dicentras. Can also be used in herbaceous and mixed borders, or in a wild garden.

**Wildlife benefits** If planted in large numbers it provides welcome colour and a rich nectar store for insects. The flowers are attractive to both bees and butterflies.

**Closely related species** Annual hedgenettle (*S. annua*) and *S. alpina* are ideal for hedge banks and wildflower areas because they are excellent nectar producers, and attract many species of bee and butterfly. Downy woundwort (*S. germanica*) is ideal for a wild garden.

*Symphytum grandiflora*
## COMFREY
Family: Boraginaceae
Native: Europe

A low-growing perennial reaching up to 30cm (1ft) high, producing a thick mat of leaves making excellent ground cover. The rich green leaves are hairy and rough. The creamy, drooping, tubular flowers appear in spring and are borne on one-sided racemes.

**Cultivation** Comfrey will grow in most soils but thrives in moist, free-draining

*Symphytum grandiflora*

ground in sun or, better still, dappled shade. Propagate by division in autumn or spring. ❀ ❀ ❀ Zone 5.

**Uses** A welcome addition to the front of the herbaceous border or group of old-fashioned roses. Annual maintenance may be required if a clump is becoming too invasive, or grow it in the wild garden.

**Wildlife benefits** The nectar-rich flowers are a magnet for bees and bumblebees. Group several plants together to create good ground cover that will encourage shy birds into the garden looking for seeds, insects and shelter.

**Closely related species** The flowers of *S. officinalis* are also good at attracting bees. It is commonly grown in vegetable gardens to make liquid tea, or is cut and added to the compost heap to provide a source of potassium.

*Solidago virgaurea*

*Stachys officinalis*

### *Taraxacum officinale*
### DANDELION
Family: Asteraceae
Native: Northern Hemisphere

Although thought of as a weed, dandelions have beautiful, round, nectar-rich flowers with sterile, golden-yellow petals around the edge. The heads can reach up to 5cm (2in) wide, and appear from spring to autumn. The mid-green leaves are oblong with toothed edges.

**Cultivation** Dandelions enjoy a sunny spot in any type of soil. The plant will naturally self-seed if the yellow flowers are left on. ❀ ❀ ❀ Zone 5.

**Uses** Leave even a small area of grass to grow long and dandelions will naturally appear, giving the area a boost of colour. They will also pop up in meadows and along hedgerow bottoms that aren't too shady, and will look completely at home in the wild garden.

**Wildlife benefits** Dandelions are a fantastic nectar and pollen plant for honeybees and bumblebees. They also provide nectar for butterflies and other insects. The leaves are eaten by caterpillars of the white ermine moth, and the seeds are eaten by birds, particularly goldfinches and greenfinches.

**Closely related species** Russian dandelion (*T. glaucanthum*) grows to 30cm (1ft) high and bears pale to bright yellow flowers striped grey underneath. *T. alpicola* grows up to 30cm (1ft) high and has orange to yellow flowers all summer.

### *Trifolium pratense*
### RED CLOVER
Family: Papilionaceae
Native: Europe

Red clover is a profuse flowering perennial, growing up to 30cm (1ft) high. The round flower heads are red to purple or pink, and occasionally cream, appearing in late spring and summer. The leaves are divided into three leaflets.

**Cultivation** Thrives in any well-drained garden soil, in a variety of types. Place in full sun for best flowering results. Propagate by seed in spring or autumn. ❀ ❀ ❀ Zone 6.

**Uses** They are used in wildflower areas for their attractive flowers and nectar. *T. pratense* can be used as a green manure in vegetable gardens, or in areas that will lie dormant for several weeks, because the roots fix nitrogen in the soil.

**Wildlife benefits** An excellent plant for providing nectar for bumblebees, and feeding several species of butterfly caterpillar. Birds also peck at the flowers, hunting pollinating insects as a quick meal. The seeds are eaten by birds, especially finches.

**Closely related species** White clover (*T. repens*) is less attractive, but is still worth including in a wildflower meadow mix. Its leaves provide food for caterpillars of the common blue and clouded yellow butterfly. It can also be used in an ornamental lawn seed mix. The sowing rate is 50 per cent clover and 50 per cent grass mix.

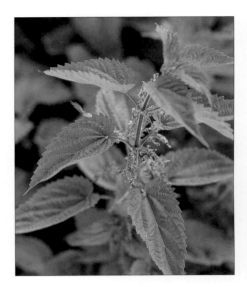

*Urtica dioica*

### *Urtica dioica*
### STINGING NETTLE
Family: Urticaceae
Native: Northern Hemisphere

One of the best herbaceous plants for attracting a large number of species into the garden. It is not every gardener's favourite, though, because of its invasive roots and stinging leaves. It will, however, attract beautiful species of butterfly into the area. It grows 1.2m (4ft) tall, and produces insignificant green flowers.

**Cultivation** The nettle is a good indicator of rich soil because it thrives in fertile areas. To attract butterflies to lay their eggs on the plant, the nettle has to be positioned in full sun. If planted in shade it's of limited use to the surrounding wildlife. Excellent spreader. ❀ ❀ ❀ Zone 5.

**Uses** Grow in wild gardens or areas of long grass. As it has insignificant flowers, plant alongside red campion and cow parsley to bring colour to a grassland area. Cut down a small patch halfway through the season and allow to regenerate because late egg-laying butterflies prefer to lay on young foliage.

**Wildlife benefits** Caterpillars of many species of garden butterfly, including peacock, red admiral and the small tortoiseshell, feed on the leaves of the plant and, in turn, attract many bird species, including the sparrow, chasing an easy meal. The seeds are eaten by bullfinches and siskins.

**Closely related species** The annual nettle (*U. urens*) has blue-green leaves that sting if touched. It flowers from summer to autumn.

*Taraxacum officinale*

*Trifolium pratense*

## *Verbascum olympicum*
## MULLEIN
Family: Scrophulariaceae
Native: Turkey

This tall, majestic plant can be classed as a biennial or perennial. Its stems are white and hairy and produce large, woolly textured, lance-shaped basal leaves. The flower heads contain hundreds of individual flowers that are bright golden-yellow.

**Cultivation**  Mullein enjoys full sun, and thrives in well-drained soil. Although it will grow in almost any type of soil, it prefers chalky ground. Propagate by seed in spring. ❀ ❀ ❀ Zone 6.

**Uses**  A brilliant border plant, giving structure and height. Use in herbaceous or mixed borders. It can be used effectively when randomly spaced around a dry garden, between grasses, globe thistles and knautias.

**Wildlife benefits**  Bees are frequent visitors to the flowers collecting pollen for their larvae. Butterflies will occasionally take nectar from the flowers.

**Closely related species**  All verbascums (except doubles) are good for visiting wildlife. Good single-flowering species include dark mullein (*V. nigrum*), which is 1.2m (4ft) high with purple-centred yellow flowers, and nettle-leaved mullein (*V. chaixii*), with yellow flowers and purple hairy anthers. The stems can reach up to 90cm (3ft).

## *Veronica spicata*
## SPIKED SPEEDWELL
Family: Scrophulariaceae
Native: Europe

A lovely herbaceous perennial that is extremely popular. It produces strong growth, reaching 60cm (2ft) tall and is a welcome addition to any border. The lance-shaped foliage knits together closely giving rise to spikes of purple-blue flowers in early summer.

**Cultivation**  Veronicas prefer full sun with their roots in any type of free-draining soil. Propagate by division in spring or autumn. ❀ ❀ ❀ Zone 3.

**Uses**  Plant in large clumps in herbaceous or mixed borders to create the best effect. *V. spicata* looks good planted next to silver-leaved plants, such as *Stachys byzantina*, and red-pink flowering plants, for example *Persicaria affinis*.

**Wildlife benefits**  A real winner with bees seeking pollen and nectar. Leave the stems uncut during winter because the tight-knit foliage offers refuge for hibernating beneficial insects. Cut back the stems in early spring.

**Closely related species**  There are many other species in the genus that benefit bees, and are ideal for ornamental borders. They include *V. gentianoides*, 60cm (2ft) high, *V. peduncularis* at 20–25cm (8–10in), and *V. austriaca* at 30cm (1ft).

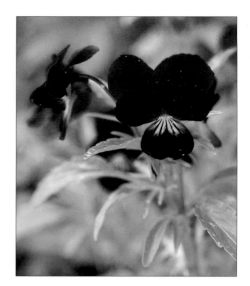

*Viola odorata*

## *Viola odorata*
## SWEET VIOLET
Family: Violaceae
Native: Europe

A pretty little woodland ground-cover plant that is named after its scented purple, lilac, white or occasionally yellow flowers that appear in early spring. The delicate flowers rise just above the deep green, heart-shaped leaves. It reaches no more than 15cm (6in) high.

**Cultivation**  Grows best in semi- or full shade in soil that contains large quantities of humus, especially leaf mould. This will help the soil to retain moisture during the summer months. Propagate by division in late spring or early autumn. ❀ ❀ ❀ Zone 8.

**Uses**  An ideal little plant for using as ground cover in the woodland garden or a shady border. Plant at the front of a border, or under trees and shrubs in large numbers to create a carpet of flowers. Inter-plant with dwarf daffodils, such as *N.* 'February Gold', for a dramatic effect.

**Wildlife benefits**  The leaves of *V. odorata* are eaten by caterpillars of several fritillary butterfly species. The flowers are visited by bumblebees in spring, and the seeds are eaten by several species of birds, including bullfinches and coal tits.

**Closely related species**  Common dog violet (*V. riviniana*) is a woodland plant that is similar in size but with smaller lilac flowers and purple leaves. It is another very important early nectar source for insects, and a caterpillar food plant for fritillary butterflies. The pansy (*V.* x *wittrockiana*) is usually grown as an annual, and is used in bedding schemes and containers.

*Verbascum olympicum*

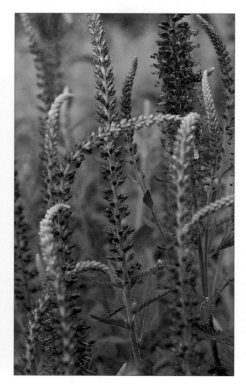

*Veronica spicata*

# HERBS

### *Allium schoenoprasum*
### CHIVES
Family: Alliaceae
Native: Europe

Chives are hardy perennials that bear gorgeous pale purple or pink flowers in early summer. This frost-tender culinary herb produces 30cm (12in) tall, thin, cylindrical leaves that, with the flowers, are used in salads.

**Cultivation** Provide an open, sunny situation and free-draining soil. Grows well if left undisturbed for several years to form large clumps. Easily propagated by seed in autumn, or by dividing the clumps in spring. ❀ ❀ ❀ Zone 5.

**Uses** Often used with foxgloves (*Digitalis*) and wallflowers (*Erysimum*) as a companion plant for apples. Chives also make excellent ornamental plants, ideal for tubs, hanging baskets (especially when grown with colourful nasturtiums and fuchsias), borders (herbaceous and mixed), and herb gardens.

**Wildlife benefits** Chives are a big draw for bees and bumblebees seeking abundant quantities of nectar. Chives are also occasionally visited by butterflies.

**Closely related species** Alliums are ideal for the wildlife garden, producing plenty of nectar, and come in a wide range of heights. At one extreme is *Allium insubricum* that flowers in summer, bearing nodding, pinkish-purple, bell-shaped flowers, and reaches 15–30cm (6–12in) high. A real gardener's favourite is *Allium cernuum*, 30–70cm (12–28in) high with pink to white cup-shaped, nodding summer flowers.

*Allium schoenoprasum*

*Anethum graveolens*

### *Anethum graveolens*
### DILL
Family: Apiaceae
Native: SW Asia

An attractive annual with a strong anise scent, and bluish-green leaves that are finely divided and look very similar to its close relation, fennel (*Foeniculum*). Dill will grow to 60cm (2ft) tall if left unpicked, and will then bear tiny yellow flowers in terminal clusters. The foliage and seed are commonly used in fish dishes, and in pickling spice mixtures.

**Cultivation** Plant in rich, well-drained soil and site in full sun. Keep watered in dry periods because it has a tendency to bolt in poor, dry soil. Propagate from seed in spring. Sow direct in the open ground as they don't transplant well. ❀ ❀ ❀ Zone 8.

**Uses** Dill is ideal in the herb or vegetable garden. It's also an attractive plant that works well in tubs and mixed borders. Looks particularly good when planted next to *Geranium phaeum* or sage (*Salvia nemorosa*).

**Wildlife benefits** The plants attract many species of hoverfly that enjoy feeding on the nectar-rich flowers. By increasing the number of hoverflies in the garden, it will decrease the number of aphids. Dill also attracts several types of bee, lacewings and ladybirds. By leaving the hollow stems intact over winter, small insects can hibernate inside; they re-emerge in spring to provide food for hungry birds.

**Closely related species** Cow parsley (*Anthriscus sylvestris*) is loved by various insects, including flies.

### *Angelica archangelica*
### ANGELICA
Family: Apiaceae
Native: N and E Europe, C Asia and Greenland

A statuesque biennial that often lives for three years. It grows 1.2–2.4m (4–8ft) high, and has hollow stems with large, deeply divided, light green leaves. The globular flower heads are magnificent, producing clusters of green flowers in early summer.

**Cultivation** Angelica thrives in rich, damp soil, but will tolerate most conditions except extreme dryness. Site in sun or partial shade. ❀ ❀ ❀ Zone 4.

**Uses** Great architectural plant for the mixed or herbaceous border. Place it at the back of the border, where staking may be necessary. Stunning if planted beside black elder (*Sambucus* 'Black Beauty') or other purple-leaved plants.

**Wildlife benefits** The large flower heads are rich in nectar and are frequently engulfed by buzzing, beneficial insects, such as lacewings, ladybirds and parasitic wasps. In turn they attract insect-eating birds, e.g. swifts and wagtails. Blue tits and greenfinches enjoy the autumn seed.

**Closely related species** All angelicas are great insect attractors. *Angelica atropurpurea*, the American angelica, has dark purple stems and white flowers, *A. sylvestris* is the wild European kind and bears white or pink flowers, and the attractive *A. gigas*, the Korean version, has purple stems and pink flowers but dies after flowering.

*Angelica archangelica*

*Carum carvi*

## *Carum carvi*
## CARAWAY
Family: Apiaceae
Native: Asia and C Europe

A pretty biennial, 30–60cm (1–2ft) tall, with clusters of white flowers in the second year of growth. The bright green feathery leaves contrast well with the flower heads. The seed is often used in culinary dishes or as an organic breath-freshener.

**Cultivation** Prefers deep, well-drained soil (although it will tolerate heavy ground) in a sunny position. Sow in its final position in spring because the seedlings dislike being moved. ❀ ❀ ❀ Zone 3.

**Uses** As with many herbs, especially those in the Apiaceae family, caraway is brilliant at attracting beneficial insects to the garden. Grow small groups every few metres throughout a mixed or herbaceous border, vegetable or fruit garden.

**Wildlife benefits** The attracted beneficial insects, such as hoverflies, ladybirds and lacewings, are major predators of aphids. The more caraway you grow, the more effective the pest control.

**Closely related species** Caraway is a near relative of the carrot, another excellent insect attractor. Its roots can be prepared and eaten in a similar way to carrot and parsnip. Note, if you want caraway to flower (which occurs in the second year), you won't get the roots because by then they'll be tasteless.

## *Coriandrum sativum*
## CORIANDER
Family: Apiaceae
Native: N Africa and Mediterranean

An aromatic annual, known as cilantro in the US, that can reach 30cm (1ft) high, with small white to mauve flowers in spring. The pungent, finely divided leaves are narrow and feathery. It has been in cultivation for thousands of years (seed was found in Tutankhamen's tomb).

**Cultivation** Succeeds in well-drained, fertile soil that is moisture retentive, in a sunny site. Young plants start producing seed if ample water is not given in periods of dry weather. ❀ ❀ ❀ Zone 3.

**Uses** If coriander is left to flower, it is one of the best plants for attracting beneficial insects. Grow clusters of coriander in mixed and herbaceous borders to provide natural pest control. Also very effective in the fruit and vegetable garden to attract pollinators.

**Wildlife benefits** Coriander is loved by ladybirds, lacewings and particularly hoverflies, which visit the small, whitish flowers laden with nectar. All (both adults and larvae) are voracious eaters of aphids. Parasitic wasps are also visitors to the flowers, seeking nectar.

**Closely related species** Many of the plants in the Apiaceae family (formerly the Umbelliferae family) attract insects, especially dill (*Anethum graveolens*), *Ferula assa-foetida* and cumin (*Cuminum cyminum*).

*Coriandrum sativum*

*Hyssopus officinalis*

## *Hyssopus officinalis*
## HYSSOP
Family: Lamiaceae
Native: S and E Europe

A lovely herbaceous perennial, growing to 60cm (2ft) high. It bears violet, blue or, occasionally, white flowers from late summer to autumn. The small, dark green leaves are pungent and, when chopped, emit a strong, peppery aroma.

**Cultivation** Needs well-drained (preferably alkaline) soil in a sunny location. Hyssop does not divide particularly well, and propagation by seed or cuttings is best. ❀ ❀ ❀ Zone 3.

**Uses** Great in pots, or borders (herbaceous or mixed), or grow as a low hedge. Beekeepers often plant such hedges near their hives because of the good-quality nectar. Also plant in the fruit and vegetable garden to attract pollinators, and for its attractive appearance.

**Wildlife benefits** Butterflies occasionally visit the plant for nectar. Spiders are also attracted, making webs between the stems and sunbathing on the sunny side of the plant. Because many insects hibernate in the foliage, delay cutting back until spring.

**Closely related species** Plants in the Lamiaceae family are renowned for their nectar. To attract bees, also grow white deadnettle (*Lamium album*), sage (*Salvia nemorosa*), and spearmint (*Mentha spicata*).

## *Lavandula angustifolia*
### LAVENDER
Family: Lamiaceae
Native: Mediterranean

An aromatic shrub with grey-green leaves, it grows 60–90cm (2–3ft) high and produces small, purple flowers rich in nectar from midsummer to autumn. Lavender is as important to wildlife as it is for its aesthetic qualities.

**Cultivation** Provide well-drained soil in plenty of sun. Best propagated by cuttings. ✽ ✽ ✽ Zone 5.

**Uses** Lavender hedges look great and smell amazing. Plants can also be used in mixed and shrub borders, in tubs and containers. Site next to silver-leaved plants, such as wormwood (*Artemisia ludoviciana* subsp. *mexicana* var. *albula*) or *Santolina chamaecyparissus*, for a cool, calming effect, or with *Perovskia atricifolia* and *Phlomis italica* for a Mediterranean look.

**Wildlife benefits** Great clouds of white butterflies are often seen in large patches of lavender in late summer, looking for nectar. They have to share it with several species of bee competing for the sugary drink. Goldfinches and other seed-eaters devour the seed from autumn on.

**Closely related species** Lavender (*Lavandula angustifolia* 'Hidcote') has neat, erect growth making it ideal for hedges or lining paths, especially of old, characterful properties. *L. a.* 'Munstead' is more compact at 30–45cm (12–18in) high, and is very effective in tubs.

*Lavandula angustifolia*

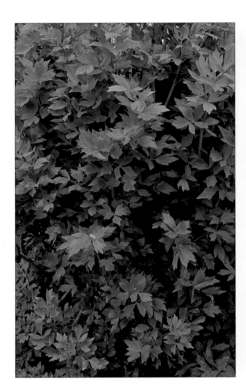

*Levisticum officinale*

## *Levisticum officinale*
### LOVAGE
Family: Apiaceae
Native: E Mediterranean

A tall, hardy, vigorous perennial reaching 1.8m (6ft) high, bearing insignificant, dull yellow flowers in summer. The leaves are deeply divided, with a pungent smell, and taste of celery. The roots are long and fleshy.

**Cultivation** It tolerates most conditions, except heavy clay, and grows best in rich, deep soil in sun or partial shade. Propagate from seed in spring, or by division in spring or autumn. ✽ ✽ ✽ Zone 4.

**Uses** Great in a herb garden or to the back of a scented border, next to red and orange flowers because the glossy green foliage brings out the vibrant colours. Due to its vigorous growth, be careful where it's planted or it'll quickly swamp less vigorous neighbours. Excellent in a wildflower meadow or wild garden.

**Wildlife benefits** Attracts hoverflies and bees to the nectar-rich flowers, and beneficial wasps seeking nectar in late summer. The lush foliage shelters ground beetles that prey on young slugs.

**Closely related species** Nectar-rich relatives include the carrot (*Daucus carota*), parsley (*Petroselinum crispum*) and one of the best wildlife plants, fennel (*Foeniculum vulgare*).

*Melissa officinalis*

## *Melissa officinalis*
### LEMON BALM
Family: Lamiaceae
Native: S and C Europe

Lemon balm is a vigorous herbaceous perennial. It has small, white flowers borne in summer on stems up to 75cm (2½ft) high. The leaves are deeply veined and smell of lemon.

**Cultivation** It grows in almost any soil in full sun or semi-shade, with shelter from strong winds. It is easily propagated by division in spring or autumn, or by seed in spring. ✽ ✽ ✽ Zone 4.

**Uses** If using in a small herb garden, grow it in a pot to restrict the root spread. The plants need to be left to flower and therefore produce nectar to be of any benefit to wildlife. Due to its vigorous growth, take care that neighbouring plants aren't swamped. The ideal solution is to let it naturalize in a wild garden.

**Wildlife benefits** Bees are attracted by the smell of the leaves and the nectar. The foliage can be used to ease the pain of insect stings or bites.

**Closely related species** Balm (*Melissa officinalis* 'Aurea') has variegated foliage and is better for a smaller garden because it is less vigorous. *M.* 'All Gold' has bright yellow leaves, and should be planted in partial shade because it can scorch in full sun.

*Mentha spicata*

## *Mentha spicata*
## SPEARMINT
Family: Lamiaceae
Native: S and C Europe

When gardeners think of planting mint, they immediately worry about root invasion, and spearmint is certainly a vigorous species, spreading everywhere and growing up to 60cm (2ft) tall. The leaves are dark green with prominent patterning, and purple flowers in summer.

**Cultivation** Mint enjoys full sun or semi-shade, and thrives in almost any fertile soil that doesn't dry out. Best to propagate by cuttings in summer, or by division in spring. ❀ ❀ ❀ Zone 3.

**Uses** Most gardeners prefer to grow mint in pots to limit its spread. Either stand it on a patio or sink a large container in the ground.

**Wildlife benefits** Predatory wasps, flies, bees and butterflies are attracted to the nectar-rich flowers all summer, and spiders find shelter beneath the leaves. The mature seed is eaten by birds.

**Closely related species** All mints are good producers of nectar, usually over summer. Pennyroyal (*Mentha pulegium*) is a smaller plant that prefers moister soil in sun or partial shade, and produces a profusion of mauve flowers in whorls, whereas the variable peppermint (*M.* x *piperita*) grows 30–90cm (1–3ft) tall and has pink flowers.

## *Myrrhis odorata*
## SWEET CICELY
Family: Apiaceae
Native: Europe

A vigorous, pleasantly scented herbaceous perennial, it has a strong taproot and grows to 90cm (3ft) tall. It bears fern-like leaves and produces clusters of fluffy white flowers in late spring. Often used to sweeten stewed fruits and rhubarb.

**Cultivation** Grows in full sun or thrives in semi-shade, being a natural hedgerow plant. Prefers moist, humus-rich soil. Propagate by seed or by root division in spring. ❀ ❀ ❀ Zone 5.

**Uses** Sweet cicely is a lovely plant, ideal in a cottage garden. It is invasive and self-seeds everywhere, so is only suitable in an unkept or wild cottage garden, or as part of a natural-looking woodland garden. It is extremely hard to eradicate once established, so think carefully before planting.

**Wildlife benefits** The nectar-rich flowers are a real winner for attracting bees in late spring. Beneficial wasps and flies are also tempted by the flat, white flower heads. Flies are often seen visiting Apiaceae flowers and, although you would not want too many in the garden, they are a vital part of the food chain and support a great number of birds and other creatures.

**Closely related species** Cow parsley (*Anthriscus sylvestris*) is closely related to sweet cicely. This herbaceous perennial is also ideal for naturalizing in long grass, attracting many insects, particularly flies.

*Myrrhis odorata*

*Ocimum basilicum*

## *Ocimum basilicum*
## BASIL
Family: Lamiaceae
Native: India and Middle East

A multi-stemmed, tender annual that grows to 40cm (16in) high. It produces bright green leaves that vary in pungency and flavour, depending on the growing conditions, with constant watering diluting the flavour. To be of value to wildlife, don't pick the foliage and leave the small, white summer flowers, a real magnet for bees.

**Cultivation** Sow seed in early spring under glass. Plant out in late spring and early summer after hardening off. Plants thrive in well-drained soil in full sun, ideally against a sheltering wall. ❀ Zone 10.

**Uses** Plant in garden containers, pots and hanging baskets, mixing it with ornamental plants, such as fuchsias, trailing lobelia and thyme (*Thymus*). Pick only some of the leaves for the kitchen, and then allow the plant to produce nectar-rich flowers.

**Wildlife benefits** Carry out several sowings over summer, and plant out when large enough. This will ensure an everlasting supply of nectar for the hungry bees.

**Closely related species** *Ocimum basilicum* 'Citriodorum' has lemon-scented leaves and *O.* 'Crispum' has leaves that are curled along the edges. *O.* 'Minimum' is ideal for growing in pots because it's just 15–30cm (6–12in) high.

*Origanum majorana*

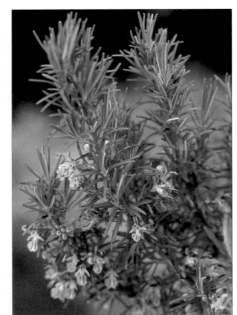

*Rosmarinus officinalis*

### *Origanum majorana*
### SWEET MARJORAM
Family: Lamiaceae
Native: Europe

A half-hardy perennial, often grown as an annual, that can reach 60cm (2ft) high in a season. It has pale green leaves and bears small, white to pink flowers in distinctive clusters from mid- to late summer.

**Cultivation** It thrives in well-drained, fertile soil in full sun. Sow seed in early spring under glass, and plant out in late spring or early summer after the last frost. ✿ ✿ ✿ Zone 7.

**Uses** Great in herb gardens and borders (herbaceous and mixed). Place to the front of a border and also use as ground cover. Alternatively, grow in pots with other herbs or in hanging baskets with a mix of ornamentals and vegetables.

**Wildlife benefits** The nectar-rich flowers are excellent for attracting bees and butterflies all summer long. Plant in a sheltered, sunny position to attract large numbers of insects. Seed-eating birds start to forage on the plant from autumn on, while the many crevices of the stems and leaves provide a good site for hibernating insects.

**Closely related species** All *Origanum* species produce plenty of nectar. Pot marjoram (*O. onites*) is a sturdier grower than sweet marjoram, and produces hairy green leaves and pinkish-purple flowers. Oregano (*O. vulgare*) is very pungent and has a thyme-like scent.

### *Rosmarinus officinalis*
### ROSEMARY
Family: Lamiaceae
Native: Mediterranean

A long-flowering evergreen shrub, rosemary has pale blue flowers all along the stems from spring to summer, and will even flower sporadically in autumn and winter. Stems reach 2m (6½ft) high if left unpruned, and produce needle-like aromatic leaves that are green on top and silvery beneath.

**Cultivation** Enjoys a sheltered, sunny location, and thrives in well-drained soil requiring little moisture. Propagate by semi-ripe cuttings taken in summer. ✿ ✿ Zone 6.

**Uses** A great plant for a splash of colour in a shrub or mixed border. Also ideal for a dry garden where little or no irrigation is used. Grow beside other drought-tolerant plants, such as the globe thistle (*Echinops ritro*), sea holly (*Eryngium alpinum*) and red hot poker (*Kniphofia caulescens*).

**Wildlife benefits** The flowers attract bees, hoverflies and the occasional butterfly. Also, the flowers often open when there are few other flowers present rich in nectar, giving a welcome meal for hungry insects. Birds forage around in the foliage looking for a quick meal, usually aphids.

**Closely related species** The dwarf *Rosmarinus officinalis* 'Blue Boy' is ideal for growing in pots, whereas 'Miss Jessop's Upright' is tall and erect, making it ideal for a shrub border. *R. eriocalyx* is a prostrate shrub rarely reaching 90cm (3ft) high, and can only be grown in frost-free conditions.

### *Salvia officinalis*
### COMMON SAGE
Family: Lamiaceae
Native: S Europe

People either love or hate the smell of the leaves that are grey-green with a rough texture. Spikes of tubular, violet-blue flowers are borne from early to late summer, reaching to 60cm (2ft) high.

**Cultivation** Best grown in light, well-drained soil in a sunny location. Propagate from seed in spring or by cuttings in summer. ✿ ✿ ✿ Zone 5.

**Uses** Sage is a good all-rounder and can be used in many different garden locations. It is a real winner at the front of a shrub border, in a herb garden, and looks superb in a pot. The foliage of box (*Buxus sempervirens*) nicely complements the pastels of sage. The latter also marries well with pink- and purple-flowering plants, such as the coneflower (*Echinacea purpurea*) and *Cirsium rivulare*.

**Wildlife benefits** Visited by bees seeking nectar and the occasional butterfly. In late summer the flowers are well known for providing a source of pollen when many other plants have finished flowering. If left uncut over winter, the intricate mass of stems creates many crevices and homes for insects.

**Closely related species** Two ornamental cultivars of sage, equally good at attracting wildlife, are *Salvia officinalis* 'Icterina', with yellow and green variegated leaves, and 'Purpurascens', with purple foliage, but both are less hardy than the species. *S.* x *sylvestris* and *Salvia nemorosa* are two of the best bee plants for an ornamental garden.

*Salvia officinalis*

*Satureja montana*

## *Satureja montana*
### WINTER SAVORY
Family: Lamiaceae
Native: Mediterranean

Winter savory was celebrated by Virgil (70–19BC) who said it was one of the most fragrant plants for growing near beehives. This semi-evergreen sub-shrub grows to 38cm (15in) tall and has dark green, aromatic leaves. The stems also bear small white flowers in summer.

**Cultivation** Thrives in well-drained soil in a sunny location. Propagate by seed or by division in spring. ❀ ❀ ❀ Zone 6.

**Uses** Plant in a nectar-rich herbaceous border, herb garden or mixed border. Can also be grown in pots with other herbs, although its growth can be a little untidy. Can be used in companion planting to ward off aphids.

**Wildlife benefits** Winter savory is still one of the best plants for attracting bees into the wildlife garden. The flowers provide an important source of nectar throughout summer. It can be brought on to flower in winter, hence its name.

**Closely related species** Summer savory (*Satureja hortensis*) is equal to winter savory in its ability to provide nectar for bees. It is a small, busy, hardy annual, slightly shorter than the winter kind. It bears small white or lilac flowers in summer.

## *Tanacetum vulgare*
### TANSY
Family: Asteraceae
Native: Europe and temperate Asia

A vigorous, popular herb, tansy grows up to 1.2m (4ft) tall. The stems bear aromatic, finely cut foliage and culminate in flower heads with button-like clusters of yellow flowers that attract many insects.

**Cultivation** Grows well in dry, free-draining soil in full sun or semi-shade. Propagate by seed, division or by cuttings in spring. ❀ ❀ ❀ Zone 4.

**Uses** Looks at home in any herbaceous border, adding bright colour from summer to early autumn. In fact tansy is one of the showiest flowers in the herb garden, and is best in a mixed border next to the dark green leaves of bay (*Laurus nobilis*) and yew (*Taxus baccata*).

**Wildlife benefits** The flowers attract many insects, including lacewings, ladybirds, parasitic wasps and hoverflies. The blooms are especially attractive to bees, bumblebees and butterflies seeking nectar. Leave the stems uncut in the winter to provide a home for hibernating insects.

**Closely related species** Feverfew (*Tanacetum parthenium*) also attracts many insects. It is a bushy, hardy perennial that grows up to 1m (3ft) high. It produces masses of white flowers with yellow centres in early to midsummer.

*Tanacetum vulgare*

*Thymus vulgaris*

## *Thymus vulgaris*
### THYME
Family: Lamiaceae
Native: W Mediterranean

Thyme is an excellent plant for attracting wildlife. This species creates a neat dome up to 30cm (1ft) high. The stems bear small, aromatic leaves and a profusion of tiny, mauve flowers.

**Cultivation** It grows well in poor, stony soil, neutral to alkaline, in a sunny position. ❀ ❀ ❀ Zone 7.

**Uses** All thymes are ideal for planting between cracks in a patio or path, and in rock gardens or dry borders. They can also be grown in a herb or vegetable plot or in a hanging basket.

**Wildlife benefits** Hoverflies and butterflies are frequent visitors to the numerous flowers seeking nectar. Bees and bumblebees are attracted to the nectar and collect pollen for their young. Plant in a sunny position for increased nectar production.

**Closely related species** *Thymus polytrichus* subsp. *britannicus* needs excellent drainage, making it ideal for growing in the cracks between paving stones. *T. serphyllum* bears small, purple-red flowers from early to midsummer and reaches 25cm (10in) tall. It is often used in tubs and hanging baskets.

# SHRUBS

### *Amelanchier lamarckii*
### JUNEBERRY
Family: Rosaceae
Native: E Canada

This beautiful plant can be classed as either a large shrub or a small tree, and can grow up to 10m (33ft) high. The white flowers are a joy to see in spring and are followed by round, juicy, dark fruit in autumn. The newly emerged leaves have white hairs that quickly fall off. They are oblong and dark green, turning orange and red in late summer.

**Cultivation** The juneberry prefers well-drained, acid soil that's fertile and moist. Site in full sun or partial shade. Sow seed when ripe or take semi-ripe cuttings in summer. ✿ ✿ ✿ Zone 4.

**Uses** It flowers all over, not just at the crown, and is best grown as a specimen in a wildflower meadow. It can also be sited in a shrub or mixed border, and is ideal for giving height in a small garden without being invasive.

**Wildlife benefits** Many pollinating insects, especially solitary bees and butterflies, are drawn to the spring flowers. The fruits are eaten by birds, particularly starlings, garden warblers, thrushes, chaffinches and greenfinches, and mammals, such as squirrels and foxes.

**Closely related species** The allegheny serviceberry (*A. laevis*), a native North American, has a spreading, shrubby habit with white flowers and good autumn colour before leaf drop. The shadbush (*A. canadensis*) is a suckering species with similar attributes.

### *Berberis darwinii*
### BARBERRY
Family: Berberidaceae
Native: Chile and Argentina

The barberries have the best shrub species for wildlife. This particular shrub is a vigorous evergreen with spine-toothed, glossy, dark green leaves. Pendulous, dark orange flowers appear in spring and occasionally in autumn. They are followed by blue to black round fruits.

**Cultivation** The shrubs grow in most well-drained soils. Nectar production, fruiting and autumn colour are best if the plants are sited in full sun. Take semi-ripe cuttings in summer. ✿ ✿ ✿ Zone 7.

**Uses** All the species are excellent when used as an informal single-species hedge. *B. darwinii* is also an excellent choice in shrub beds and mixed borders because of its many attributes, which include attractive flowers, late-summer fruits and evergreen foliage.

**Wildlife benefits** The nectar-rich flowers are loved by bees and bumblebees. The fruits are eaten by birds, particularly blackbirds, thrushes, nuthatches, tits, garden warblers and finches. And small birds often nest amongst the thorny branches because they offer protection from predators.

**Closely related species** *B. julianae* is one of the species' best nectar producers and, like *B. darwinii*, makes a fantastic hedge. It is an evergreen and bears yellow flowers with a red tinge. *B. thunbergii* is deciduous and can be used in informal or formal hedging.

*Buddleja davidii*

### *Buddleja davidii*
### BUTTERFLY BUSH
Family: Buddlejaceae
Native: China and Japan

If you want to attract clouds of adult butterflies, plant *B. davidii* in the garden. It is a large, fast-growing shrub which can easily reach 3m (10ft) high, with tall, arching shoots bearing lance-shaped green to grey leaves. The lilac to purple honey-scented flowers are borne in 30cm (12in) long panicles from summer to autumn.

**Cultivation** The butterfly bush likes fertile, well-drained soil in full sun. Propagate by semi-ripe cuttings in summer, or hardwood cuttings in autumn. ✿ ✿ ✿ Zone 5.

**Uses** *B. davidii* is great in mixed and shrub borders. It has many cultivars in a range of colours, making it easy to select for a colour-themed border. In North America research indicates that butterflies prefer to visit pink- and lilac-coloured flowers more frequently than the dark purple- and white-flowering cultivars.

**Wildlife benefits** The large panicles of nectar-rich flowers are a magnet for many butterfly species, particularly peacocks, red admirals, commas and small tortoiseshells, and are also visited by several species of bees. The seeds are eaten in winter by birds and small mammals.

**Closely related species** *B. alternifolia* and *B. crispa* also attract butterflies and other insects.

*Amelanchier lamarckii*

*Berberis darwinii*

*Calluna vulgaris*

## *Calluna vulgaris*
### LING
Family: Ericaceae
Native: N and W Europe to
Russia, Turkey and Morocco

A wonderful evergreen shrub that is extremely popular with gardeners, and provides excellent ground cover if planted in large groups. Ling produces flower spikes of bell-shaped flowers in many different colours including red, purple, pink and white. The leaves lie flat along the stem and are short, linear and dark green.

**Cultivation** Ling prefers an open site in full sun. These ericaceous plants enjoy humus-rich, well-drained acid soil. Propagate by semi-ripe cuttings in midsummer. ❁ ❁ ❁ Zone 4.

**Uses** *C. vulgaris* has over 500 different cultivars with a wide colour range. They are best planted close together in large groups to create drifts of colour. Once knitted together, they provide excellent ground cover for small mammals and insects.

**Wildlife benefits** The bell-shaped flowers are very popular with bees and bumblebees seeking nectar. Butterfly larvae of the silver-studded blue butterfly and the emperor moth eat the foliage, and the seeds are eaten by siskins, crossbills and other finches.

**Closely related species** Do not select double-flowering varieties, such as 'Elsie Purnell', because the double pale pink flowers are inaccessible to bees. Recommended cultivars include 'Allegro' with ruby red flowers, and 'Beoley Gold' with yellow foliage and white flowers.

## *Caryopteris* x *clandonensis*
### BLUEBEARD
Family: Verbenaceae
Native: Garden origin

A delicate shrub grown for its grey-green, silver-haired foliage and soft blue, nectar-rich flowers carried in terminal heads from late summer to autumn. The shrub reaches up to 90cm (3ft) high, and is ideal in the small garden but needs careful siting because it is extremely prone to frost damage.

**Cultivation** Likes moderately fertile, free-draining soil. Site in full sun; it thrives in colder areas against a sunny, warm wall. Propagate by softwood cuttings in late spring. ❁ ❁ ❁ Zone 7.

**Uses** Ideal for a mixed or shrub border, planted beside silver or purple foliage plants, particularly *Cotinus coggygria* 'Royal Purple' and *Elaeagnus angustifolia* 'Quicksilver'. Other good planting combinations include *Perovskia atriplicifolia* and lavender cultivars.

**Wildlife benefits** The blue flowers are an excellent late-season source of nectar, and are very popular with a number of insects, especially honeybees and butterflies. Leave the seed heads untouched during the winter months because they provide a snack for small birds.

**Closely related species** One of the best cultivars is the erect 'Heavenly Blue' with dark blue flowers and 'Worcester Gold' with yellow leaves. The species *C. incana* is slightly larger with bright violet-blue flowers, and makes a dense mound-forming shrub.

*Caryopteris* x *clandonensis*

*Ceanothus thyrsiflorus*

## *Ceanothus thyrsiflorus*
### CALIFORNIAN LILAC
Family: Rhamnaceae
Native: California and S Oregon

The Californian lilac is one of the best shrubs (occasionally classed as a tree) to attract huge numbers of bees. It is a large, vigorous, evergreen shrub growing to 6m (20ft) high in a relatively short space of time. The arching branches sport ovate, glossy, mid-green leaves and, in spring, it bears pale to dark blue flowers in large panicles.

**Cultivation** Grow in full sun in a sheltered location, protected from cold winter winds. The roots favour fertile, well-drained soil. Propagate by semi-ripe cuttings in mid–late summer. ❁ ❁ ❁ Zone 8.

**Uses** Ideal for planting in a large shrub border, or train against a sunny wall where it provides a valuable source of food for insects. Also, several species of birds are likely to nest in the network of branches. Clematis can be trained up through the stems.

**Wildlife benefits** A huge favourite with bees and bumblebees seeking mainly pollen and, occasionally, nectar. The leaves are eaten by caterpillars of several common butterflies and moths. Songbirds feast on the numerous visiting insects that take refuge in the dense foliage.

**Closely related species** Research has shown that *C.* 'Ray Hartman' is a fantastic plant to attract bees. *C. impressus* is another favourite, attracting several species of insect. It is an evergreen shrub with dark blue flowers in mid- to late spring. *C. dentatus* bears dark blue flowers in spring.

### *Chaenomeles japonica*
### JAPANESE QUINCE
Family: Rosaceae
Native: Japan

The early flowers borne by Japanese quince are a joy to see after the dull winter months. This deciduous thorny shrub can reach up to 90cm (3ft) high, and produces clusters of orange-red, scarlet or crimson flowers in spring before leaf burst. The small leaves are oval with serrated edges. The flowers are followed by yellow-flushed, apple-shaped fruit.

**Cultivation** Japanese quince enjoys fertile, well-drained soil. Position in sun for optimum flowers and fruits, though the shrub will also grow well in partial shade. Propagate by semi-ripe cuttings in summer. ❀ ❀ ❀ Zone 5.

**Uses** Excellent in a shrub border or as an informal hedge. A good companion plant is common ivy (*Hedera helix*), which can be used for the under-planting; it makes good ground cover and helps show off the brightly coloured flowers.

**Wildlife benefits** In spring, the flowers are pollinated by early bees and butterflies that welcome the nectar. Birds, especially bullfinches, are known to eat the sugar-rich flowers, and the fruits are eaten by blackbirds and starlings.

**Closely related species** Insects and birds also use *C. speciosa*, a more vigorous shrub that easily reaches 2.5m (8ft). Very effective in large shrubberies or for training against walls. A valued garden plant is *C.* x *superba* 'Crimson and Gold' with deep red flowers and showy yellow stamens.

*Chaenomeles japonica*

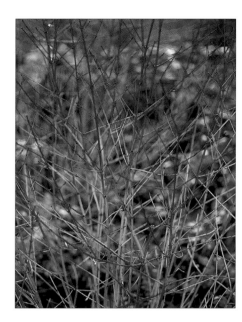

*Cornus sanguinea*

### *Cornus sanguinea*
### DOGWOOD
Family: Cornaceae
Native: Europe

A large, deciduous shrub generally grown for its attractive, reddish-green winter stems, but it needs coppicing annually to promote the attractive new growth. Alternatively it can be left to grow into a large shrub. The latter is the most beneficial to wildlife, and if allowed to grow for two years or more it bears white flowers in summer, followed by dull blue-black fruits in autumn.

**Cultivation** To achieve the best winter stem colour, grow *C. sanguinea* in free-draining soil in full sun. Propagate by hardwood cuttings in autumn. ❀ ❀ ❀ Zone 5.

**Uses** To allow dogwood to flower and fruit freely, it needs to be planted in a shrub or mixed border where it grows without annual pruning. Dogwood is also ideal in a wild garden, and is commonly used in a mixed hedge.

**Wildlife benefits** The flowers are popular with bees and other pollinating insects. Caterpillars of the green hairstreak butterfly eat the leaves, and the blue-black berries are eaten by birds, especially thrushes, tits, woodpeckers and finches, and small mammals.

**Closely related species** Cornelian cherry (*C. mas*) is a vigorous, deciduous shrub, or small tree, that bears nectar and pollen-rich yellow flowers on bare branches in late winter. On acid soils, *C. canadensis* provides excellent ground cover for birds and small mammals.

### *Cytisus scoparius*
### COMMON BROOM
Family: Papilionaceae
Native: W Europe

A terrific garden plant providing plenty of colour when in flower. It is a relatively short-lived shrub, usually reaching its peak in 8–10 years. Upright and deciduous, it can reach 1.5m (5ft) in a short period of time. The stems bear bright yellow, pea-like flowers in late spring, and leaves that are small and palmate.

**Cultivation** Brooms like basking in full sun and will thrive in well-drained, poor, acid soil, although most are lime tolerant. Plant when small because they do not transplant well. Take semi-ripe cuttings in summer. ❀ ❀ ❀ Zone 5.

**Uses** Excellent in a shrub border or dry garden. Brooms look at their best if planted next to other Mediterranean species, such as rock roses (*Cistus*), lavender (*Lavandula*) and *Phlomis*. Mulch with various grades of pebbles to create a dry-garden look.

**Wildlife benefits** Flowers are pollinated by bees and the occasional butterfly seeking nectar. They are also eaten by waxwings, and the black seed pods are devoured by rooks, greenfinches and hawfinches. The leaves are eaten by the larvae of the green hairstreak butterfly.

**Closely related species** Pineapple broom (*C. battandieri*), with scented yellow flowers and silvery leaves, is a tall, vigorous species that is ideal at the back of a very large shrub border, or it can be trained against a wall. *C. decumbens* is a prostrate deciduous shrub with yellow flowers.

*Cytisus scoparius*

*Corylus avellana*

### *Corylus avellana*
### HAZEL
Family: Betulaceae
Native: Europe and Turkey

A natural woodland plant that bears beautiful, pendent, yellow male catkins 4–6cm (1½–2¼in) long in late winter and early spring. The female flowers are small and insignificant, but produce edible nuts. Though a deciduous shrub, it can be sometimes classed as a multi-stemmed tree and produces heart-shaped leaves with rounded ends.

**Cultivation**  Hazels thrive in fertile, well-drained soil in full sun or partial shade. They grow in most soils, but favour chalky ones. Propagate by seeds when ripe, or layer in autumn. ❀ ❀ ❀ Zone 4.

**Uses**  An excellent shrub for structure planting in a woodland garden or shrub border. The corkscrew hazel ('Contorta') has twisting shoots that look fantastic in winter. The plant can also be grown in a mixed-species hedge.

**Wildlife benefits**  An important plant for wildlife, it supports up to 70 different species. Bees feed on the early source of pollen, while the nuts are eaten by small mammals and birds including nuthatches, tits, great spotted woodpeckers, hawfinches and crossbills.

**Closely related species**  The filbert (*C. maxima*) is similar to *C. avellana* except it is slightly taller, growing up to 6m (20ft). An excellent purple cultivar is *C. maxima* 'Purpurea' with dark purple foliage, and purple-tinged catkins and fruit husks.

### *Cotoneaster lacteus*
### COTONEASTER
Family: Rosaceae
Native: China

An extremely ornamental evergreen shrub, it can reach up to 4m (13ft) high and produces arching branches bearing thick ovate, dark green, deeply veined leaves. The milky white flowers with pink anthers are abundant, with up to 100 per branch. They are followed in the autumn by red berries that can stay on the plant if uneaten over the winter.

**Cultivation**  Cotoneasters enjoy fertile, well-drained soil, and tolerate dry soil in sun or partial shade. Propagate by semi-ripe cuttings in late summer. ❀ ❀ ❀ Zone 6.

**Uses**  Excellent in a shrub border, giving height, while the berries and evergreen foliage provide winter colour. It can also be used to form a single-species hedge, or be trained against a wall to help soften the hard structure.

**Wildlife benefits**  Honeybees and bumblebees seek out the nectar-rich flowers. The overhanging foliage and branches favour birds – especially shy ones such as wrens and dunnocks – that like to use the branch system to roost and hide in. The berries are eaten by many species of birds, particularly thrushes, starlings, tree sparrows and finches.

**Closely related species**  All cotoneasters are good for wildlife, one of the best being *C. horizontalis*, a spreading, deciduous shrub with pink-tinged flowers produced in late spring, followed by red fruit in late summer.

*Cotoneaster lacteus*

*Daphne mezereum*

### *Daphne mezereum*
### MEZEREON
Family: Thymelaeaceae
Native: Europe, Caucasus and Turkey

Fragrant, sweet-smelling flowers adorn this deciduous shrub in late winter and early spring. The flowers range from pink to light purple, and are borne on bare stems before the pale green, lance-shaped leaves appear. The flowers are followed by round, red, fleshy fruits in summer. The shrub will ultimately reach 1.2m (4ft) high, making it ideal for the small garden.

**Cultivation**  Daphnes thrive in humus-rich soil, which should be well drained without drying out for long periods. Site in sun or partial shade. Propagate by semi-ripe cuttings in late summer. ❀ ❀ ❀ Zone 4.

**Uses**  Use *D. mezereum* to provide late winter colour in a shrub border, or use in a special winter border. Under-plant with snowdrops and dwarf daffodils to add interest when in flower. Also plant next to an evergreen to act as background for the flowers.

**Wildlife benefits**  The flowers are a great source of early pollen and nectar for insects, especially bees. Blackcaps have also been known to drink the nectar from the flowers. The red fruits are eaten by finches, thrushes, starlings, tits and warblers.

**Closely related species**  *D. blagayana*, a prostrate evergreen (sometimes semi-evergreen), bears sweet-smelling, cream-white flowers in spring. Spurge laurel (*D. laureola*) is a bushy evergreen, flowering in late winter.

*Fuchsia magellanica*

## *Fuchsia magellanica*
## LADIES EAR DROPS
Family: Onagraceae
Native: Chile and Argentina

A wonderful, floriferous shrub that produces small, tubular flowers with red petals that are occasionally pink or white, with large sepals and long, purple corollas. Oblong red-purple fruits follow the flowering. The branches can reach up to 3m (10ft) high, and bear ovate leaves.

**Cultivation** Fuchsias enjoy fertile, well-drained soil that retains some moisture. For this reason, when planting smaller cultivars in pots use a loam-based compost instead of peat. Site in sun or partial shade. Propagate by softwood cuttings. ❋ ❋ Zone 6.

**Uses** *F. magellanica* will make a fantastic single-species hedge in areas that do not encounter severe frosts. The hedge doubles as a barrier, and flowers throughout summer. Also ideal in a shrub or mixed border.

**Wildlife benefits** The pollen and nectar-rich flowers of fuchsias are extremely popular with bees and bumblebees, so do not select fancy double-flowering varieties. Butterflies also seek the nectar, and the leaves are eaten by the caterpillars of elephant hawk moths.

**Closely related species** 'Riccartonii' is an extremely hardy, upright shrub with single flowers, scarlet tubes and sepals, and dark purple corollas. Use as a hedge, as a shrub, or in mixed borders. 'Mrs Popple' is popular in borders and containers.

## *Hebe salicifolia*
## HEBE
Family: Scrophulariaceae
Native: New Zealand

An important genus with many ornamental species. *H. salicifolia* is a tall species, which grows up to 2.5m (8ft) high and bears narrow, pointed, lance-shaped leaves. The flowers are white or pale blue-lilac, and are borne in drooping racemes up to 20cm (8in) long all summer.

**Cultivation** Grow in any well-drained soil that is neutral to alkaline. Grows best in a sunny, sheltered position but will also tolerate partial shade. Propagate by semi-ripe cuttings in late summer. ❋ ❋ ❋ Zone 7.

**Uses** Hebes are an excellent choice for use at the back of a shrub or mixed border. This species can be used as a tall hedging plant in coastal locations, although it can become bare at the bottom through age. It can be incorporated in a specialist butterfly border to provide evergreen colour and height.

**Wildlife benefits** A popular plant with bees and bumblebees seeking nectar. Several species of butterfly, particularly small tortoiseshells and red admirals, will visit the flowers looking for nectar.

**Closely related species**
*H. brachysiphon* and *H.* 'Great Orme' are great plants for an informal hedge.

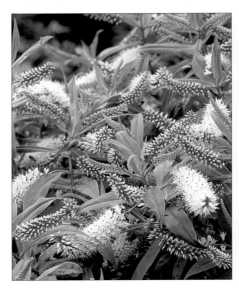

*Hebe salicifolia*

## *Helianthemum nummularium*
## ROCK ROSE
Family: Cistaceae
Native: Europe and Asia Minor

A pretty, evergreen, bushy shrub that grows to 10–50cm (4–20in) high and flowers from late spring to late summer. The flowers are saucer-shaped and light yellow, golden yellow, pink or orange. The attractive, grey-green leaves are lance-shaped and slightly hairy underneath, and cover the whole of the stem.

**Cultivation** The rock rose prefers an open, sunny site in well-drained soil. Cut back plants after flowering to promote a second flush of flowers in late summer. Propagate by softwood cuttings in late summer, and after the cuttings have rooted, pinch them back to produce bushy plants. ❋ ❋ ❋ Zone 5.

**Uses** *H. nummularium* is excellent for use in dry gardens because it has naturally adapted to grow in areas of low rainfall with free-draining soil. It is also well suited to rock gardens because of its low-growing, mound-forming habit.

**Wildlife benefits** The flowers attract bees and other insects, including butterflies. The small shrub produces a dense mat of stems and foliage providing an ideal environment for small invertebrates to hunt and forage in.

**Closely related species** All rock roses are good nectar producers. *H. appeninum* is a sub-shrub reaching 50cm (20in) high, and produces linear, grey leaves and yellow-white flowers. *H. croceum* is a compact shrub reaching 30cm (1ft) high, with white, yellow or apricot flowers.

*Helianthemum nummularium*

*Ilex aquifolium* 'J. C. van Tol'

*Mahonia aquifolium*

## *Ilex aquifolium*
### COMMON HOLLY
Family: Aquifoliaceae
Native: S and W Europe, N Africa and W Asia

A tall shrub or tree, it can grow up to 25m (82ft) high and produces prickly, dark green leaves. The nectar-rich flowers are small and white, and are borne in spring. To obtain a show of late summer and autumn red berries, you'll need to plant separate male and female plants.

**Cultivation** Holly will tolerate most soils, except ones that are waterlogged. Site in any position, including full sun to full or partial shade. Propagate by cuttings in late summer. ❀ ❀ ❀ Zone 6.

**Uses** A popular plant for a wildlife garden because it has so many uses. It is also excellent in a woodland garden in deep shade or sun, a shrub border, or as a formal hedging or windbreak plant.

**Wildlife benefits** Honeybees feast on the nectar-rich flowers in spring. After the flowers finish, the plant attracts a great number of bird species. In particular, robins, finches and thrushes feed on the berries, as well as nesting in the branches. The holly blue butterfly is a widespread species throughout the Northern Hemisphere that feeds upon holly for some of the year. The adults that emerge in spring nectar upon the holly flowers and lay eggs on the plant. Once the spring brood have become adults, however, they mate and lay their eggs on ivy for the overwintering brood.

**Closely related species** *I. aquifolium* 'J. C. van Tol' is a good producer of berries and does not require cross-pollination. It reaches 6m (20ft) high and produces oval, slightly spiny leaves. Use as a hedge or in a container. *I. x altaclerenis* is similar, with much broader leaves and smaller spines.

## *Lavatera olbia*
### TREE LAVATERA
Family: Malvaceae
Native: W Mediterranean

A highly floriferous shrub producing showy, solitary, red-purple flowers similar to a hollyhock. The flowers are borne throughout summer on stems that can easily reach up to 2m (6½ft) high, and bear 3–5 lobed, semi-evergreen, sage-green leaves that are slightly hairy.

**Cultivation** Site is full sun, sheltered from cold winds, in poor, free-draining soil. Propagate by softwood cuttings in early summer. ❀ ❀ ❀ Zone 5.

**Uses** *L. olbia* is a welcome addition to any shrub border because of its long flowering period and abundant clusters of flowers. It can also be used in mixed borders where it mixes well with perennials, such as blue delphiniums and purple aconitums.

**Wildlife benefits** The bright nectar-producing flowers attract bees, butterflies and a host of other insects. Leave the

*Lavatera olbia*

foliage uncut over winter before hard pruning in spring because several beneficial insects hibernate amongst the stems.

**Closely related species** *L. trimestris*, to 1.2m (4ft) high, is an annual that produces an abundance of foliage and white-pink flowers from spring to autumn. *L.* 'Silver Cup' and *L.* 'Mont Blanc' are popular cultivars, and *L. arborea*, a tree-like biennial, is ideal for the wild garden.

## *Mahonia aquifolium*
### OREGON GRAPE
Family: Berberidaceae
Native: NW North America

A pretty evergreen shrub producing fragrant, bell-shaped, golden flowers in tight clusters during spring. They are followed by blue-black berries in late summer. The stems, up to 1.2m (4ft) high, have deeply fissured bark and produce bright glossy green leaflets that often turn red-purple in winter.

**Cultivation** Plant in partial shade in moist, well-drained soil and protect from strong winds. Propagate by semi-ripe cuttings in summer. ❀ ❀ ❀ Zone 5.

**Uses** It is a valuable, medium-high ground-cover plant because it tends to sucker. Use for its evergreen foliage in a woodland edge or in the dappled shady area of a shrub border. Plant yellow daffodils beside it because the colours complement each other.

**Wildlife benefits** The flowers are a welcome source of early nectar for bees. Birds, particularly house sparrows and blue tits, attack the flowers seeking nectar and pollen. The blue-black berries are eaten by mistle thrushes and blackbirds.

**Closely related species** *M. japonica* grows to 1.8m (6ft) high and produces highly fragrant yellow flowers.

*Morus nigra*
## BLACK MULBERRY
Family: Moraceae
Native: SW Asia

A long-lived, round-headed shrub or tree that has been cultivated since at least ancient Egyptian times. It can reach up to 12m (40ft) high and is grown for its attractive, heart-shaped foliage and edible fruits. The tree produces inconspicuous flowers in spring but, by late summer and early autumn, it bears edible, dark purple fruits.

**Cultivation** Requires full sun and fertile, well-drained soil. Protect from cold winds and frost. Propagate by softwood cuttings in midsummer. ❀ ❀ ❀ Zone 5.

**Uses** *M. nigra* is best shown off as a specimen tree, for example on a lawn, but avoid a shrub border where it can easily be lost amongst other plants. In colder areas grow against a south-facing wall to provide extra heat and protection.

**Wildlife benefits** The twisted, gnarled bark provides a home for overwintering insects taking refuge in the cracks. The fruits are eaten by birds, particularly finches, sparrows, tits and waxwings, and the windfalls are taken by small mammals.

**Closely related species** The white mulberry (*M. alba*) is a deciduous tree growing to 15m (50ft), with oval, pink-red or purple fruits that ripen in summer. The fruits are less palatable than *M. nigra*. Red mulberry (*M. rubra*) is a native of North America and grows to 15m (50ft) high with orange to red fruits.

*Morus nigra*

*Olea europaea*

*Olea europaea*
## OLIVE
Family: Oleaceae
Native: Mediterranean

Olives are one of the most important economic plants of hot, dry regions because they provide oil, fruit and timber. *O. europaea*, reaching 7m (23ft) high, is grown for its attractive, narrow, grey-green leaves with silvery undersides and large, oval, green fruits that turn purple. The flowers are tiny, fragrant and white.

**Cultivation** *O. europaea* thrives in a frost-free environment and will be severely damaged if temperatures hit -10°C (14°F). Site in full sun and in deep, fertile soil with good drainage. ❀ ❀ Zone 8.

**Uses** Old gnarled and twisted plants are fantastic, and are best used as a specimen tree. They are often planted as a central focal point in a herb garden, under-planted with annuals, or grown in terracotta containers on terraces.

**Wildlife benefits** The flowers are wind pollinated, but the mature fruits are eaten by many species of birds, particularly blackbirds, tits, sparrows, starlings, song thrushes and many finches. Several species use the narrow leaves for nesting material.

**Closely related species** Black ironwood (*O. capensis*) is a large tree, reaching 20m (66ft). The leaves are lance-shaped and the flowers are small and white, with round, black fruits to follow.

*Perovskia atriplicifolia*

*Perovskia atriplicifolia*
## RUSSIAN SAGE
Family: Lamiaceae
Native: Afghanistan and Pakistan

Grown for its deeply cut, silver-green, aromatic foliage with serrated edges, and its strong, erect, silvery stems. This upright, deciduous sub-shrub produces grey-white stems that reach 1.5m (5ft) high. The long flower spikes bear numerous violet to soft blue flowers from late summer through to autumn.

**Cultivation** Russian sage is completely hardy and requires full sun in free-draining soil. Cut back, almost to the base of the plant, each spring. Propagate by softwood cuttings in late spring. ❀ ❀ ❀ Zone 6.

**Uses** It's a versatile plant that can be used in several areas around the garden, including dry gardens, shrub and mixed borders, herb gardens and fragrant borders. It is extremely floriferous, and is ideal planted next to herbs such as lavender and sage.

**Wildlife benefits** The open flower spikes are a real favourite with bees and bumblebees collecting nectar. Hoverflies are also frequent visitors to the flowers, as they too are seeking nectar.

**Closely related species** Another excellent nectar producer is the sub-shrub *P. abrotanoides* that grows to 90cm (3ft) high, and bears panicles of pink-violet flowers in late summer. Its grey-green leaves are deeply divided.

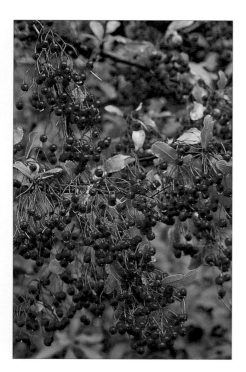

*Pyracantha coccinea*

## *Pyracantha coccinea*
## FIRETHORN
Family: Rosaceae
Native: Italy to Asia Minor

A stunning large shrub that bears autumn fruits after a profusion of small white flowers in spring. Cultivars of this species bear fruits in colours ranging from yellow and orange to bright red. They stand out in winter against the shrub's lance-shaped, dark evergreen foliage.

**Cultivation** Although firethorn can tolerate poor soil, it grows best in any fertile, well-drained soil. Propagate by semi-ripe heel cuttings in autumn. ❀ ❀ ❀ Zone 6.

**Uses** It is extremely versatile and can be grown as a freestanding shrub in a border if given plenty of room. It is probably more commonly grown as a wall shrub, being pruned back annually to keep it under control.

**Wildlife benefits** In spring, bees and bumblebees visit the flowers for pollen and nectar. The autumn fruits are devoured by birds, particularly blackbirds and songbirds. The thorny branches make ideal safe nesting sites for birds.

**Closely related species** Another evergreen, *P. rogersiana* is slightly less vigorous than *P. coccinea*, and bears fruits in the same colour range. The gardener's favourite must be *P.* 'Flava' with interesting, bright yellow fruits, one of the last berried plants to be eaten by birds because they usually go straight for red and orange berries.

## *Rhamnus frangula*
## ALDER BUCKTHORN
Family: Rhamnaceae
Native: Europe, Turkey and
N Africa

Alder buckthorn is classed as either a deciduous shrub or tree, and is grown for its beautiful autumn colour and wildlife value. The plant grows 2–5m (6½–17ft) high and bears oblong to lance-like leaves and flowers borne in clusters from late spring to early summer. The ornamental fruits are red, maturing to black.

**Cultivation** Grows best in sun or semi-shade, in moist, relatively fertile soil. Propagate by seed in spring or by softwood cuttings in early summer. ❀ ❀ ❀ Zone 3.

**Uses** Alder buckthorn is not a classic ornamental plant, and is therefore not usually included for use in a shrub border unless it is required just for greenery. It is mainly used in a mixed hedgerow or allowed to mature as a specimen tree. It is often included in wild, natural planting schemes.

**Wildlife benefits** In spring, the brimstone butterfly lays its eggs on the foliage, and the caterpillars eat the leaves before emerging as adults. The flowers provide early nectar for insects, particularly bees, and the berries are eaten by birds.

**Closely related species** Similar wildlife is attracted to common buckthorn (*R. cathartica*), which has dull green, ovate leaves with insignificant yellow-green flowers, followed by glossy black fruit. *R.* 'Tall Hedge' is often used as a screen or hedge.

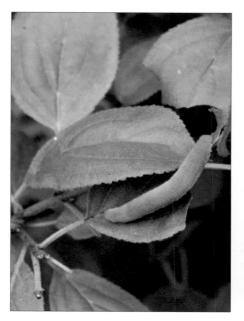

*Rhamnus frangula*

## *Rhododendron luteum*
## DECIDUOUS AZALEA
Family: Ericaceae
Native: E Europe to Caucasus

*R. luteum* is one of the main species used in hybridization to produce many of the modern cultivars of *Azalea*. This deciduous shrub reaches from 1.5–2.5m (5–8ft) high and bears heavily scented, funnel-shaped yellow flowers in spring, and green, oblong, lance-shaped leaves with a wonderful rich autumn colour.

**Cultivation** Azaleas demand acid soil with plenty of organic matter to help retain moisture in dry periods, and a site in semi-shade. Propagate by seed or semi-ripe cuttings in late summer. ❀ ❀ ❀ Zone 5.

**Uses** Azaleas are ideal for using at the edge of a woodland, but not inside because it'll be too shady. Plant in large, bold groups for a striking effect, both in terms of flower and autumn colour. Do not under-plant because of the shallow root system.

**Wildlife benefits** The sweetly scented flowers are frequently visited by bees and bumblebees seeking nectar. Honey made largely from rhododendron nectar contains a substance called andromedotoxin, a potent toxin that causes terrible vomiting if ingested.

**Closely related species** All rhododendron flowers are real favourites with bees. Spring-flowering species include *R. williamsianum*, an evergreen shrub reaching 1.5m (5ft) high with pink flowers, and *R. yakushimanum*, to 90cm (3ft), an evergreen, dome-shaped shrub bearing pink flowers.

*Rhododendron luteum*

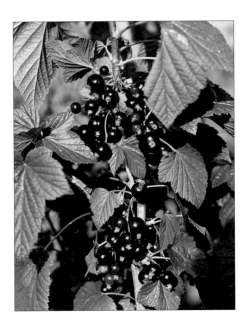

*Ribes nigrum*

## *Ribes nigrum*
### BLACKCURRANT
Family: Grossulariaceae
Native: Europe to C Asia, the Himalayas and Russia

A wide-spreading, aromatic, deciduous shrub that grows up to 1.8m (6ft) high, grown for its round, black, edible fruit. The leaves have 3–5 lobes and a distinct aroma, especially if crushed. Hanging racemes of 4–10 flowers are produced in spring. They are small and bell-shaped, green on the outside, and red-white inside.

**Cultivation** Blackcurrants thrive in full sun and fertile, well-drained soil. Cut the older stems hard back, by one-third, in winter. Propagate by hardwood cuttings in winter. ❀ ❀ ❀ Zone 5.

**Uses** When used in a vegetable garden, expose the excess fruits for the birds when you've had your fill. Alternatively they can be planted in a shrub, mixed or herb border where the fruits can be left solely for the birds and mammals.

**Wildlife benefits** Honeybees and particularly bumblebees (especially at low temperatures) visit the flowers for pollen. The fruits are eaten by birds, including thrushes, tits, warblers and blackbirds. The stem structure is ideal for several species of birds to nest in.

**Closely related species** The redcurrant (*R. silvestre*) is also grown for its fruits that are palatable to many species of birds. It bears hanging racemes of green or red cup-shaped flowers in spring, followed by red berries.

## *Ribes sanguineum*
### FLOWERING CURRANT
Family: Grossulariaceae
Native: W North America

A wonderful ornamental plant for the wildlife garden. A medium-sized shrub reaching 1.8m (6ft) or more, it produces 3–5 lobed leaves that are dark green and slightly hairy. The rose-red, tubular flowers are borne in hanging clusters in spring. This species has produced many cultivars.

**Cultivation** Plant in full sun in moderately fertile, moisture-retentive, well-drained soil. Mulching aids healthy growth. Propagate by nodal hardwood cuttings in late autumn–early winter. ❀ ❀ ❀ Zone 6.

**Uses** An extremely useful plant for the shrub or mixed border, providing a valuable source of early nectar. Use 'Brocklebankii' if golden foliage is required, or 'Tydemans White' for bright white flowers.

**Wildlife benefits** The nectar is popular with bees and bumblebees, while sparrows and tits feed on visiting insects. *R. sanguineum* often fails to fruit whereas buffalo currant (*R. odoratum*) bears dark fruits eaten by songbirds and small mammals.

**Closely related species** *R. odoratum* is an excellent ornamental shrub for wildlife. The fragrant yellow flowers provide an early source of nectar for insects, particularly bees and butterflies, and its dense framework gives good nesting cover for birds.

*Ribes sanguineum*

*Ribes uva-crispa*

## *Ribes uva-crispa*
### GOOSEBERRY
Family: Grossulariaceae
Native: NE and C Europe

The gooseberry is a short, spreading shrub that should reach 1.2m (4ft) high, being grown for its large, green to yellow hairy fruits. The stems bear groups of thorns up to 1cm (⅓in) long, and 3–5 lobed leaves that are slightly hairy underneath. Clusters of up to three, green to pink-green, cup-shaped flowers are borne in spring.

**Cultivation** The gooseberry prefers well-drained garden soil in full sun, but will also grow in partial shade. Mulch to keep the roots moist. Propagate by hardwood cuttings in winter. ❀ ❀ ❀ Zone 5.

**Uses** It is nearly always grown in a kitchen garden for its delicious crop. When you've taken what you want for the family (and frozen some), let the wildlife take the surplus berries. Alternatively, plant in a wildlife border where all the fruit can be eaten.

**Wildlife benefits** The small, white, nectar-rich spring flowers are extremely popular with bees because they are borne before the main burst of spring blossom. Several birds, particularly blue tits, drink the nectar from the flowers, while the fruits are eaten by the likes of blackbirds.

**Closely related species** Bees and birds also like American gooseberry (*R. hirtellum*), a native of northern North America. It is a deciduous shrub that grows to 2m (6½ft) high, and produces small green flowers and round purple-black fruits in summer.

*Rosa canina*

## *Rosa canina*
## DOG ROSE
Family: Rosaceae
Native: Europe, SW Asia and
NW Africa

A vigorous shrub that will reach 1.5–5.5m (5–18ft) high, it bears arching stems with leaves divided into leaflets, and fierce, hooked thorns. The large, fragrant flowers are borne in summer, being followed by juicy red autumn hips. The dog rose is also called the common briar rose and dog briar rose.

**Cultivation** Thrives best in full sun although it will tolerate a degree of partial shade. Grow in any fertile, well-drained soil. Propagate by hardwood cuttings in early autumn. ❄ ❄ ❄ Zone 3.

**Uses** Dog rose is a useful plant for including in a mixed hedge with other species such as *Acer campestre*, common holly (*Ilex aquifolium*), hazel (*Corylus avellana*) and common hawthorn (*Crataegus monogyna*). It is also ideal in a wild garden where the arching stems can ramble.

**Wildlife benefits** The pollen-bearing flowers are a favourite with bees, bumblebees, flies and beetles. The rose hips that follow are popular with birds, small mammals and several species of gall wasps. Birds use the thorny branches as protection when nesting.

**Closely related species** Sweet briar (*R. rubiginosa*) bears single, pale to deep pink flowers, and can be used in borders or a mixed hedgerow. The Japanese rose (*R. rugosa*) is often used as a single-species hedge or in an ornamental border.

## *Rosa glauca*
## SHRUB ROSE
Family: Rosaceae
Native: Mountains of C and
S Europe

A tall, statuesque rose that produces small pink flowers that complement its attractive, greyish-purple foliage. The flowers are followed by spherical red hips. The almost thornless stems can reach up to 1.5–3m (5–10ft) tall and bear deciduous leaves, each one divided into 5–9 leaflets.

**Cultivation** Grows best in full sun and tolerates extremely low temperatures over winter. Plant in any well-drained soil. Propagate by hardwood cuttings in autumn. ❄ ❄ ❄ Zone 2.

**Uses** *R. glauca* is best grown as a specimen rose in a mixed or shrub border, and should be sited where the attractive foliage can be viewed easily. The pink flowers and greyish foliage mix well with purple-leaved shrubs.

**Wildlife benefits** Bees and hoverflies seek out pollen from the small pink flowers, and the hips are eaten by birds and small mammals. Do not prune any old growth until spring to allow the hips to be completely stripped off.

**Closely related species** 'Geranium' is best grown as a specimen rose and has single red flowers with a creamy centre, followed by beautiful, bright scarlet hips. *R. gallica* bears beautifully scented, single or semi-double, rose to crimson flowers.

*Rosa glauca*

*Rubus fruticosus*

## *Rubus fruticosus*
## BRAMBLE
Family: Rosaceae
Native: Unknown

A semi-deciduous shrub with arching to erect thorny stems that can grow several metres high. The leaves are dark green and deeply divided, and the flowers are white-pink. The plant *Rubus fruticosus* covers at least 14 different but closely related species, some of which may be hybrids and have become known as bramble or blackberry.

**Cultivation** Site in full sun to attract a large number of nectaring insects, or in semi-shade. Propagate by division of suckers in autumn or spring. ❄ ❄ ❄ Zone 6.

**Uses** Definitely not for the formal garden, but excellent in a wild garden. Plant on sunny banks to encourage nectar production, also enabling invertebrates to bask in the sun. A large plant will encourage birds to nest here.

**Wildlife benefits** The flowers are a fantastic nectar source for bees, bumblebees and many different species of butterfly. The caterpillars of the grizzled skipper and ringlet butterfly will devour the leaves, and the berries are a favourite with birds and small mammals.

**Closely related species** The raspberry (*R. idaeus*) is a woodland plant that can thrive in full sun or semi-shade. The white flowers are prized by bees, especially honeybees seeking nectar and particularly pollen. Small mammals and several species of birds enjoy the fruit.

## *Sambucus nigra*
## ELDERBERRY
Family: Caprifoliacae
Native: Europe, N Africa and
SW Asia

Elderberry is a fast-growing plant reaching to 10m (33ft) high, and can be classed as a shrub or small tree. Each leaf is divided into 3–9 leaflets. The stems must be two years old before they produce cream, musk-scented, summer flowers in flat-topped umbels. They are followed by round, shiny black fruits.

**Cultivation** Grows best in full sun or dappled shade in rich, moist soil. Elderberry can tolerate atmospheric pollution and coastal conditions. Propagate by hardwood cuttings in winter. ❀ ❀ ❀ Zone 5.

**Uses** Elderberry is too rampant for the small garden, but is ideal in large shrub or mixed borders, and in a wild garden. Do not carry out annual pruning because the plants will not flower and berry that year.

**Wildlife benefits** A fantastic plant for wildlife, attracting many species of insects, including bees, flies and hoverflies, and a range of insect-eating birds. The berries are eaten by small mammals and birds, particularly finches, thrushes, starlings and garden warblers.

**Closely related species** American elder (*S. canadensis*) grows to 4m (13ft) high and produces ivory flowers followed by dark fruits. Red-berried elder (*S. racemosa*) is a shrub that'll grow to 3.5m (11½ft) high, and bears green to white-yellow flowers in spring and scarlet berries.

*Sambucus nigra*

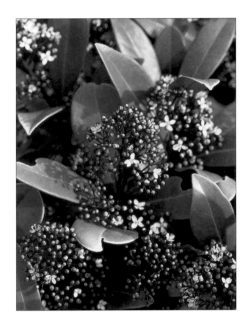

*Skimmia japonica*

## *Skimmia japonica*
## SKIMMIA
Family: Rutaceae
Native: Japan and China

An attractive, erect or low-growing evergreen shrub reaching 0.6–1.5m (2–5ft) high, grown for its flowers and berries. *S. japonica* has separate male and female plants, and both need to be grown in close proximity to produce berries. The white, female flowers are fragrant and appear in late spring, being followed by numerous red autumn berries.

**Cultivation** Best grown in dappled or full shade in well-drained soil that is neutral to acidic, with plenty of organic matter. Propagate by semi-ripe cuttings in late summer. ❀ ❀ ❀ Zone 7.

**Uses** Excellent for growing in a woodland garden. Plant in large groups along the side of a path to create an impressive, evergreen swathe of colour. Also grow beside rhododendrons and *Enkianthus*.

**Wildlife benefits** The flowers are popular with bees and hoverflies seeking nectar. Many species of birds are attracted to the autumn fruits when insect numbers decrease. The dense, evergreen foliage provides great ground cover for insects and small mammals.

**Closely related species** *S. anquetilia* is a creeping or erect shrub that grows from 30cm–1.8m (1–6ft). The evergreen leaves are strongly aromatic and it has separate male and female plants. The flowers are green to yellow and have an unpleasant smell.

## *Symphoricarpos albus*
## SNOWBERRY
Family: Caprifoliaceae
Native: W North America

A suckering, deciduous shrub that can become invasive if it is not checked. The arching stems can grow 1.2m (4ft) long and bear oval, dark green leaves and pink flowers in clusters over summer. Snow white, large round fruits follow the flowers and can persist through winter.

**Cultivation** Snowberry tolerates a wide range of soil types, and will cope with urban pollution and maritime conditions. Site in sun to full shade. Propagate by softwood cuttings in summer. ❀ ❀ ❀ Zone 3.

**Uses** It's probably best sited in a wild garden where it can spread freely and produce a dense stand that birds might use for nesting. In an ornamental garden it will need a large space, and will require annual pruning to keep the size of the clump in check.

**Wildlife benefits** Bees, bumblebees and wasps visit the shrub seeking out the nectar-rich flowers. The leaves are occasionally eaten by the marsh fritillary butterfly and the berries are eaten by birds, especially robins, garden warblers, tits, blackbirds and finches.

**Closely related species** *S.* x *chenautii* 'Hancock' provides excellent ground cover for foraging insects and small mammals. Coralberry (*S. orbiculatus*), a native to eastern North America, produces ivory-flushed pink flowers in summer followed by large, grey-white fruits.

*Symphoricarpos albus*

*Syringa vulgaris*

*Ulex europaeus*

## *Syringa vulgaris*
### COMMON LILAC
Family: Oleaceae
Native: SE Europe

Lilac is a beautiful, sweetly scented large shrub that can grow to 7m (23ft) high. The ovate leaves are up to 12cm (5in) long, and the flowers are borne in pyramidal, large, terminal panicles. There are many different hybrids with colours ranging from white to shades of pink, mauve and blue.

**Cultivation**  Lilacs grow in most locations but prefer full sun with their roots in well-drained, fertile soil. Propagate by semi-ripe cuttings in late summer. ❀ ❀ ❀ Zone 5.

**Uses**  Great for the back of a border to give height, and will also provide a blaze of colour and wonderful scent when in flower. Plant in a shrub or mixed border, though lilac is occasionally used as an informal hedge or screen.

**Wildlife benefits**  Many insects are drawn to the flowers seeking nectar, particularly bees and butterflies. The seeds are eaten by siskins and other finches, and the dense branches are often used by blackbirds and thrushes for nesting.

**Closely related species**  Single-flowering species lilacs are ideal for wildlife gardens. The compact, 1.5m (5ft) high *S. meyeri* is a real favourite, being well suited to the small garden or even tubs. The pink *S. villosa* grows up to 4m (13ft) high.

## *Ulex europaeus*
### GORSE
Family: Papilionaceae
Native: W Europe

Gorse is an exceptionally spiny, evergreen shrub with yellow-golden flowers that are strongly scented and smell of coconut. The shrub can reach up to 1.8m (6ft) high, and produces extremely dense young stems. The leaves are linear or reduced to sharp spines, an excellent adaptation enabling the plant to tolerate low rainfall.

**Cultivation**  Thrives in free-draining soil that is acidic to neutral. Best in full sun, but will tolerate dappled shade. Propagate by seed or from semi-ripe cuttings in summer. ❀ ❀ ❀ Zone 6.

**Uses**  Gorse is ideal in a dry garden if enough space is available. It can also be used in a woodland edge or for naturalizing in a wild garden, particularly on poor, dry sandy soils or old heathland.

**Wildlife benefits**  The long flowering period from summer to autumn makes gorse an extremely important nectar and pollen source for bees and bumblebees. The thorny stems provide excellent protection for nesting birds, such as long-tailed tits, against predators.

**Closely related species**  Spanish gorse (*Genista hispanica*) is used more frequently in ornamental and smaller gardens than *U. europaeus*. The stems reach up to 60cm (2ft) and produce a dense network of branches. The golden-yellow flowers appear in summer.

## *Viburnum* x *bodnantense*
### WINTER-FLOWERING VIBURNUM
Family: Caprifoliaceae
Native: Garden origin

A thicket-forming, medium-sized, upright, deciduous shrub that can grow to 3m (10ft) high. The stems bear ovate leaves from spring to autumn, and flowers that appear on naked stems from autumn to spring. The flowers are white with a strong flush of pink and appear in clusters.

**Cultivation**  Grows well in any type of soil that is fertile and free draining. Viburnums prefer sun but will also grow in partial shade. Propagate by hardwood cuttings in autumn. ❀ ❀ ❀ Zone 7.

**Uses**  Can be grown in an ornamental shrub or mixed border. Site next to an entrance or path because of the beautiful scent. Ideal for using in a wild garden where it is best planted in large groups, particularly if trying to encourage birds to nest.

**Wildlife benefits**  The flowers provide a welcome source of nectar for early flying insects, especially bumblebees. The dense network of stems provides good cover for nesting songbirds. The dark blue fruits in spring are eaten by birds if insect numbers are low.

**Closely related species**  Other *Viburnum* species that are excellent for wildlife include *V.* x *burkwoodii* and *V. lantana*. *V. tinus* flowers from late winter to early spring, and is a winner with early flying insects.

*Viburnum* x *bodnantense*

# MIXED HEDGES

*Crataegus monogyna*
## HAWTHORN
Family: Rosaceae
Native: Europe

Hawthorn is widely known as the May tree, being named after the month in which it flowers. It is typically thought of as a hedgerow shrub, and is named after the Saxon word for hedge. The thorns form an excellent barrier but, if left uncut, an individual hawthorn eventually develops into a strong tree with a dense crown.

**Cultivation** An easily cultivated plant, it thrives in a variety of soil types and a range of settings, including hedgerow, scrub, thicket and woodland. Best raised from seed. ❀ ❀ ❀ Zone 5.

**Uses** An excellent hedging plant that grows rapidly, is long-lived and provides abundant blossom and fruit. Prune after flowering to aid flower and fruit production next season. In natural settings it protects seedlings of other broadleaved trees, particularly oak (*Fagus*), from being grazed, and aids natural regeneration.

**Wildlife benefits** Hawthorn provides food for over 150 different species of insect. The spring blossom is an excellent source of nectar for bees, and the berries are eaten by mice and many birds, including finches, blue tits, starlings and thrushes. Blackbirds and finches nest in the dense branches.

**Closely related species** *C. aestivalis* is grown in North America for similar purposes, and Midland hawthorn (*C. laevigata*) is very similar but has pink or red blossom and is often grown as a street tree, while blackthorn is a related shrub used in hedgerows.

*Crataegus monogyna*

*Euonymus europaeus*

*Euonymus europaeus*
## SPINDLE TREE
Family: Celastraceae
Native: E and W Asia

This deciduous shrub or small tree can grow to 5m (17ft) high, and is frequently found in hedges although it naturally inhabits the edges of forest and gentle slopes. The rather inconspicuous flowers are produced in late spring, followed by red to purple or pink fruit with orange seeds that tend to persist until late autumn.

**Cultivation** It tolerates a wide range of soils, although it tends to perform best on nutrient-rich, chalky and salt-poor soil. It is best raised from stratified seed sown in spring. ❀ ❀ ❀ Zone 3.

**Uses** The bright pink or purple capsules that contain the seeds, and the attractive autumn colouring of the foliage against the green bark, have made it a popular ornamental plant in gardens and parks. It has also been used extensively as a hedging plant, especially in cold, windswept places.

**Wildlife benefits** The plant provides light cover for roosting birds and the flowers, though insignificant, provide nectar for insects. The autumn fruits are eaten by birds, particularly starlings, sparrows, wood pigeons, garden warblers and finches.

**Closely related species** The winged spindle (*E. alatus*) is a deciduous, spreading shrub native to eastern Asia, its stems being notable for their four corky ridges or "wings". *E. fortunei* is an Asian species that is widely planted in gardens, and climbs by small rootlets on the stems.

*Ilex aquifolium*

*Ilex aquifolium*
## HOLLY
Family: Aquifoliaceae
Native: S and W Europe and W Asia

With its bright red berries (found only on female plants), and shiny, evergreen leaves, the holly has been a symbol of midwinter festivals since pre-Christian times, and of Christmas. It grows as a shrub or tree with a narrow, conical crown, smooth silver-greyish bark and spiny leaves, and is often found in hedges.

**Cultivation** Though it tolerates shade, it grows best in full sun. It prefers neutral to slightly acid, moist, well-drained soil. Sow fresh seed in autumn, but note it can take 18 months to germinate. ❀ ❀ ❀ Zone 6.

**Uses** Slow-growing holly takes a number of years to form a hedge-sized plant, but is still well worth including in a mixed hedge. It increases the security aspect, and its shade-tolerance means it can be grown under the canopy of deciduous trees.

**Wildlife benefits** The small white spring flowers are packed with nectar that attracts many insects, including holly blue butterflies and honeybees. The holly blue butterfly caterpillars also eat the flower buds. The berries are eaten by the likes of robins and thrushes during winter.

**Closely related species** American holly (*I. opaca*) – native to eastern and central North America – is a small to medium evergreen tree with red berries that persist into winter. Yaupon holly (*I. vomitoria*) is an evergreen from south-east North America.

## *Prunus spinosa*
## BLACKTHORN
Family: Rosaceae
Native: Europe to Iran and
SW Siberia

Blackthorn has a long history as a
hedgerow plant because of its thorns. The
beautiful white blossom tends to appear
early in the year before the leaves, often in
a very cold period following a false spring
(widely known as "blackthorn winter").
The bitter bluish-black fruits, or sloes,
have a whitish bloom and contain a
single, hard-shelled seed.

**Cultivation** An easily grown deciduous
shrub that will grow in most well-drained,
moisture retentive soils. Site in a sunny
position for the best fruiting. Raise from
seed after stratification. ❀ ❀ ❀ Zone 4.

**Uses** It grows very well in exposed
seaside locations, although it can be rather
bare in winter and does not provide very
good shelter if grown as a single-species
hedge. It does have early blossom, though,
and the fruit (sloes) are used to flavour gin,
jellies, conserves and syrups.

**Wildlife benefits** The flowers provide
nectar and pollen for early emerging bees
and other insects. The leaves are important
for caterpillars of several species, including
the emperor moth and brown hairstreak
butterfly. Dense branches shelter nesting
birds, especially nightingales. The berries
are eaten by birds, particularly thrushes
and starlings.

**Closely related species** Blackthorn
is related to the plums, and the most similar
is possibly the damson, an edible, cultivated
variety of the plum tree, *P. domestica*, also
known as the damask plum. *P. d.* subsp.
*institia* is another form of the plum, often
found growing in hedges.

*Prunus spinosa*

*Ulmus glabra*

## *Ulmus glabra*
## WYCH ELM
Family: Ulmaceae
Native: Europe and W Asia

This large deciduous tree was once
common across its range but its
susceptibility to Dutch elm disease means
that it is now rare, except as suckering
growth in hedges. It survives there because
the elm bark beetles that transmit the
disease fly at a height of 4m (13ft) in search
of healthy elms. If unaffected by disease it
can live for up to 500 years.

**Cultivation** An easily grown tree,
succeeding in any moist soil, but it does
not thrive if the soil is too acidic or chalky.
Grow in sun or dappled shade. Propagate
from ripe seed. ❀ ❀ ❀ Zone 5.

**Uses** Was once a common sight in
hedgerows, and often grew as part of
mixed woodlands. Its use has declined
since the outbreak of Dutch elm disease,
although it may still be used in a mixed
hedge, particularly in windy locations.

**Wildlife benefits** The tiny red flowers
that appear in spring provide pollen for
bees. The leaves are eaten by the
caterpillars of moths and butterfly species,
including the large tortoiseshell and white
hairstreak butterflies. The seeds may also
be eaten by birds, including sparrows,
siskins and other finches.

**Closely related species** Many
species of elm are similarly affected by
disease and are therefore rare. *U. procera*
is similar but the leaves have bristly hairs on
the upper surface and are generally smaller,
with fewer veins.

*Viburnum lanata*

## *Viburnum lanata*
## WAYFARING TREE
Family: Caprifoliaceae
Native: S and C Europe to N Africa

This attractive deciduous shrub is found
on chalk and limestone areas as part of
woodland edges, or in hedgerows. The
undersides of the leaves are covered with
dense, white, silky hairs and, in midsummer,
the whole bush is covered in fragrant white
flowers that are followed in autumn by
oblong red berries, which turn black as
the season progresses.

**Cultivation** This bush does well in any
soil, although it is best on chalk and
limestone. It is wind-tolerant and grows
happily in sun or partial shade. Propagate
from ripe seed. ❀ ❀ ❀ Zone 3.

**Uses** *V. lanata* is an excellent garden
specimen that can be used as a freestanding shrub, and in hedges and
woodland-edge borders. The young growth
and even winter twigs are covered in a
woolly bloom, giving added interest to
a mixed hedge throughout the season.

**Wildlife benefits** All viburnums are
a good source of nectar for bees, and are
excellent for attracting hoverflies, effective
predators of aphids. The fruit is also an
important food for many birds, particularly
members of the thrush family, as well as
a number of mammals.

**Closely related species** The guelder
rose (*V. opulus*) is native to Europe and
Asia, and is very closely related to the
North American species *V. trilobum*.
Possum haw (*V. acerifolium*) is also
common in eastern North America.

# SINGLE-SPECIES HEDGES

*Berberis thunbergii*
**JAPANESE BARBERRY**
Family: Berberidaceae
Native: Japan

Barberry is a dense, deciduous, spiny shrub that, if left untrimmed, grows 1–2m (3½–6½ft) tall. In its natural habitat or in areas where it has become naturalized, it can be found beside roads, along field margins, in hedgerows or in open woods. It has deeply grooved, brown branches with a single spine at each leaf cluster.

**Cultivation** Grows best in full sun or light shade on moist, loamy soil, but will also succeed on thin, dry, shallow or heavy clay ground. Sow seed as soon as it is ripe, or take cuttings of half-ripe wood. ❀ ❀ ❀ Zone 4.

**Uses** Makes a good medium-sized hedge because it's very tolerant of trimming and re-sprouts well from the base. Its dense, prickly nature makes an effective barrier, and since deer find the leaves unpalatable it has become a popular landscape species.

**Wildlife benefits** Excellent for providing shelter for a number of smaller species of nesting birds, with the thorns preventing attacks from cats and larger birds. The flowers are visited by honeybees and bumblebees seeking nectar, and the berries are eaten by birds and small mammals.

**Closely related species**
*B. canadensis* is a North American species with sharply toothed leaves and three-pronged spines. *B. vulgaris*, native to central and southern Europe, can be distinguished from *B. thunbergii* by its spiny, toothed leaves and flowers in a long raceme.

*Berberis thunbergii*

*Buxus sempervirens*

*Buxus sempervirens*
**COMMON BOX**
Family: Buxaceae
Native: W and S Europe, N Africa and W Asia

This evergreen, small tree is rather slow-growing but long-lived. It reaches a maximum height of 6m (20ft), with a trunk about 15cm (6in) in diameter, covered by rugged, greyish bark and yellowish branches. It is more familiar as a clipped, shrubby specimen, and is most commonly used as a hedging plant.

**Cultivation** Box naturally prefers chalk and limestone, although it tolerates a wide variety of soils and thrives in sun or part shade. Can be grown from seed or, more commonly, cuttings. ❀ ❀ ❀ Zone 5.

**Uses** Box is a popular ornamental plant, partly due to its small, scented flowers and deep green leaves, although it is most valued for topiary and hedging because of its dense habit and tolerance of close clipping. It is also notably resistant to honey fungus and pests in general.

**Wildlife benefits** If just clipped lightly and allowed to flower in early spring, the tiny blooms will attract a number of pollinators, especially any early emerging bees and flies. The dense growth makes an excellent dry hibernation site for many overwintering insects.

**Closely related species** Several cultivars have variegated foliage. *B. balearica*, from the Balearic Isles, is hardy to Zone 8 and *B. henryi* has a neat, vase-shaped habit. Small-leaved box (*B. microphylla*) is often used as edging.

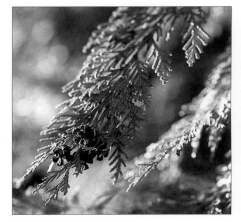

*Chamaecyparis lawsoniana*

*Chamaecyparis lawsoniana*
**LAWSON CYPRESS**
Family: Cupressaceae
Native: California and Oregon

This large, coniferous, evergreen tree is also called Port Orford cedar (despite its not being a cedar) in its native range, where it can reach 60m (200ft) tall. It has blue-green, feathery foliage in flat sprays of scale-like leaves, with narrow white markings on the underside, and makes an excellent hedge.

**Cultivation** Thrives in neutral to slightly acid, moist, well-drained soil, prefers full sun, and is pollution-tolerant. Propagate by cuttings, taken in winter from tips of large branches of the lower crown of young trees. ❀ ❀ ❀ Zone 6.

**Uses** Lawson cypress is popular in gardens, and has given rise to many named cultivars. 'Elwoodii' is very popular, being suitable for both hedging and growing as a specimen tree, and is an excellent substitute.

**Wildlife benefits** The dense, evergreen foliage is used as either a roost or a nesting site by many bird species, such as blackbirds, starlings and greenfinches. When grown as a hedge, the base provides cool, dry shelter for many insect species, small mammals, birds, spiders, reptiles and amphibians.

**Closely related species** Hinoki cypress (*C. obtusa*) and *C. pisifera* (Sawara cypress) are slow-growing trees that, if left uncut, grow to 35m (115ft) tall. Both make fine specimens but are less suited for hedging. Western red cedar (*Thuja plicata*) makes an excellent hedge.

*Escallonia rubra* var. *macrantha*
## REDCLAWS
Family: Escalloniaceae
Native: Chile

This evergreen shrub has bright, attractive, glossy green leaves and, in favourable locations, may reach 1.8m (6ft) or more. From mid- to late summer the branch tips become clothed in deep red, tubular flowers. When it's grown in warm, seaside regions, it makes an excellent windbreak, and often grows taller than specimens growing inland.

**Cultivation** Thrives in most well-drained soils and tolerates lime quite well. It'll establish best if planted out when young. Propagate from cuttings of short side shoots, in mid- to late summer. ❀ ❀ ❀ Zone 8.

**Uses** Redclaws makes an excellent informal hedge or windbreak, and can be clipped or hard-pruned to restrict the growth, although this reduces the amount of flower. It is an ideal seaside plant, tolerant of wind and salt. If cut back by frost, it'll reshoot from the base.

**Wildlife benefits** Good for providing nesting sites for birds and shelter for insects and small mammals, while the nectar-rich flowers are favoured by bees and some butterfly species. It also attracts aphids which, in turn, attract predators. In Australia, the white-brow hawkmoth feeds on the leaves.

**Closely related species** *E. rubra* has pink rather than red flowers. *E. virgata* is a deciduous shrub with slender branches, tiny leaves and tiny white flowers, but doesn't tolerate alkaline soil. *E.* 'Langleyensis' is a popular garden hybrid.

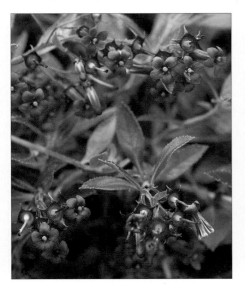

*Escallonia rubra* var. *macrantha*

*Rosa rugosa*
## RAMANAS ROSE
Family: Rosaceae
Native: E Asia

This native of coastal sand dunes is a dense, vigorous, suckering shrub that forms packed thickets of thorny stems. The flowers that appear from summer to autumn are dark pink to white, sweetly scented, and are followed by large, flattened hips; the bush often simultaneously bears fruit and flowers. The leaves turn bright yellow in autumn.

**Cultivation** It tolerates wind and salty conditions, in shade or full sun, and thrives in poor soil provided it's well drained. Easily propagated by seed, softwood cuttings or hardwood cuttings. ❀ ❀ ❀ Zone 2.

**Uses** Widely used as an ornamental plant across Europe and North America, and is valued by rose breeders for its considerable resistance to rose rust and black spot. Its tolerance of salt spray makes it ideal for planting beside roads that are treated with salt.

**Wildlife benefits** The attractive, strongly scented flowers attract many pollinators, especially bumblebees and malachite beetles. The large, red, tomato-like hips are extremely rich in vitamin C, and are eaten by small mammals and birds, such as finches, thrushes and waxwings.

**Closely related species** Numerous cultivars have been selected for garden use, with flower colour varying from white to dark red-purple. The dog rose (*R. canina*) has smaller but equally nutritious hips, and the burnet or Scots rose (*R. pimpinellifolia*) is also a good choice for seaside planting.

*Rosa rugosa*

*Taxus baccata*

*Taxus baccata*
## YEW
Family: Taxaceae
Native: Europe, NW Africa and SW Asia

Yew is a slow-growing, evergreen tree, reaching 10–20m (33–66ft) high, and can be very long-lived, with the oldest approximately 2–4,000 years old. The soft, needle-like leaves are arranged spirally around the stem, and the highly modified seed cones are surrounded by a bright red berry-like structure called an aril, the only non-poisonous part of the plant.

**Cultivation** An easy plant to grow, it tolerates cold and heat, sunny and shady sites, wet and dry soils, and a range of pH. Propagate from seed or cuttings of half-ripe terminal shoots. ❀ ❀ ❀ Zone 6.

**Uses** Yew is widely used in gardens, and there are over 200 named cultivars, the most popular of which is the upright Irish yew (*T. baccata* 'Fastigiata'). They are popular subjects for topiary, and make highly attractive, long-lived hedges that are very resistant to honey fungus.

**Wildlife benefits** The berry-like arils ripen over 2–3 months and are eaten by thrushes, waxwings and other birds. The foliage is toxic to most mammals, but is eaten by deer because they can break down the poisons. The larvae of some moth species, including willow beauty, also eat the leaves.

**Closely related species** All yews are closely related, and some botanists treat them all as the subspecies or varieties of one widespread species. Good examples include the Pacific yew (*T. brevifolia*) from north-west North America, Canada yew (*T. canadensis*) and Japanese yew (*T. cuspidata*).

# TREES

*Acer campestre*
**FIELD MAPLE**
Family: Aceraceae
Native: Europe, Near East and Africa

The field maple is a relatively small tree that can sometimes be found in semi-natural woods and, most frequently, in hedgerows. Its small leaves have 3–5 lobes, are greyish-green turning to gold in autumn, while the grey to yellowish-brown bark has a rough texture. It never achieves the size of its relative, the sycamore (*A. pseudoplatanus*), but can reach a great age.

**Cultivation**  Easily grown in full sun or partial shade, it prefers moist, well-drained soil and tolerates urban conditions much better than most maples. Sow seed as soon as it is ripe. ❀ ❀ ❀ Zone 4.

**Uses**  Field maple makes a strong, very durable hedge thanks to its dense foliage with well-developed branches, but it can also make an attractive freestanding tree. The young foliage is initially reddish before turning dark green and then yellow in autumn.

**Wildlife benefits**  Field maple supports over 50 species of wildlife, being the food plant for many moths including the winter moth, maple pug, mocha and small yellow wave. Nectar and pollen attract bees and other insects, and the strong, dense growth makes an ideal haven for nesting birds.

**Closely related species**  The taller sycamore (*Acer pseudoplatanus*) is well known for its ability to make a fine specimen, and for the nuisance value of its seedlings. If space is limited, try growing the 8m (25ft) high Japanese maple (*A. palmatum*).

*Acer campestre*

*Alnus glutinosa*

*Alnus glutinosa*
**COMMON ALDER**
Family: Betulaceae
Native: Europe

Its native habitat is wet ground, and it can certainly withstand regular immersion in water. The oval leaves are distinctive, with a notch at the tip of the main vein, and the buds appear on short stalks. In winter, small, persistent, woody "cones" appear near the branch tips.

**Cultivation**  Grows in most soils, including the waterlogged, and because it fixes nitrogen in its root nodules it can grow on quite infertile ground. Propagate by seed in late autumn. ❀ ❀ ❀ Zone 3.

**Uses**  Its ability to withstand poor soil has made it a tree of choice for land reclamation and waterside planting. In time it makes a handsome specimen, growing 25m (85ft) high, making it best suited to large gardens.

**Wildlife benefits**  The seeds attract finches, such as redpolls and siskins, and tits. The caterpillars of around 30 moth species, including alder kitten, brindled beauty, large emerald, and the waved carpet, feed on the leaves, as do alder sawfly and alder leaf-miners.

**Closely related species**  There are approximately 35 species of alder, and many are quite similar to the common alder. *A. rubra* is an American species, also suited to wet ground, while the grey alder (*A. incana*) and Italian alder (*A. cordata*) are better suited to drier sites. All are useful wildlife trees.

*Betula pendula*

*Betula pendula*
**SILVER BIRCH**
Family: Betulaceae
Native: Europe and Asia Minor

Silver birch is a common, widely used tree that's grown for its graceful habit provided by the thin, whip-like twigs that are pendulous at the tips. Its silvery, attractive bark becomes rugged, with black patches appearing as the tree ages. A fast-growing tree (though quite short-lived with a life expectancy of around 90 years), it quickly colonizes open areas, such as unmanaged heaths and abandoned land.

**Cultivation**  Silver birch grows in a wide range of habitats, and is incredibly tolerant of a wide-ranging soil pH, from 3.5–7. It is usually best in dry, sandy soils or harsh settings where other trees fail. Propagate by seed in late autumn. ❀ ❀ ❀ Zone 1.

**Uses**  Often called "lady of the woods" because of its outstanding elegance, it is a wonderful landscape tree, especially when young. Despite its rapid growth rate, it rarely dominates or shades the garden too much.

**Wildlife benefits**  Birch seeds are a food source for overwintering birds, such as tits and finches, and older trees provide nesting sites in cracked trunks for the likes of tree creepers. The leaves are a food source for well over 100 kinds of moth caterpillar, as well as birch leaf miners.

**Closely related species**  While silver birch grows best on drier soils, the closely related downy birch (*B. pubescens*) is chiefly associated with damper soils and grows well with alder.

*Carpinus betulus*

## *Carpinus betulus*
## COMMON HORNBEAM
Family: Carpinaceae
Native: Europe and Asia Minor

This large, attractive forest tree closely resembles beech (*Fagus*), and has a pyramidal shape that later becomes more rounded. It produces flowers in the form of catkins, which remain on the tree until early autumn when the small "nutlets" hang in clusters of green, three-pointed, papery wings. During winter, dead leaves remain on the lower branches until spring.

**Cultivation** Hornbeam is especially good in chalky and clay soil, though it will tolerate wet ground, and likes both dense shade and exposed, windy sites. It is raised from seed, which remains dormant in the soil for 18 months. Propagate by seed in spring or autumn. ❀ ❀ ❀ Zone 5.

**Uses** Hornbeam makes an excellent hedge because of its ability to retain its withered, tan or light brown leaves until spring, a characteristic called *marcescence*. It also makes a fine specimen tree, although it's only suited to larger gardens.

**Wildlife benefits** Hornbeam supports many insects, including caterpillars of the small white wave and copper underwing moths. The nuts are eaten in winter by birds, such as hawfinches, while hares, rabbits and field mice eat the young leaves. It provides good bird cover when grown as a hedge.

**Closely related species** There are a number of species that are similar to, and as handsome as, the European hornbeam. American hornbeam (*C. caroliniana*) is a tree or large shrub from eastern North America, and the Japanese *C. japonica* is a medium-sized tree with deep, flaking, fissured bark.

## *Castanea sativa*
## SWEET CHESTNUT
Family: Fagaceae
Native: Mediterranean

It has been cultivated for over 3,000 years, and was widely spread beyond its original range by Roman legionaries who used the nuts as a staple food. It grows into a tall tree with deep, spirally fissured bark, has distinctively large, tough, serrated leaves, and slim, cream-coloured flower panicles followed, in autumn, by chestnuts held in prickly cases.

**Cultivation** Sweet chestnut does best on deep, moist, sandy soil and well-drained clay, and suffers if grown on very wet or lime-rich ground. It fruits best in areas with long, hot summers. Propagate by seed in autumn. ❀ ❀ ❀ Zone 5.

**Uses** It ultimately grows into a beautiful tree, but you'll need a huge garden. It is tolerant of drought, grows fast when young and is quite showy in bloom, making it a popular choice where space permits.

**Wildlife benefits** The long yellow catkins are attractive to many pollinating insects, especially bees. The nuts that follow are eaten by mammals, including squirrels, badgers and dormice. The tree is also a good nesting site for woodpeckers, nuthatches and nightingales, while waved carpet moths eat the leaves.

**Closely related species** The Japanese *C. crenata* and Chinese *C. mollisima* are widely planted in North America with the American chestnut (*C. dentate*) because they are blight-resistant. Note that *C. alnifolia* is a suckering, dwarf, American native just 1m (3ft) high.

*Castanea sativa*

## *Cercis siliquastrum*
## JUDAS TREE
Family: Caesalpiniaceae
Native: E Mediterranean

A handsome, small, deciduous, ornamental tree reaching 6m (20ft) high, it gradually develops a rounded crown and needs well-drained soil and a sunny location. In early summer, lilac pea-like flowers clothe both the branches and the main trunk, and are followed by conspicuous, purple-tinted, bean-like seed pods later in summer.

**Cultivation** It prefers deep, fertile, moist but well-drained soil in full sun or light shade, and needs hot summers to flower. Plant when young because it resents root disturbance. Propagate seed when ripe. ❀ ❀ ❀ Zone 6.

**Uses** The Judas tree makes an excellent freestanding specimen, although it can also be planted towards the back of a shrub border or trained against a wall. It is nitrogen-fixing and very drought-tolerant once established, and is notably resistant to honey fungus.

**Wildlife benefits** The nectar and pollen provide an excellent source of food for insects, especially bees. In the spring the flowers often appear quite early, preceding the foliage. This gives a valuable boost to early, emerging bees, and to some early flying butterfly species.

**Closely related species** California or Western redbud (*C. occidentalis*) is a large Californian shrub quite similar to the Judas tree, and grows well in a sunny, well-drained site. The Chinese redbud (*C. chinensis*) forms a fine specimen shrub or small tree, and bears lavender to crimson flowers.

*Cercis siliquastrum*

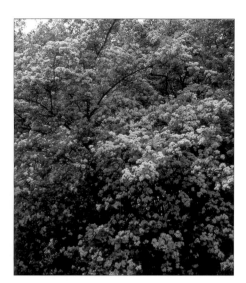

*Crataegus monogyna*

## *Crataegus monogyna*
### COMMON HAWTHORN
Family: Rosaceae
Native: Europe

This short, deciduous, long-lived, thorny tree is dense with leaves, and is regularly found in naturally regenerating woodland. Its reddish new shoots and leaves are most attractive in late spring or early summer when the distinctive, white, scented blossom appears. The autumn red berries are called haws.

**Cultivation** It occurs on a wide range of soil types, including very dry and wet ground, and isn't in the least bit fussy, being resistant to both exposure and pollution. Propagate by seed in autumn after stratification. ❀ ❀ ❀ Zone 5.

**Uses** Hawthorn has long been used to create stock-proof hedges, and is still widely used for this purpose. Cultivars or hybrids are often grown in the garden, but the wild species forms a fine, small specimen tree, with an attractive, deep, rounded dome shape.

**Wildlife benefits** Hawthorn supports many insects including the caterpillars of over 70 species of moth, and is an important nectar source for others early in the year. The berries provide vital winter food supplies for small mammals and especially birds, such as redwings, fieldfares and waxwings.

**Closely related species** The red-flowering Midland hawthorn (*C. laevigata*) is similar to *C. monogyna*. The south-east American *C. aestivalis* has large fruit enjoyed by birds, and Washington thorn (*C. phaenopyrum*) has fragrant blooms.

## *Fagus sylvatica*
### BEECH
Family: Fagaceae
Native: Europe

This large forest tree eventually forms a large specimen with smooth, metallic grey bark. The rounded crown is very dense and often casts such deep shade that little else can grow beneath it. The spring flowers are followed by triangular nuts with edible kernels in late summer. In autumn, the leaves turn amber and bronze.

**Cultivation** Beech is usually happiest on moist, alkaline soil, but is very tolerant of a wide range of soils and conditions, and will grow in quite acidic conditions. Young trees are very shade-tolerant. Propagate by seed in late autumn. ❀ ❀ ❀ Zone 5.

**Uses** Forms a beautiful specimen tree with smooth, grey bark and copper and russet autumn foliage, but it's too large for all but the biggest gardens. It makes a superb hedge however, retaining its foliage through winter, and is useful in a rather shady setting.

**Wildlife benefits** The nuts are attractive to many small mammals, including mice, voles, squirrels and badgers, with birds such as bramblings, chaffinches and parakeets also eating the seed. The leaves provide food for caterpillars of over 20 moth species, including the green silver-lines and large emerald.

**Closely related species** American beech (*F. grandifolia*) is also useful for wildlife, and is the only member of the genus found in North America. It makes a fine specimen with leaves initially a light blue, turning golden-bronze in autumn.

*Fagus sylvatica*

*Larix decidua*

## *Larix decidua*
### EUROPEAN LARCH
Family: Pinaceae
Native: Continental Europe

From the alpine regions of Europe, it is somewhat unusual for a conifer because it is deciduous, shedding its leaves each autumn. The foliage is also less needle-like than most conifers, being soft and light green. In spring the female, rose-coloured cones appear with the more yellowish male ones towards the end of the branches.

**Cultivation** Larch tends to do well in wetter, hilly districts on well-drained, acidic soil where it can withstand high winds and exposure. Propagate by seed when ripe. ❀ ❀ ❀ Zone 4.

**Uses** Ultimately forming a large, spreading, handsome tree, with a conical crown when young, becoming broader on maturity, it is too large for smaller gardens. The dwarf, weeping selections, such as *L. decidua* 'Puli,' are better suited to smaller gardens.

**Wildlife benefits** The light shade cast by larch provides good cover for birds and animals sheltering from the elements. Seed- and bud-eating birds, such as tree creepers, crested tits, redwings and fieldfares, rely on the larch, as do the caterpillars of larch pug and small engrailed moths.

**Closely related species** Japanese larch (*L. kaempferi*) is probably the most similar species, growing to 45m (145ft), and makes a good shelter, best for a large garden. This species attracts small finches, tits and treecreepers. The European larch (*L. x marschlinsii*) thrives on less fertile soils.

*Malus sylvestris*

## *Malus sylvestris*
## CRAB APPLE
Family: Rosaceae
Native: Europe and W Asia

The crab apple is a small, thorny, deciduous tree, common in oak woods and hedges, and is most highly visible in spring when its abundant blossom – pink in bud and white-pink when open – clothes the branches. The flowers are followed by small, hard fruits that are quite bitter and unpalatable to humans, but are quickly taken by wildlife.

**Cultivation** Grows most prolifically on chalky soils, and needs to be situated in sun to thrive. It is best planted on well-drained soil, and will grow happily even in heavy clay provided it has been opened up so that it is free-draining. ❀ ❀ ❀ Zone 4.

**Uses** Besides being an attractive specimen tree in its own right, the crab apple is a good pollinator for fruiting apples. While the wild form can grow up to 10m (33ft) tall, there is also a wide selection of cultivated varieties, with some for small gardens.

**Wildlife benefits** Crab apples support over 100 different animal species, including crevice-living insects. The caterpillars of over 20 moth species, including the eyed hawkmoth, eat the leaves while the flowers support many insects, and the fruits are eaten by birds, rodents and various insects.

**Closely related species** Orchard apples are very closely related to *M. sylvestris*, although the fruit is much larger and sweeter. Hall's crab apple (*M. halliana*) is a Chinese species with pink flowers and purple fruits, and the Nagasaki crab apple (*M. cerasifera*) has white flowers and red fruit.

## *Nothofagus antarctica*
## SOUTHERN OR ANTARCTIC BEECH
Family: Nothofagaceae
Native: S Chile and Argentina

This native of the temperate rainforests of South America is naturally quite variable, making tall bushes from 2–3m (6½–10ft) high in some places, and in others making 25m (85ft) high trees. It has a slender trunk with attractive, scaly bark while its branches, arranged in a herringbone formation, are covered by small, heart-shaped leaves that turn yellow in autumn.

**Cultivation** A fast-growing tree that does best in a sunny position on acid loam. It will not tolerate lime but is very hardy, and tolerates wind and drought once properly established. Propagate by seed in autumn. ❀ ❀ ❀ Zone 7.

**Uses** The large forms make a remarkably attractive tree that is too big for all but the biggest gardens. 'Puget Pillar' is a good example of the dwarf form with more upright branches, and is better suited to medium-sized gardens.

**Wildlife benefits** Antarctic beech is excellent at supporting wildlife, even in areas where it is not native. It is the larval food plant for many species of ghost moth, and its deep-fissured bark provides shelter for many insects, especially overwintering butterflies. The seeds are eaten by birds.

**Closely related species** *N. moorei*, found in Australia (and also called Antarctic beech), is somewhat less hardy than its namesake. Two other species, *N. procera* and *N. obliqua*, are also South American, from the same area as *N. antarctica*, and are large, deciduous trees.

*Nothofagus antarctica*

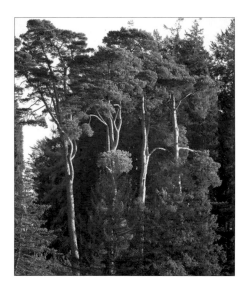

*Pinus sylvestris*

## *Pinus sylvestris*
## SCOTS PINE
Family: Pinaceae
Native: Europe

This conifer normally grows up to 25m (85ft) high, although it is variable across its range and can even reach 45m (145ft). The bark is thick, scaly and dark grey-brown on the lower trunk and changes to thin, flaky and orange higher up. The mature tree's habit is distinctive due to its long, bare, straight trunk topped by a rounded or flat-topped mass of foliage.

**Cultivation** Whilst Scots pine grows on a wide range of soils, it prefers light, dry sands and gravels, and tolerates poor soils, often colonizing areas of heath land. Propagation is by seed. ❀ ❀ ❀ Zone 2.

**Uses** Although its main use is for forestry, it makes a very attractive specimen, and is used as an accent plant because of its distinctive mature shape. It is too large for most gardens, but try cultivars 'Glauca Nana' and 'Compressa' where space is limited.

**Wildlife benefits** Scots pine provides nesting sites for many birds, and the seeds are the preferred food of red squirrels and crossbills. A number of moth caterpillars, including the pine beauty, pine carpet and pine hawkmoth, live on it, and the deep-fissured bark provides shelter for many insects.

**Closely related species** The lodge-pole pine (*P. contorta*) is from western North America where it grows on much wetter soils than Scots pine. The black pine (*P. nigra*) is a southern European relative which grows to 40m (130ft) and has many cultivars.

## *Prunus avium*
### WILD CHERRY, GEAN
Family: Rosaceae
Native: Europe, N Africa and
W Asia

The wild cherry can grow to an impressive size, sometimes reaching 30m (100ft) although 15m (50ft) is more common. The flowers appear in clusters on short shoots along the twigs of established wood in spring, and are often spectacular, but the fruits are much less conspicuous than those of cultivated varieties.

**Cultivation** Easily grown in most fertile soils, but it does not do well on acidic ground. Propagation is usually from seed, though it can be grown from cuttings when taken from young trees. ❀ ❀ ❀ Zone 3.

**Uses** A stately and very attractive tree, both when in bloom and for the rest of the year. It looks good in naturalistic, mixed planting and is an ideal back-of-the-border specimen for a woodland-edge border. Many cultivated forms are available.

**Wildlife benefits** During the flowering season the blossom is a good nectar source for a variety of insects, especially bees. The fruits are eaten by numerous bird species that quickly strip them from the trees almost as soon as they are ripe. Green pug moth caterpillars eat the leaves.

**Closely related species** Wild cherry is one of the parents of most European cultivated cherries, and is very similar to most of them. The bird cherry (*P. padus*) is a small, deciduous tree with flowers in short, branched inflorescences, followed by black, egg-shaped fruit. It prefers moist sites.

*Prunus avium*

## *Pyrus communis*
### COMMON PEAR
Family: Rosaceae
Native: C and E Europe and
SW Asia

A medium-sized tree that is likely to reach 10m (33ft) high but can, if conditions are ideal, double that. It has glossy, oval leaves that turn from dark green to orange and red in autumn. The conspicuous, white, star-shaped flowers with five petals appear in spring. A mass of white flowers open in April.

**Cultivation** Grows in full sun on most fertile, well-drained soil, although a sandy or clay loam with a pH of 5–7 is best. It has strong, vertical branches and requires little pruning. Propagate by seed in spring. ❀ ❀ ❀ Zone 4.

**Uses** Its narrow and rather conical form, coupled with the fact that it casts fairly light shade, means it can be grown in a lawn without badly affecting the grass. It is very attractive when flowering in spring, and the glossy, bright green leaves sometimes colour up well in autumn.

**Wildlife benefits** Finches may attack young shoots, and blossom and green pug moths also feed on the flowers. The open flowers are an excellent source of nectar, especially for bees. Hawkmoths feed on the leaves, and many species eat the overripe fruit in autumn.

**Closely related species** The European pear probably descended from two species of wild pear, *P. pyraster* and *P. caucasica*, both of which hybridize with the domestic species. Willow-leaved pear (*Pyrus salicifolia*) is grown widely as an ornamental tree.

*Pyrus communis*

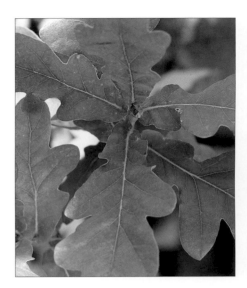

*Quercus robur*

## *Quercus robur*
### ENGLISH OAK
Family: Fagaceae
Native: Europe, Asia Minor and
N Africa

A large, long-lived, deciduous tree that reaches 25–35m (85–115ft) in height, with a large, wide-spreading head of rugged branches. While it may naturally live to a few hundred years old, some coppiced oaks are known to be over 1,000 years old and the whole tree, including the deadwood, is an extremely valuable habitat for wildlife.

**Cultivation** The oak grows on a range of soils, including heavy clay, and has a pH tolerance ranging from 4.5–7.5. Mature trees are very robust and will tolerate flooding, even by seawater. Propagate by seed in late autumn. ❀ ❀ ❀ Zone 6.

**Uses** Oaks are ultimately large trees that dominate the landscape. In the garden, they need plenty of space and are only really suited to a large site. The variety 'Fastigiata' has erect branches and a narrow, pyramidal form, and is useful if you want to limit the amount of shade cast.

**Wildlife benefits** Mature trees can support over 300 species of insects that, in turn, feed birds such as woodpeckers, tree creepers and nuthatches. Acorns feed small mammals and the likes of jays, and the leaves are a larval food source for over 100 moth and butterfly species.

**Closely related species** The sessile oak (*Q. petraea*) shares much of the English oak's range, and the two often hybridize in the wild, creating *Q. x rosacea*. The white oak (*Q. alba*), from America, is very similar, but slightly taller.

*Salix caprea*
## GOAT WILLOW
Family: Salicaceae
Native: Europe and NW Africa

Also known as the pussy willow or great sallow, this deciduous shrub or small tree reaches a height of 6–14m (20–45ft), or more rarely 20m (66ft). The leaves are broader than those of most other willows, and the spring catkins emerge before the foliage and resemble animal fur, hence the name pussy willow.

**Cultivation** Goat willow grows in both wet and dry ground, wherever bare soil is available. Unlike almost all other willows, goat willow does not take root readily from cuttings. Propagate by seed. ❀ ❀ ❀ Zone 5.

**Uses** The species is not often planted because of its somewhat unruly nature in the garden. 'Kilmarnock' is a cultivated variety with pretty catkins borne in early spring, and a weeping habit. It is normally grafted on to a rootstock to give height to what would otherwise be a small tree.

**Wildlife benefits** Goat willow is visited by early emerging bees that collect the abundant pollen, which also provides larval food for the poplar hawkmoth, puss moth and many other insects. Many invertebrates hide in the cracks and splits that appear in the bark and stems of older trees.

**Closely related species** Willow is a variable and widespread genus with many closely related species. White willow (*S. alba*), crack willow (*S. fragilis*) and bay willow (*S. pentandra*) all occur naturally in the same area as the goat willow, and introduced species readily naturalize.

*Salix caprea*

*Sorbus aucuparia*
## MOUNTAIN ASH
Family: Rosaceae
Native: Europe and W Asia

This small- to medium-sized deciduous tree, also known as rowan, grows up to 20m (66ft) high but is often smaller, and is common in temperate European regions. It has divided leaves, bunches of white flowers and red, edible berries. It is very tolerant of cold, and is often found at high altitude on mountains, hence its common name.

**Cultivation** Grows best in humus-rich, lime-free, moderately fertile soil, provided it isn't waterlogged. It is also pollution-tolerant, although it dislikes shading. Propagate seed when ripe. ❀ ❀ ❀ Zone 2.

**Uses** Mountain ash is ideal for a wide variety of gardens, usually being medium height and relatively compact growing. It is ideal for birds or a forest-edge border, and is extremely decorative when adorned with blossom in spring, or autumn berries.

**Wildlife benefits** In early summer the abundant, small, white, nectar-rich flowers are extremely popular with bees. The berries that follow are especially liked by starlings, finches, waxwings and thrushes, with leaves being eaten by several moths, including the brimstone and orange underwing.

**Closely related species** Over 60 species of *Sorbus* are closely related to mountain ash, including the sargent's rowan (*S. sargentiana*) and the small-leaf rowan (*S. microphylla*), both from China, and American mountain ash (*S. americana*) and showy mountain ash (*S. decora*).

*Sorbus aucuparia*

*Tilia cordata*

*Tilia cordata*
## SMALL-LEAVED LIME
Family: Malvaceae
Native: Europe

Lime trees are a highly variable genus, and are mostly deciduous, medium to large trees. *T. cordata* typically grows 15–18m (50–60ft) high but can reach 25–28m (85–90ft). They are pyramidal or conical when young, gradually becoming ovate when mature with a dense, compact nature consisting of upright and spreading branches.

**Cultivation** Lime prefers moist, deep, fertile, well-drained soil but also tolerates poor ground, drought, a range of pH and air pollution, and is easy to transplant. Propagate by seed in autumn. ❀ ❀ ❀ Zone 3.

**Uses** Small-leaved lime has sweet-smelling flowers and is an attractive tree that has been widely planted along roads and in parks where it can be pollarded or heavily pruned. It can also be grown as a large hedge.

**Wildlife benefits** Lime is an excellent nectar source, especially for bees, and unlike many large forest trees is pollinated by insects rather than the wind. Numerous moths eat the foliage, including the lime hawkmoth and orange sallow, and the seeds are taken by some birds.

**Closely related species** Limes hybridize very freely, with common lime being a hybrid of *T. cordata* and large-leaved lime (*T. platyphyllos*), a widely grown street tree. Small-leaved lime is widely cultivated in North America as a substitute for the American linden (*T. americana*), which has a larger leaf.

# CLIMBERS

### *Clematis tangutica*
### CLEMATIS
Family: Ranunculaceae
Native: Mongolia and NW China

A vigorous, summer-to-autumn-flowering clematis that grows to 3m (10ft) high. The drooping, lantern-shaped, golden-yellow flowers are borne on new shoots, and are followed by gorgeous, decorative, fluffy, silvery seed heads. The abundant, bright green leaves are deeply divided into lance-shaped leaflets.

**Cultivation** Grow in shade or full sun. It prefers its roots in rich, free-draining soil in shade. Propagate by semi-ripe cuttings in summer. ❀ ❀ ❀ Zone 5.

**Uses** Like many other clematis, it is grown for its flowers and seed heads, and is best displayed when trained on walls and trellises. It can also be trained up trees or grown through other climbers, such as roses, to add extra interest.

**Wildlife benefits** Bees and bumblebees visit the flowers seeking nectar, and the flower buds are eaten by bullfinches. The seed heads are eaten by birds and used to make nests. The mass of unpruned, twining stems are ideal places for birds to secure their nests.

**Closely related species** Old man's beard (*C. vitalba*) is a rampant climber with small, white, nectar-rich flowers visited by bumblebees, bees, hoverflies and night-flying moths, and seeds eaten by birds. *C. montana* is used in ornamental gardens where bees visit the flowers for pollen.

*Clematis tangutica*

*Hedera helix*

### *Hedera helix*
### COMMON IVY
Family: Araliaceae
Native: Europe, Scandinavia and Russia

This vigorous, evergreen, self-clinging climber grows to 10m (33ft) high. It has two distinct phases, the juvenile and adult, the main difference being the leaf shape. The juvenile leaves are small and 5-lobed whereas the adult foliage is simple and ovate. The yellow-green flowers are borne from autumn, and are followed by black berries from winter to spring.

**Cultivation** Site in sun or semi- to full shade, in any well-drained, alkaline soil. Propagate by softwood cuttings of new growth in summer. ❀ ❀ ❀ Zone 5.

**Uses** Ivies are excellent for covering large areas, such as walls, sheds and tree stumps. They are also frequently used as ground cover in gardens where the evergreen foliage acts as a foil for the border plants, especially in winter and spring.

**Wildlife benefits** The flowers provide late nectar for bees, hoverflies and butterflies. The flower buds are eaten by the caterpillar of the holly blue butterfly. The berries provide valuable winter food for birds, particularly thrushes and finches. Birds, such as wrens and blackbirds, nest in the foliage.

**Closely related species** Persian ivy (*H. colchica*) and Irish ivy (*H. hibernica*) are two of the best species for covering large areas. *H. c.* 'Dentata Variegata' has attractive variegated, cream-yellow leaves.

### *Humulus lupulus*
### HOP
Family: Cannabaceae
Native: Northern temperate regions

This herbaceous, twining climber can reach up to 6m (20ft) each year. It displays hairy, rough stems and deeply divided, 3–5 lobed leaves. There are separate male and female plants, and it is the female that is grown ornamentally. It produces green-yellow fruits that hang in clusters from autumn.

**Cultivation** Thrives in full sun or semi-shade in deep, fertile, well-drained soil. Grow the golden 'Aureus' in full sun for the best foliage colour. Propagate by tip cuttings in spring. ❀ ❀ ❀ Zone 5.

**Uses** Hops are traditionally used to make beer, but in gardens they are brilliant for clothing a pergola or arch, and for screening a fence or wall. Grow 'Aureus' with large, purple-flowering clematis to create a striking colour combination.

**Wildlife benefits** The caterpillars of the comma butterfly and the buttoned snout moth (also recorded on the cultivar 'Aureus') feed on the leaves. Small birds will use the dried hop fruits as nesting material. If left uncut, the stems will harbour overwintering insects.

**Closely related species** Most gardeners grow 'Aureus' because of its beautiful lime-green leaves. The Japanese *H. japonicus* is normally grown as an annual in temperate climates, and 'Variegatus' has blotched and streaked white foliage.

*Humulus lupulus*

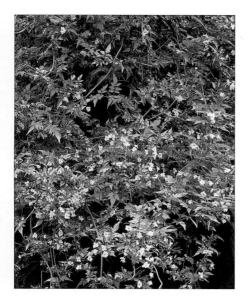

*Jasminum officinale*

## *Jasminum officinale*
### COMMON JASMINE
Family: Oleaceae
Native: Asia Minor, Himalayas and China

This semi-evergreen (sometimes deciduous) twining climber can reach up to 12m (40ft) high. The dark green leaves are deeply divided, each leaf comprising 7–9 leaflets. Clusters of white, tubular flowers are borne from summer to autumn. Common jasmine is one of the best fragrant plants.

**Cultivation**  Plant in a sunny, sheltered position that is protected from harsh winds. Grow in moist, fertile, free-draining soil. Propagate by semi-ripe cuttings in late summer. ❀ ❀ Zone 7.

**Uses**  Common jasmine is ideal for growing up a pergola, trellis or archway. Also plant next to a path, door or seating area because of its amazing scent. Frequently selected for a specialist moth border.

**Wildlife benefits**  The sweetly scented flowers are excellent at attracting bees and butterflies by day, while at night the visiting moths will attract bats to the area. The dense mat of twining stems is ideal for birds to nest in, and for foraging. Roosting insects are frequent visitors.

**Closely related species**
*J. polyanthum*, to 3m (10ft) high, is an evergreen, twining climber that produces clusters of scented white flowers from late summer to winter. Winter jasmine (*J. nudiflorum*) is a deciduous arching shrub bearing bright yellow flowers in winter.

## *Lathyrus latifolius*
### PERENNIAL PEA
Family: Fabaceae
Native: C and S Europe

This herbaceous, perennial climber dies down every winter and re-emerges in spring. The stems climb by tendrils and can reach up to 3m (10ft) in a season. The pea-like, rose-pink flowers are borne from summer to autumn but aren't scented. The leaflets are borne in pairs, and are grey-green terminating in a 3-branched tendril.

**Cultivation**  For best results, plant in full sun although it can stand partial shade, and grow in moderately fertile, well-drained soil. Propagate by seed or division in spring. ❀ ❀ ❀ Zone 5.

**Uses**  Peas are often grown up an ornate wigwam of bamboo canes or, better still, on pollarded hazel stems. They are also ideal for covering and rambling across hot, sunny banks. Can also be planted in informal hanging baskets to cascade over the sides.

**Wildlife benefits**  The pollen-rich flowers, complete with two large nectar glands, attract many insects including bees, bumblebees, butterflies and beetles. The leaves are eaten by the caterpillar of the long-tailed blue butterfly. Site in full sun for optimum insect visits.

**Closely related species**  The everlasting pea (*L. grandiflorus*), to 1.5m (5ft) high, is a herbaceous perennial with pink-purple and red flowers in summer. The sweet pea (*L. odoratus*) is a hardy annual climber with large, fragrant flowers from summer to early autumn.

*Lathyrus latifolius*

*Lonicera periclymenum*

## *Lonicera periclymenum*
### COMMON HONEYSUCKLE
Family: Caprifoliaceae
Native: Europe, Asia Minor, Caucasus and W Asia

Beautiful fragrant flowers adorn this twining climber that can reach up to 4m (13ft) high. The opposite green-bluish leaves are rounded and slightly hairy. The scented, tubular flowers are red and yellow-white, and can extend to 5cm (2in) long, being followed by spherical red fruits.

**Cultivation**  Plant in moist but well-drained soil enriched with organic matter, such as leaf mould. Grow in full sun or part shade. Propagate by semi-ripe cuttings in summer. ❀ ❀ ❀ Zone 4.

**Uses**  Ideal for growing on a trellis, wall, pergola, fence, or over an old tree stump. Plant a honeysuckle every 3–5m (10–17ft) along a mixed hedgerow to enrich the habitat. Keep the roots in the shade and the top growth in full sun.

**Wildlife benefits**  The nectar-rich flowers attract moths, particularly hawkmoths, in midsummer. The shiny red berries are eaten by birds, especially song thrushes, blackbirds, tits, robins and finches. Old bark is stripped off by pied flycatchers and dormice to use as nesting material.

**Closely related species**  *L. nitida* makes an excellent hedge. *L. n.* 'Baggescens Gold' is an attractive golden-leaved cultivar. The dense foliage attracts many nesting birds. *L. x purpusii* is a semi-evergreen shrub with nectar-rich flowers from winter to spring, providing food for early emerging insects.

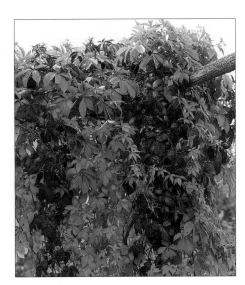

*Parthenocissus quinquefolia*

## *Parthenocissus quinquefolia*
## VIRGINIA CREEPER
Family: Vitaceae
Native: E North America to Mexico

A self-clinging climber that hauls itself up by tendrils and adhesive pads. The stems can reach to 30m (100ft) high, and bear deciduous, dull green leaves, each with 3–5 leaflets. The foliage produces spectacular autumn colour when it turns flashy rich crimson. The summer flowers are insignificant, but are followed by small blue fruits.

**Cultivation**  Virginia creeper enjoys deep, moist soil with plenty of organic matter. Plant in partial shade for the best autumn colour. Propagate by sowing fresh seed. ❀ ❀ ❀ Zone 3.

**Uses**  Ideal for growing over pergolas, walls, buildings and fences, and for growing up through trees. Only use where you have room, and where it can be trimmed regularly and prevented from snaking under and disturbing the roof tiles.

**Wildlife benefits**  The mass of stems host a variety of wildlife, sheltering insects and nesting birds, while the leaves are eaten by the Virginia creeper sphinx moth caterpillar. The round, blue berries are eaten by birds, including mistle thrushes, blackcaps and magpies.

**Closely related species**  *P. henryana*, which can reach up to 5m (17ft) high, is more suited to a small garden. The green-pink, veined, compound leaves are its most striking feature. Boston ivy (*P. tricuspidata*) is another rampant species that should be used with caution.

## *Phaseolus coccineus*
## SCARLET RUNNER BEAN
Family: Fabaceae
Native: Tropical America

Often just called runner bean, this is a tender, twining, perennial vine with bright red flowers. Due to its tenderness to frost, it is usually grown as an annual. The stems can reach a height of 4m (13ft) in a year, and produce edible seed pods 10–30cm (4–12in) long. The round seeds are red to purple.

**Cultivation**  It enjoys a warm, sheltered spot in free-draining soil. Sow outdoors in mid-spring, or sow under glass and harden off before planting outside. ❀ Zone 10.

**Uses**  Traditionally used in the vegetable garden, but why not try growing it up a wigwam of hazel stems in the ornamental garden, either in the herbaceous or mixed border, or in pots. It can also be used to clothe archways or a trellis.

**Wildlife benefits**  Runner beans are pollinated by bees as they manoeuvre into the bright red flowers to reach the nectar. Bumblebees have been observed eating part of the flower near the nectaries to gain easy access to the sugary drink.

**Closely related species**  An alternative, but not as good for wildlife, is the self-fertile French bean (*Phaseolus vulgaris*). Research indicates that only 8 per cent of a yield is caused by bee pollination. Beekeepers do not consider this crop an important source of nectar and pollen.

## *Pisum sativum*
## GARDEN PEA
Family: Fabaceae
Native: S Europe

The garden pea is an annual grown for its edible seed pods. The climber grows to 2m (6½ft) high using its tendrils. The leaves are deeply divided into 1–4 pairs of leaflets. The pretty flowers are white, and sometimes stained with red-purple markings. The thin, oblong seed pods that follow can grow to 15cm (6in) long.

**Cultivation**  It grows best in an open but sheltered site, and the soil should be deep and fertile. Ideally, manure or compost should have been added the previous autumn. Sow seeds outside in spring. ❀ ❀ ❀ Zone 5.

**Uses**  Netting usually protects the garden peas, and can be lifted after cropping has finished to allow the wildlife to move in. Alternatively, grow in pots or up ornamental wigwams.

**Wildlife benefits**  Although pea flowers produce nectar and pollen, it is rarely in large quantities, making the pea seeds the big benefit to wildlife. The seeds are eaten by birds, especially wood pigeons, blue tits, siskins, linnets, crossbills and other finches.

**Closely related species**  The everlasting pea (*Lathyrus grandiflorus*) is a perennial reaching 2m (6½ft) high. The violet flowers are borne in summer. *L. laetiflorus*, a native to western North America, is a perennial with white-pink flowers.

*Phaseolus coccineus*

*Pisum sativum*

*Rosa banksiae*

## *Rosa banksiae*
### BANKSIA ROSE
Family: Rosaceae
Native: W and C China

A strong climber, it can grow up to 12m (40ft) high. The yellow or white, fragrant flowers are borne in umbels in early summer. The flowers are usually single but occasionally double, and are followed by dull red fruits. The glossy, evergreen leaves are divided into 3–7 leaflets.

**Cultivation** Plant in full sun for the best results where it will tolerate a range of soils, but the ground must be free-draining. Mulch in winter to protect the roots. Propagate by hardwood cuttings in autumn. ❀ ❀ ❀ Zone 7.

**Uses** A tall species rose that can be used to grow up the front of large houses, fences and walls, but it will only thrive in a sunny, sheltered location. Grow a red or pink large-flowering clematis through the rose for added interest.

**Wildlife benefits** Bees and bumblebees are attracted to the flowers seeking pollen. The flowers are followed by hips that, when mature, are eaten by small mammals and birds. Many insects, including ladybirds and lacewings, overwinter in the stems and foliage.

**Closely related species** If choosing a cultivar or variety to plant, select *R. b.* var. *normalis* or the cultivar *R. b.* 'Lutescens' for their single, scented flowers. Do not select double-flowering cultivars, or varieties such as *R. banksiae* var. *banksiae* or the cultivar 'Lutea' with double yellow flowers, because these are of little use to wildlife.

## *Vitis vinifera*
### COMMON GRAPE VINE
Family: Vitaceae
Native: S and C Europe

The common grape vine is a deciduous, woody-stemmed climber that can grow up to 7m (23ft). The pale green, insignificant flowers borne in clusters from late spring to early summer are followed by bunches of green or purple fruits. The leaves are palmate with 3–5 lobes, and are slightly hairy when young.

**Cultivation** Thrives in fertile, free-draining, chalky soil in sun or semi-shade. Produces best fruits in full sun. Propagate by hardwood cuttings in late winter. ❀ ❀ ❀ Zone 6.

**Uses** A valuable plant used for clothing a pergola or planted against a sunny wall. It will give a tropical feel to a garden, especially around a seating area. A purple-leaved cultivar, such as 'Purpurea', stands out well against a white wall.

**Wildlife benefits** The fruits are eaten by birds, including collared doves, green woodpeckers, tits, starlings, thrushes, warblers and finches. The intricate branch work is an ideal habitat for roosting and hibernating insects, and for birds to use as nesting sites.

**Closely related species** *V. coignetiae* is a rampant climber that can grow to 15m (50ft) high. It is grown solely for its luscious foliage. 'Brant' has bright green leaves that turn a lovely red autumn colour, and produces green or purple fruits.

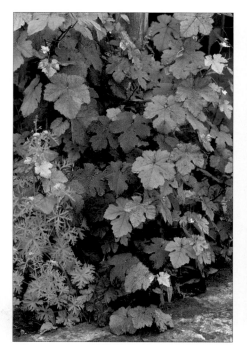

*Vitis vinifera*

## *Wisteria sinensis*
### CHINESE WISTERIA
Family: Fabaceae
Native: China

A vigorous climber that twines anticlockwise, and reaches up to 10m (33ft) high. The deep-green leaves are deeply divided into 7–13 leaflets, and the faintly scented blue-lilac flowers are borne in hanging racemes from late spring. The flowers are followed by seed pods that can be up to 15cm (6in) long.

**Cultivation** Wisteria thrives in full sun and in fertile, free-draining soil. It is best to buy or propagate plants by grafting rather than from seed because the latter often have poor flowers. ❀ ❀ ❀ Zone 5.

**Uses** Wisteria is a beautiful climber that looks fantastic on the front of a period property. It can also look elegant on pergolas, walls and fences, but avoid planting in a restricted space because it is rampant.

**Wildlife benefits** Visited by insects, including bees for nectar and pollen, and several species of butterfly seeking nectar. The unruly network of stems provides excellent roosting and nesting sites for birds and many insects. Take care not to select double-flowering varieties.

**Closely related species** Japanese wisteria (*W. floribunda*), with clockwise-turning stems, is a deciduous, woody climber that grows to 9m (30ft) high, and produces scented, lilac flowers. *W. venusta* bears white scented flowers in early summer.

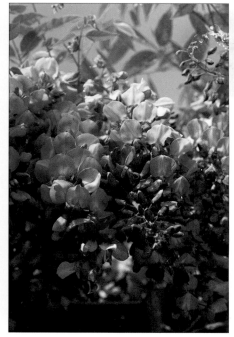

*Wisteria sinensis*

# POND AND BOG PLANTS

*Butomus umbellatus*
## FLOWERING RUSH
Family: Butomaceae
Native: Eurasia

A deciduous perennial ideally suited to marginal water areas. It is grown for its colourful display of delicate pink to rose-red flowers borne in flower-packed umbels in summer. The rush-like leaves are bronze-purple when young, becoming green, narrow and twisted, and the plant can grow up to 1.5m (5ft) high.

**Cultivation and uses** Site in soil that is immersed in water around the pond margins, or plant in aquatic containers and grow in up to 15cm (6in) of water. Propagate by division in spring, or by seed in spring or late summer. ❄ ❄ ❄ Zone 5.

**Wildlife benefits** The plant attracts insect-eating birds that seek out water lily aphids, and other insects that use the leaves for cover and also visit the flowers. Birds visiting the pond for a drink use the foliage as protection.

**Closely related species** There are no closely related species to the flowering rush (it's a one-species genus). Bogbean (*Menyanthes trifoliate*) fills a similar niche and is very effective in bogs and shallow, marginal areas. It attracts elephant hawkmoths and bees seeking nectar.

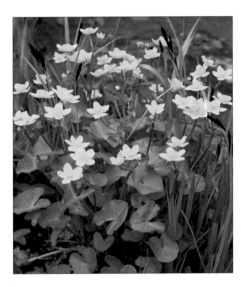

*Caltha palustris*

*Caltha palustris*
## MARSH MARIGOLD
Family: Ranunculaceae
Native: Northern temperate regions

The beautiful, single, bright golden-yellow flowers are a welcome sight in early spring. As the common name suggests, it is a marginal water plant that has a small, domed habit, and bears dark green leaves that act as an effective foil for the bright flowers. It is a compact plant, to 60cm (2ft) high.

**Cultivation and uses** The marsh marigold is one of the most popular marginal pond plants. Site in soil, or around the pond edges in water no deeper than 23cm (9in). It can also be grown in a bog garden in full sun or light shade. Propagate by seed in autumn, or division in autumn or early spring. ❄ ❄ ❄ Zone 3.

**Wildlife benefits** Being one of the first spring flowers to bloom, it offers a welcome source of early nectar for bees and butterflies emerging from hibernation. The dense foliage provides welcome shelter for small insects such as beetles, and amphibians.

**Closely related species**
*C. leptosepala* grows to 30cm (1ft) high and is a fantastic little marginal water plant with white, buttercup-like flowers. Take care not to select the double-flowering cultivars of *Caltha palustris*, such as 'Flore Pleno' or 'Monstrosa', because they are of little benefit to wildlife.

*Eupatorium cannabinum*
## HEMP AGRIMONY
Family: Asteraceae
Native: Europe

This vigorous, herbaceous perennial sports the prettiest pink flower heads, made up of small, starry flowers in late summer. It grows up to 2m (6½ft) a season, so avoid in small spaces. The leaves are lance-shaped and up to 12cm (5in) long.

**Cultivation and uses** Bog gardens are ideal sites because the roots thrive in moist soil. Site in partial shade as prolonged periods of strong sunlight cause wilting and, in severe cases, permanent cell damage occurs, especially if the soil dries out. Propagate by division or seed in spring. ❄ ❄ ❄ Zone 5.

**Wildlife benefits** One of the best plants for a wildlife garden because the flowers are always heaving with insects, particularly the small tortoiseshell, red admiral and peacock butterflies. Bees are also frequent visitors searching for pollen and nectar.

**Closely related species** 'Album' bears soft white flowers, but avoid the double flowers of 'Flore Pleno' because it will not provide the insects with sufficient nectar. The North American Joe Pye weed (*E. maculatum*) is also suited to bog gardens.

*Butomus umbellatus*

*Eupatorium cannabinum*

*Filipendula ulmaria*

## *Filipendula ulmaria*
### MEADOW SWEET
Family: Rosaceae
Native: W Asia and Europe

Meadow sweet bears clusters of creamy white flowers with a sweet almond scent in midsummer. The stems bear deeply divided, feathery foliage (which also has a slight fragrance), and grow to 90cm (3ft) high. Small, shiny seeds appear in autumn, and are taken by several species of birds and small mammals.

**Cultivation and uses** Best grown in a bog garden where the roots will be moist but not waterlogged. It is also suited to a woodland garden if the soil holds plenty of moisture. Plant in full sun or semi-shade, but it must be an open area so that bats can capture the moths taking the nectar in the evening. Propagate by division in autumn or winter. ❀ ❀ ❀ Zone 2.

**Wildlife benefits** The plants attract many summer insects, especially the bees, hoverflies and moths attracted to the scented flowers, and they in turn attract insectivorous birds. The seeds are again eaten by birds, especially finches, and the foliage provides good cover.

**Closely related species** Queen of the prairie (*F. rubra*), a native of eastern North America, is an excellent plant for the bog garden. It is an erect, vigorous perennial bearing large, soft pink flower heads in summer, and can reach up to 2m (6½ft) high.

## *Geum rivale*
### WATER AVENS
Family: Rosaceae
Native: Europe

This herbaceous perennial naturally occurs at the side of ponds and streams. It bears small clusters of pendent, white to dull purplish-pink, cup-shaped flowers from late spring to summer. The long sepals are reddish-brown and the oblong leaves dark green.

**Cultivation and uses** Grow at the front of a bog garden where the flowers and foliage soften the edge of the area. It can also be used in wildflower meadows and naturalistic plantings provided the soil is moisture-retentive. Site in full sun for best results. Propagate by seed in autumn, or division in spring or autumn. ❀ ❀ ❀ Zone 3.

**Wildlife benefits** The flowers are popular with bees seeking pollen. If planted in small or large groups, the foliage will provide cover for amphibians and invertebrates and create a moist, shady place that is essential in hot summer weather for frogs and toads.

**Closely related species** Many cultivars of *Geum rivale* are available. 'Album' sports delightful white flowers with light green leaves and 'Leonardii', formerly 'Leonard's Variety', has gorgeous copper-pink-tinted orange flowers. Do not select *G. rivale* 'Leonardii Double' because the number of petals on each flower will greatly affect the amount of pollen produced.

*Geum rivale*

*Iris pseudacorus*

## *Iris pseudacorus*
### YELLOW FLAG IRIS
Family: Iridaceae
Native: Europe to W Siberia, Turkey, Iran and N Africa

A robust, rhizomatous, beardless iris that can easily grow to 2m (6½ft) high. From early to midsummer each branched stem produces from 4–12 yellow-golden flowers with brown or violet veins, and a blotch of deeper yellow. The dull green leaves are broad and ridged, and display a prominent mid-rib. The foliage forms a dense thicket for wildlife to hide in.

**Cultivation and uses** Use as a marginal pond plant as it will grow in water up to 15cm (6in) deep, or it can also be planted in a bog garden. It thrives in full sun or semi-shade. Propagate by division of clumps in early autumn or mid-spring. ❀ ❀ ❀ Zone 5.

**Wildlife benefits** In summer, bees and hoverflies visit the flowers seeking nectar. Dragonfly larvae will also use the tall leaves to climb out of the water and pupate on, before emerging and flying off as adults. The dense foliage provides cover for birds visiting nearby water, and amphibians are often seen sheltering between the leaves.

**Closely related species** 'Variegata' has yellow- and green-striped foliage in spring, but can turn all-green later in the season. Japanese flag (*I. ensata*), with red-purple flowers, is ideal for marginal or bog gardens.

*Lychnis flos-cuculi*

## *Lychnis flos-cuculi*
## RAGGED ROBIN
Family: Caryophyllaceae
Native: Europe, Caucasus
and Siberia

Ragged robin sports pale to bright pink-purple, large flowers with deeply divided petals, giving it a ragged look. They are borne from late spring to early summer and measure 5cm (2in) across, which is large considering that the plant is 45cm (18in) tall. The basal leaves are green and lance-shaped.

**Cultivation and uses** Ragged robin naturally grows in water meadows and is ideally suited to damp areas of grassland. Alternatively it can be planted in a bog garden where the soil is not waterlogged permanently, but holds moisture all year round. Best grown in full sun, but it will tolerate semi-shade. Propagate by seed or division in autumn or spring. ❀ ❀ ❀ Zone 6.

**Wildlife benefits** The nectar-rich flowers attract many species of insect, including hoverflies, bees, several species of long-tongued bee and butterflies, from late spring onwards. In Europe the caterpillars of the campion and lychnis moths feed on the flower buds.

**Closely related species** The single-flowering white form, *L. f.* 'Alba', is an excellent choice, but avoid any cultivar with 'Plena' in the name because it means double flowering (as in 'Alba Plena' or 'Rosea Plena'). Too many petals inhibit creatures seeking the nectar.

## *Lythrum salicaria*
## PURPLE LOOSESTRIFE
Family: Lythraceae
Native: NE North America

A "must" when planting a pond. Tall spikes of bright reddish-purple flowers are produced from midsummer to early autumn, and extend up to 1.2m (4ft) high. The mid-green leaves are lance-like, and are usually opposite each other.

**Cultivation and uses** An ideal candidate for a marginal pond area or a bog garden because the roots thrive in soil that is moist or wet. Purple loosestrife is also suited to a dappled shady area in a woodland garden, provided plenty of organic matter has been incorporated to increase the moisture content of the soil. Site in full sun, though it will tolerate semi-shade. Propagate by division of clumps in autumn or by seed in spring. ❀ ❀ ❀ Zone 3.

**Wildlife benefits** The flowers attract bees and butterflies, and the leaves are eaten by the caterpillars of hawkmoths. Leave the stems uncut over winter to allow beneficial insects to hibernate in the dead foliage during the dormant season.

**Closely related species** *L. virgatum* is a clump-forming perennial, and is less vigorous than *L. salicaria*. *L. v.* 'Rose Queen' sports light pink flowers and reaches 90cm (3ft) high, and *L. v.* 'The Rocket', again to 90cm (3ft) high, produces a mass of rose-red flowers in summer.

*Lythrum salicaria*

## *Mentha aquatica*
## WATER MINT
Family: Lamiaceae
Native: Eurasia

In amongst the rampant stem growth of water mint, the most dainty, delicate, lilac-pink flowers can be found in late summer. The round flower heads are numerous, and start to flower from the bottom of the reddish-purple stems upwards. The stems can reach to 90cm (3ft) high, and bear scented, dark green leaves tinged purple.

**Cultivation and uses** Water mint is a marginal plant that is normally sited around the peripheral area of a pond. It can be grown in slightly deeper water if it is no more than 15cm (6in) above the roots. Site in full sun or semi-shade. Because water mint can become invasive, regularly check its growth after flowering. Not recommended for a small pond. Propagate by removing and replanting the rhizomes in spring. ❀ ❀ ❀ Zone 6.

**Wildlife benefits** The nectar-rich flowers are often covered with bees and butterflies. The foliage is eaten by caterpillars of moths, including water ermine and large ranunculus. The leaves and stems soon make dense cover and offer shelter to amphibians and insects.

**Closely related species** Try the dwarf form, *M. aquatica* var. *crispa*, which is more suited to a small pond. This ornamental cultivar has crinkled, curled, scented leaves.

*Mentha aquatica*

*Myosotis palustris*

## *Myosotis palustris*
### WATER FORGET-ME-NOT
Family: Boraginaceae
Native: Europe, Asia and
N America

A deciduous, herbaceous perennial, it forms neat, spreading mounds and produces narrow, mid-green leaves that complement the pretty, powder-blue summer flowers.

**Cultivation and uses** Ideal for very shallow marginal pond areas or a bog garden because the roots need permanently wet soil to grow successfully. Also effective along a straight edge of a pond to soften the boundary. Place in full sun or semi-shade. Propagate by seed in autumn. ❀ ❀ ❀ Zone 4.

**Wildlife benefits** The flowers are visited by bees and bumblebees seeking nectar and pollen, and by butterflies after the nectar. The tiny seeds produced are loved by the likes of finches, while many small invertebrates and amphibians hide out in the dense foliage.

**Closely related species**
*M. scorpioides* and *M. laxa* also like shallow water or bog gardens. The former has bright blue flowers and reaches 1m (3ft) high, while the latter is less vigorous, growing to 50cm (20in) high, again bearing bright blue flowers.

## *Nymphaea alba*
### WHITE WATER LILY
Family: Nymphaeaceae
Native: Eurasia and N Africa

The flowers of water lilies are exquisite. The summer blooms produce semi-double, pure white flowers with beautiful golden centres and can grow up to 10cm (4in) wide. The abundance of shiny, dark green, rounded leaves, up to 30cm (1ft) wide, set off the pale-coloured flowers. They are red when young, and tend to hug the water surface.

**Cultivation and uses** Water lilies enjoy an open, sunny position in still, deep water, the depth depending on the species. *N. alba* thrives when planted at a depth of 60cm (2ft). Propagate by dividing and replanting the roots, which are tuber-like rhizomes, every 3–4 years. ❀ ❀ ❀ Zone 5.

**Wildlife benefits** The flowers are visited by insects, including beetles. The dense foliage is used by basking frogs and dragonflies, and by foraging water birds. Water invertebrates hide in the shade of the leaves during the hot summer months.

**Closely related species** *N. citrina* has open, yellow, scented flowers and is a good choice for small ponds. *N.* 'Mexicana' is similar to *N. citrina*, with a slightly smaller flower. *N. odorata*, from eastern North America, bears fragrant white flowers.

## *Typha minima*
### MINIATURE REED MACE
Family: Typhaceae
Native: Eurasia

Miniature reed mace is grown for its decorative, poker-like, cylindrical seed heads that appear in late summer. The rounded leaves can reach up to 45–60cm (18–24in) high, and the roots bear needle-like tips that can easily pierce pond liners. Care should be taken when selecting reed mace for your pond.

**Cultivation and uses** Use miniature reed mace in marginal areas of a pond,

*Typha minima*

either planted in soil or in a basket. Place it on a pond shelf at a maximum of 30cm (1ft) of water. Site in sun or part-shade. Due to the intricate root system it can be used as a soil stabilizer on banks of soil. Propagate by seed or by division of the rootstock in spring. ❀ ❀ ❀ Zone 6.

**Wildlife benefits** The fluffy seed heads are often used by birds for nesting material. The intricate root system collects pond silt and debris, making it a rich breeding ground for pond invertebrates and overwintering amphibians.

**Closely related species** *T. latifolia* is a large, herbaceous perennial that can grow to 2.5m (8ft) high, but can be invasive in a small pond. It produces spikes of light brown flowers in late summer, followed by decorative, dark brown, cylindrical seed heads in autumn.

*Nymphaea alba*

# FUNGI AND DECOMPOSERS

## *Agaricus campestris*
### FIELD MUSHROOM
Family: Agaricaceae
Native: Eurasia and America

This common wild mushroom is closely related to the cultivated mushroom *A. bisporus*, one of the most important of all edible mushroom crops. *A. campestris* is most frequently encountered in meadows, but also grows in gardens.

**Appearance** The mushroom is 3–10cm (1¼–4in) in diameter, with a creamy white cap, sometimes developing small scales as it matures. The cap margin is down-turned when fully expanded.

**Role in garden habitats** The field mushroom is a decomposing organism, with the mushroom cap being only part of the fungus. The rest – a mass of white threads called *mycelium* – remains beneath the soil, breaking down organic matter and recycling nutrients.

**Wildlife benefits** Rather surprisingly, and in spite of its edibility for humans, the field mushroom is actually eaten by comparatively few garden creatures, although the caps often become heavily infested with maggots. On the whole, though, its benefits are mostly as a decomposer and recycler.

**Closely related species** There are several other similar species, including some poisonous mushrooms with which it can easily be confused. The yellow staining mushroom (*A. xanthodermus*) can cause serious stomach upsets, and is distinguished by the fact that it turns yellow when cut or bruised.

*Agaricus campestris*

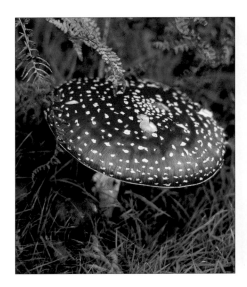

*Amanita muscaria*

## *Amanita muscaria*
### FLY AGARIC
Family: Amanitaceae
Native: Northern Hemisphere

This distinctive fungus, native to birch (*Betula*), pine (*Pinus*), spruce (*Picea*) and fir woodlands of the Northern Hemisphere and high elevations of central North America, is generally encountered in autumn. The common name is thought to derive from its European use as a crude insecticide, when sprinkled in milk.

**Appearance** Fly agaric is a large, imposing, white-gilled, white-spotted, red mushroom, making it one of the most recognizable of any fungus. It features in many folk- and fairytales.

**Role in garden habitats** Fly agaric is a type of fungus called a *mycorrhiza*, and is important because a plant's roots and the fungus form a mutual association. The plant supplies the fungus with food (sugars) and, in return, the fungus helps the root absorb mineral nutrients from the soil.

**Wildlife benefits** While fly agaric is poisonous and therefore eaten by very few species of wildlife, its benefit as a *mycorrhiza* on the roots of some trees is extremely important to the trees' long-term health. It is therefore an important part of the soil and wider garden ecology.

**Closely related species** *A. muscaria* is very variable and can be mistaken for other species, such as the edible Mexican *A. basii*, and *A. caesarea* of Europe.

*Armillaria mellea*

## *Armillaria mellea*
### HONEY FUNGUS
Family: Marasmiaceae
Native: Worldwide

Honey fungi are parasitic, living on trees and woody shrubs. They are long-lived organisms and include some of the largest living organisms in the world, with *A. ostoyae* said to be thousands of years old and covering more than 8.9sq km (3.4sq miles). They are a serious pest and can affect ornamental trees.

**Appearance** The yellow-brown coloured mushrooms that appear at, or just above, the base of the infected plant have caps from 3–15cm (1¼-6in) across, and are covered with small, dark scales.

**Role in garden habitats** Although honey fungus is a naturally occurring species, it is disliked by most gardeners because of its ability to kill otherwise apparently healthy trees and shrubs. Once present, it can easily spread to other neighbouring woody plants, but it does not affect herbaceous specimens.

**Wildlife benefits** Honey fungus generally has limited importance to other species of wildlife, despite its edibility. Some flies lay eggs in the caps of the mushrooms but, on the whole, its benefits are limited.

**Closely related species** The *Armillaria* genus includes about 10 species that were formerly lumped together as *A. mellea*. They are all quite similar and occur widely throughout the world.

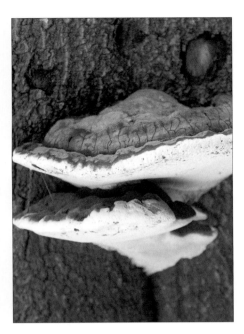

*Ganoderma adspersum*

## *Ganoderma adspersum*
## ARTIST'S FUNGUS
Family: Ganodermataceae
Native: Europe and America

This bracket fungus is widespread and parasitic on deciduous trees. *G. adspersum* is one of the commonest species and is called artist's fungus because it is possible to make pictures or drawings on the white pore surface.

**Appearance** The large, brown brackets have a white underside and develop a new layer each year, resulting in a heavily ridged upper surface as the annual growth remains visible and becomes a permanent structure.

**Role in garden habitats** It is generally thought of as an unwelcome guest in the garden because its long-lived brackets often grow one above the other, on the lower part of tree trunks. They gradually weaken the woody tissue, and the trunks can snap in high winds.

**Wildlife benefits** The fungus is an important element of forest habitats. Though it can be devastating for an individual tree, it often results in large amounts of deadwood that is consumed by other species, and helps maintain diversity.

**Closely related species** The closely related *G. resinaceum* has large brackets with an upper surface that starts out yellow, before maturing to a chestnut or blackish colour. The surface is covered with a glossy, resinous layer, and the white underside turns pale brown or cinnamon with age.

## *Marasmius oreades*
## FAIRY RING CHAMPIGNON
Family: Marasmiaceae
Native: Widely distributed, especially in temperate Northern Hemisphere

There are a number of fungi that make "fairy rings", i.e. a ring or arc of mushrooms. In time these rings may grow over 10m (33ft) in diameter, although they are usually most evident when much smaller than this. This species forms conspicuous "toadstools" between late spring and early autumn in a dead circle of grass.

**Appearance** They are most apparent when the pale brown toadstools appear, although the bare ring, just inside a ring of dark green grass, is visible in turf all year round.

**Role in garden habitats** There are two types of fairy ring fungus. One type is found in woods, being formed by *mycorrhiza* living on tree roots in a mutually beneficial partnership (see fly agaric). The meadow fairy rings live on decaying material but do not form an association with another plant.

**Wildlife benefits** Fairy ring champignon generally has a limited importance to other species of wildlife, despite its edibility. Some flies do lay eggs in the caps of the toadstools but, on the whole, its benefits seem to be as a decomposer.

**Closely related species** Most *Marasmius* species are small, nondescript brown mushrooms that do not form rings. There are somewhere in the region of 40–60 mostly unrelated species however, which do form fairy rings, although many of them only really become apparent once the toadstools appear.

*Marasmius oreades*

Slime mould

## *Various species*
## SLIME MOULD
Family: Many related groups
Native: Worldwide

Slime moulds are extraordinary organisms that show some features of fungus, and some of protozoa. They were formerly thought to be a fungus but are now classed as a group on their own, and should not be confused with true moulds that are actually fungi. Although cosmopolitan in distribution, they are mostly small and rarely noticed.

**Appearance** Slime moulds form a resting organ consisting of a stalk and a head of spores that may, in some cases, be brightly coloured.

**Role in garden habitats** Slime moulds are naturally found in damp, shady habitats, such as dark forest floors, where they tend to grow over rotted wood after it has rained. They occur widely, with the most visible species occasionally prominent on lawns where they live among dead grass.

**Wildlife benefits** They are generally of limited importance to other species of wildlife because few other species feed on them. They feed mostly on bacteria, and are usually very beneficial in helping to break down decaying plant remains and other organic matter in the garden.

**Closely related species** There are several different groups of slime mould, all of which differ in their complex life cycles. While some can easily be seen, some – such as clubroot disease (*Plasmodiophora brassicae*) of cabbages – cannot.

# SUPPLIERS

## UNITED KINGDOM

### Field guides
Field Studies Council Publications
The Annexe
Preston Montford Lane
Shrewsbury
Shropshire SY4 1DU
Tel: 01743 852 140
Email: publications@field-studies-council.org

### Organizations
Field Studies Council
Head Office
Montford Bridge
Preston Montford
Shrewsbury
Shropshire SY4 1HW
Tel: 01743 852 100
Email: enquiries@field-studies-council.org
www.field-studies-council.org

The Wildlife Trusts
The Kiln
Waterside
Mather Road
Newark
Nottinghamshire NG24 1WT
Tel: 0870 036 7711
Email: enquiry@wildlifetrusts.org
www.wildlifetrusts.org

### Information on growing native plants
Flora locale
Denford Manor
Hungerford, Berkshire RG17 0UN
Tel: 01488 680 457
Email: info@floralocale.org
www.floralocale.org

### Habitat and nesting boxes, feed and food supplements
Wiggly Wigglers
Lower Blakemere Farm
Blakemere, Herefordshire HR2 9PX
Tel: 01981 500 391
www.wigglywigglers.co.uk

CJ WildBird Foods Ltd
The Rea
Upton Magna
Shrewsbury SY4 4UR
Tel: 01743 709 545
www.birdfood.co.uk

The Specialist Bird Food Company
Gravel Hill Road
Holt Pound
Farnham, Surrey GU10 4LG
Tel: 01420 23986
www.wild-bird-food.co.uk

### Plants and seeds
Emorsgate Seeds
Limes Farm, Tilney All Saints
King's Lynn, Norfolk PE34 4RT
Tel: 01553 829 028
Email: enquiries@emorsgate-seeds.co.uk
www.wildseed.co.uk

British Wildflower Plants
Burlingham Gardens
North Burlingham, Norwich NR13 4TA
Tel: 01603 716 615
Email: paul@wildflowers.co.uk

John Chambers Wild Flower Seeds
15 Westleigh Road, Barton Seagrave
Kettering, Northamptonshire NN15 5AJ
Tel: 01933 652 562

## UNITED STATES

### Field guides
Audubon Field Guides
Knopf Publishing Group
201 East 50th Street
New York, NY 10022
Tel: (800) 733-3000
www.audubon.org

### Organizations
National Wildlife Federation
11100 Wildlife Center Drive
Reston, VA 20190
Tel: (800) 822-9919
www.nwf.org

### Information on growing native plants
Lady Bird Johnson Wildflower Center
4801 La Crosse Avenue
Austin, TX 78739
Tel: (512) 232-0100
www.wildflower.org

### Habitat and nesting boxes, feed and food supplements
Rachel's Robin
GregRobert Enterprises, LLC
PO Box 3152
Farmington Hills, MI 48333
www.rachelsrobin.com

Backyard Wildlife Refuge
9463 Hwy 377 South
Suite 146
Benbrook, TX 76126
www.backyardwildlife.com

Woodland Habitat
Gayle Pille
3495 Feeley Road
Burlington, KY 41005
Tel: (859) 586-0077
Email: gaylepille@yahoo.com
www.woodlandhabitat.com

### Plants and seeds
Easyliving Wildflowers
PO Box 522
Willow Springs, MO 65793
Tel: (417) 469-2611
Email: john@easywildflowers.com
www.easywildflowers.com

The Wildflower Seed Company
PO Box 406
St. Helena, CA 94574
Tel: (800) 456-3359
Email: sales@wildflower-seed.com
www.wildflower-seed.com

Prairie Frontier
W281 S3606 Pheasant Run
Waukesha, WI 53189
Tel: (414) 544-6708
Email: wildflower@prairiefrontier.com
www.prairiefrontier.com

## CANADA

### Field guides
Audubon Field Guides
Knopf Publishing Group
201 East 50th Street
New York, NY 10022
Tel: (800) 733-3000
www.audubon.org

Nature Study Guild Publishers
PO Box 10489
Rochester, NY 14610-0489
Tel: (800) 954-2984
Email: naturebooks@worldnet.att.net
www.naturestudy.com

## Organizations
Canadian Wildlife Federation
350 Michael Cowpland Drive
Kanata, Ontario K2M 2W1
Tel: 1-800-563-WILD or (613) 599-9594
www.cwf-fcf.org

## Information on growing native plants
North American Native Plant Society
(formerly the Canadian Wildflower Society)
NANPS, PO Box 84, Station D
Etobicoke, Ontario M9A 4X1
Tel: (416) 631-4438
Email: nanps@nanps.org
www.nanps.org

## Habitat and nesting boxes, feed and food supplements
Bird Feeders Direct
Editor, Bird Feeders Direct
Geosign Technologies Inc.
503 Imperial Road North, Units 5–9
Guelph, Ontario N1H6T9
Tel: (866) 436-7446, ext. 2295
Fax: (519) 837-1288

The Wildbird Habitat Store
8810-C Young Road
Chilliwack, British Columbia V2P 4P5
Tel: (604) 792-1239
Fax: (604) 792-3436
Email: jasono@imag.net
www.wildbirdstore.com

## Plants and seeds
Prairie Habitats Inc.
Box 1, Argyle, Manitoba R0C 0B0
Tel: (204) 467-9371
Fax: (204) 467-5004
Email: jpmorgan@mb.sympatico.ca
www.prairiehabitats.com

Nature's Garden Seed Co.
PO Box 32105, 3651 Shelbourne Street
Victoria, British Columbia V8P 5S2
Tel: (250) 595-2062 or 1-877-302-7333
Email: mail@naturesgardenseed.com
www.naturesgardenseed.com

# AUSTRALIA

## Field guides and gardening
CSIRO Publishing
PO Box 1139
(150 Oxford Street)
Collingwood
VIC 3066
Tel: (03) 9662 7500
Email: publishing@csiro.au
www.publish.csiro.au

## Organizations
Wildlife Preservation Society of Australia Inc.
PO Box 42
Brighton Le Sands
NSW 2216
Tel: (02) 9556 1537
Email: wildlifepreservation@optusnet.com.au
www.wpsa.org.au

## Information on growing native plants
Australian National Botanic Garden
GPO Box 1777
Canberra, ACT 2601
Tel: (02) 6250 9540
Email: anbg-info@anbg.gov.au
www.anbg.gov.au/anbg

## Habitat and nesting boxes, feed and food supplements
Melbourne Wildlife Sanctuary
La Trobe University
VIC 3086
Tel: (03) 9479 1206
Email: wildlife@latrobe.edu.au
www.latrobe.edu.au/wildlife

Hollow Log Homes
PO Box 144
Kenilworth
QLD 4574
Tel: (07) 5472 3142
www.hollowloghomes.net

## Plants and seeds
Native Growth Holdings
6/15 Marine Parade
St Kilda
VIC 3182
Tel: (03) 9593 9665
Email: tim@nativenursery.com.au
nativegrowth.c3.ixwebhosting.com

Australian Seed Company
PO Box 67
Hazelbrook, NSW 2779
Tel: (02) 4758 6132

Nindethana Seed Service
PO Box 2121
Albany, WA 6330
Tel: (08) 9844 3533
Email: nindseed@iinet.net.au
www.nindethana.iinet.net.au

# NEW ZEALAND

## Field guides
Mobil New Zealand Nature Series
Reed Publishing (NZ)

## Organizations
Royal Forest and Bird Protection Society
of New Zealand
Wellington Central Office
Level One
90 Ghuznee Street
PO Box 631
Wellington
Tel: (04) 385 7374
www.forestandbird.org.nz

## Information on growing native plants
New Zealand Plant Conservation Network
PO Box 16-102
Wellington
Email: info@nzpcn.org.nz
www.nzpcn.org.nz

New Zealand Gardens Online
www.gardens.co.nz

## Plants and seeds
Oriata Native Plant Nursery
625 West Coast Road
Oratia
Auckland
Tel: (09) 818 6467
www.oratianatives.co.nz

Country Cottage Nursery
205 A Godley Road
Titirangi
Auckland
Tel: (09) 817 7806
homepages.ihug.co.nz/~shrubs

New Zealand Tree Seeds
PO Box 435
Rangiora 8254
Tel: (03) 312 1635
www.nzseeds.co.nz

# INDEX

## A

*Acer campestre* 106
*Achillea filipendula* 11, 35, 66
*Achillea millefolium* 39
aconite, winter 63
*Agaricus campestris* 120
*Agastache*
  *A. foeniculum* 66
  *A. nepetoides* 37
*Agrostemma githago* 52
*Agrostis stolonifera* 41
*Ajuga reptans* 35, 66
*Alcea rosea* 52
alder 106
alder buckthorn 97
*Allium giganteum* 62
*Allium schoenoprasum* 84
*Alnus glutinosa* 106
alpine cinquefoil 35
alyssum, yellow 68
*Amanita muscaria* 120
amaranth 15
*Amaranthus caudatus* 15, 52
*Amelanchier lamarckii* 13, 90
amphibians 26–7
*Anethum graveolens* 39, 84
*Angelica archangelica* 84
anise hyssop 66
*Anthemis tinctoria* 67
*Antirrhinum majus* 53
ants 46–7
apple, crab 109
aquatic life 28–9
  *Elodea* (pond weed) 29
  water mint 29
  water soldier 29
  white water lily 29
*Aquilegia vulgaris* 67

*Armillaria mellea* 120
*Asclepias tuberosa* 33, 67
*Aster novi-belgii* 68
*Aubrieta deltoidea* 68
*Aurinia saxatilis* 68
azalea, deciduous 97

## B

backswimmers 28, 29, 34
badgers
  blackberry 23
  blackcurrant 23
  elderberry 23
  English oak 23
  mulberry 23
balm, bee 37, 76
balm, lemon 11, 86
*Baptisia australis* 69
barberry 90
  Japanese 104
basil 87
bats
  evening primrose 19
  heliotrope 19
  honeysuckle 19
  jasmine 19
  night scented stock 19
  tobacco plant 19
bean, scarlet runner 114
beech 108
beech, southern 109
bee balm 37
bees 36–7
  bee balm 37
  blackberry 37
  catmint 37
  giant yellow hyssop 37
  laurustinus 37
  lavender 37
beetles 34–5
bellflower 69
*Berberis*
  *B. darwinii* 90
  *B. thunbergii* 104
bergamot 37, 76
betony 39, 81
*Betula pendula* 106
bilberry 25
birch, silver 106
birds, fruit-eating
  blackcurrant 17
  elderberry 17
  guelder rose 17

herringbone cotoneaster 17
  holly 17
  mezereon 17
  rowan 17
  wild strawberry 17
birds, insect-eating
  evening primrose 11
  flowering rush 11
  golden rod 11
  honesty 11
  lavender 11
  lemon balm 11
  tansy 11
  yarrow, fern-leaved 11
birds, omnivorous
  blackthorn 13
  bramble 13
  evening primrose 13
  gooseberry 13
  hawthorn 13
  ivy 13
  juneberry 13
birds, seed-eating
  amaranth 15
  dandelion 15
  fat hen 15
  field forget-me-not 15
  millet 15
  red clover 15
  sunflower 15
  teasel 15
bistort 78
black-eyed Susan 39, 79
blackberry 13, 23, 37, 99
blackcurrant 17, 23, 98
blackthorn 13, 31, 103
bluebeard 91
bluebell, English 64
bogbean 43
borage 53
*Borago officinalis* 53
box 104
bramble 13, 23, 37, 99
brooklime 43, 83
broom, common 92
*Buddleja davidii* 33, 90
bugle 35, 66
bugs 34–5
bulrush 43, 119
burr weed 43
*Butomus umbellatus* 11, 43, 116
butterflies 32–3
  butterfly bush 33, 90

  butterfly weed 33
  gillyflower 33
  ice plant 33
  *Phlox paniculata* 33
  tobacco plant 33
  *Verbena bonariensis* 33
  *Zinnia elegans* 33
butterfly bush 33, 90
butterfly flower/weed 33, 67
*Buxus sempervirens* 104

## C

*Calendula officinalis* 53
*Callitriche stagnalis* 43
*Calluna vulgaris* 25, 91
*Caltha palustris* 27, 116
*Campanula latifolia* 69
campion, red 80
candytuft 57
caraway 85
*Cardamine pratensis* 69
carnivores 18–19
*Carpinus betulus* 107
carrot 39, 54
*Carum carvi* 85
*Caryopteris* x *clandonensis* 91
*Castanea sativa* 21, 107
catmint 37, 77
*Ceanothus thyrsiflorus* 51, 91
*Centaurea montana* 70
centipedes 47
*Centranthus ruber* 70
*Ceratophyllum demersum* 43
*Cercis siliquastrum* 107
*Cerinthe major* 'Purpurascens' 54

*Chaenomeles japonica* 92
*Chamaecyparis lawsoniana*
    31
chamomile, yellow 67
*Chenopodium album* 15
cherry, wild 110
chestnut, sweet 21, 107
chicory 70
*Chionodoxa luciliae* 62
chives 84
*Cichorium intybus* 70
*Cirsium rivulare* 71
*Clematis tangutica* 112
clover, red 15, 82
cockroaches 46
cock's foot 41
columbine 67
comfrey 81
coneflower (*Echinacea*) 72
coneflower (*Rudbeckia*)
    79, 80
*Coreopsis tinctoria* 71
coriander 39, 85
*Coriandrum sativum* 39, 85
corn cockle 52
cornflower 70
*Cornus sanguinea* 92
*Corylus avellana* 21, 93
cotoneaster, herringbone
    17
*Cotoneaster lacteus* 93
cowslip 78
cranberry 25
*Crataegus monogyna* 13,
    31, 102
creeping bentgrass 41
crested dog's tail 41
crickets 40–1
*Crocus chrysanthus* 62
cross-leaved heath 25
crown imperial 63
curled pondweed 43
currant, flowering 98
cypress, Lawson 31

*Cynosurus cristatus* 41
*Cytisus scoparius* 92

**D**
*Dactylis glomerata* 41
daffodil, autumn 65
daffodil, wild 55
*Dahlia* Collerette Group 7, 71
damselflies 42–3
dandelion 15, 82
*Daphne mezereum* 17, 93
*Daucus carota* 39, 54
dead nettle, white 75
*Deschampsia flexuosa* 72
*Dianthus barbatus* 54
*Digitalis purpurea* 55
dill 39, 84
*Dipsacus fullonum* 15, 55
directory use 51
dogwood 92
dragonflies 7, 42–3
    bogbean 43
    brooklime 43
    bulrush 43
    burr reed 43
    curled pondweed 43
    Eurasian water milfoil 43
    floating pondweed 43
    flowering rush 43
    frogbit 43
    hornwort 43
    pickerel weed 43
    water crowfoot 43
    water forget-me-not 43
    water horsetail 43
    water lilies 43
    water mint 43
    water smartweed 43
    water starwort 43
    yellow flag 43
duck weed 27

**E**
earwigs 38–9
*Echinacea purpurea* 72
*Echinops nitro* 72
elderberry 17, 23, 100
elm, wych 103
*Elodea* (pond weed) 29
English oak 21, 23
*Equisetum fluviatile* 43
*Eranthis hyemalis* 63
*Eremurus stenophyllus* 63
*Erica tetralix* 25
*Eryngium alpinum* 73
*Erysimum cheiri* 55
*Escallonia rubra* var.
    *macrantha* 105

*Eschscholzia californica* 56
*Euonymus europaeus* 102
*Eupatorium cannabinum*
    116
Eurasian water milfoil 43
evening primrose 11, 13,
    19, 59

**F**
*Fagus sylvatica* 108
fairy ring champignon 121
fat hen 15
fennel 39, 73
fescue 41, 73
*Festuca glauca* 73
*Festuca rubra* 41
*Filipendula ulmaria* 117
firethorn 97
flag iris 27
flatworm, New Zealand
    44, 45
flies 38–9
floating pondweed 43
flowering rush 11, 43
fly agaric 120
*Foeniculum vulgare* 39, 73
forget-me-not, field 15, 58
forget-me-not, water
    43, 119
foxglove 55
*Fragaria vesca* 17
French marigold 35
*Fritillaria imperialis* 63
*Fritillaria meleagris* 64
frogbit 43
frogs
    duck weed 27
    flag iris 27
    marsh marigold 27
    water mint 27
    white water lily 27
*Fuchsia magellanica* 94
fungi 120–1

**G**
*Ganoderma adspersum*
    121
gayfeather 75
gean 110
*Geranium maculatum* 74
*Geum rivale* 117
giant yellow hyssop 37
gillyflower 33
glory of the snow 62
golden rod 11, 81
gooseberry 13, 98
gorse 101
grape hyacinth 64

grape vine 115
grasses 41, 72
grasshoppers 40–1
    cock's foot 41
    creeping bentgrass 41
    crested dog's tail 41
    red fescue 41
guelder rose 17

**H**
hawthorn 13, 31, 102, 108
hazel 21, 93
heath, cross-leaved 25
*Hebe salicifolia* 94
*Hedera helix* 13, 31, 112
*Helenium autumnale* 49, 74
*Helianthemum nummularium*
    94
*Helianthus*
    *H. annuus* 15, 56
    *H. maximiliani* 35
heliotrope 19
*Heliotropium arborescens*
    (heliotrope) 19, 56
hemp agrimony 116
herringbone cotoneaster 17
*Hesperis matronalis* 57
*Holcus lanatus* 74
holly 17, 95, 102
hollyhock 52
honesty 11, 58
honey fungus 120
honeysuckle 19, 113
honeywort 54
hop 112
hornbeam 107
hornwort 43
hoverflies
    black-eyed Susan 39
    carrot 39
    coriander 39
    dill 39
    fennel 39
    lobelia 39

wood betony 39
yarrow 39
*Humulus lupulus* 112
*Hyacinthoides non-scripta*
64
*Hydrocharis morsus-ranae*
43
*Hylotelephium spectabile* 80
hyssop, giant yellow 37
*Hyssopus officinalis*
(hyssop) 85

**I**
*Iberis amara* 57
ice plant 33, 80
*Ilex aquifolium* 17, 95, 102
indigo, false 69
invertebrates 46–7
*Iris pseudacorus* (flag iris)
27, 43, 50, 117
ivy 13, 31, 112

**J**
jasmine 19, 113
*Jasminum officinale*
19, 113
Judas tree 107
juneberry 13, 90

**K**
*Knautia macedonia* 83, 80

**L**
ladies ear drops 94
lady's smock 69
ladybirds
alpine cinquefoil 35
bugle 35
French marigold 35
*Penstemon strictus* 35
prairie sunflower 35
speedwell 35
tansy 35
yarrow, fern-leaved 35

*Lamium album* 75
*Larix decidua* (European
larch) 108
*Lathyrus latifolius* 113
laurustinus 37
lavender 11, 37, 86
*Lavandula* (lavender)
*L. angustifolia* 11, 86
*L. officinale* 86
*L. stoechas* 37
*Lavatera olbia* (tree lavatera)
95
Lawson cypress 31
leaf insects 46
leeches 44, 45
lemon balm 11
*Liatris spicata* 75
lilac
Californian 51, 91
common 101
lily, foxtail 63
lime, small-leaved 111
*Limnanthes douglasii* 57
*Linaria vulgaris* 76
ling 25, 91
Linnaeus, Carl 50
lobelia 39, 58
*Lobelia erinus* 39, 58
*Lonicera periclymenum*
19, 113
loosestrife, purple 118
lovage 86
love-lies-bleeding 15, 52
*Lunaria annua* 11, 58
lungwort 79
*Lupinus nootkatensis* (lupin)
49, 76
*Lychnis flos-cuculi* 118
*Lythrum salicaria* 118

**M**
*Mahonia aquifolium* 95
*Malus sylvestris* 109
mammals
carnivorous 18–19
herbivorous 20–1
insectivorous 18–19
omnivorous 22–3
mantises 46
maple, field 106
*Marasmius oreades* 121
marigold
English 53
French 35, 60
marsh 27, 116
marjoram 88
marsh marigold 27
*Matthiola bicornis* 19

*Matthiola incana* 33
meadowsweet 117
*Melissa officinalis* 11, 86
*Mentha*
*M. aquatica* 27, 29, 43,
118
*M. spicata* 87
*Menyanthes trifoliata* 43
mezereon 17, 93
Michaelmas daisy 68
millet (*Panicum*) 15
millipedes 47
*Monarda didyma* 37, 76
*Morus nigra* 23, 96
moths 32–3
butterfly bush 33
butterfly weed 33
gillyflower 33
ice plant 33
*Phlox paniculata* 33
tobacco plant 33
*Verbena bonariensis* 33
*Zinnia elegans* 33
mountain ash 17, 111
mulberry 23, 96
mullein 83
*Muscari armeniacum* 64
mushrooms 120–1
*Myosotis*
*M. arvensis* 15, 58
*M. palustris* 119
*M. scorpioides* 43
*Myriophyllum spicatum* 43
*Myrrhis odorata* 87

**N**
*Narcissus pseudonarcissus*
65
nasturtium 61
*Nepeta racemosa* 37
*Nepeta x faassenii* 77
nettle, stinging 82
*Nicotiana*
*N. affinis* 19

*N. sylvestris* 33, 59
night scented stock 19
*Nothofagus antarctica* 109
*Nymphaea* 43
*N. alba* 27, 29, 119

**O**
oak, English 21, 23, 110
*Ocimum basilicum* 87
*Oenothera biennis* 11, 13,
19, 59
*Olea europaea* (olive) 96
onions 62
Oregon grape 95
*Origanum majorana* 88

**P**
*Panicum miliaceum* 15
*Papaver orientale* 77
*Papaver rhoeas* 59
*Parthenocissus*
*quinquefolia* 114
pea, garden 114
pea, perennial 113
pear 110
*Penstemon barbatus* 77
*Penstemon strictus* 35
*Perovskia atriplicifolia* 96
*Petunia x hybrida* 60
*Phaseolus coccineus* 114
*Phlox paniculata* 33, 78
pickerel weed 43
pied currawong 13
pine, Scots 21, 109
*Pinus sylvestris* 21, 109
*Pisum sativum* 114
poached egg plant 57
*Polygonum amphibium* 43
*Polygonum bistorta* 78, 80
pondweed (*Potamogeton*)
43
*Pontederia cordata* 43
poppy 59, 77
California 56
*Potamogeton crispus* 43
*Potamogeton natans* 43
*Potentilla crantzii* 35
prairie sunflower 35
*Primula veris* 78
*Prunus avium* 110
*Prunus spinosa* 13, 31, 103
*Pulmonaria officinalis* 79
*Pyracantha coccinea* 97
*Pyrus communis* 110

**Q**
*Quercus robur* 21, 23, 110
quince, Japanese 92

## R

ragged robin 118
*Ranunculus aquatilis* 43
red clover 15, 82
red fescue 41
redclaws 105
reed mace, miniature 43, 119
reptiles 24–5
  bilberry 25
  cranberry 25
  cross-leaved heath 25
  ling 25
*Rhamnus frangula* 97
*Rhododendron luteum* 97
*Ribes*
  *R. nigrum* 17, 23, 98
  *R. sanguineum* 98
  *R. uva-crispa* 98
rock rose 94
*Rosa* (roses)
  *R. banksiae* (banksia
    rose) 115
  *R. canina* (dog rose) 99
  *R. glauca* (shrub rose) 99
  *R. rugosa* (ramanas rose)
    50, 105
rosemary 88
*Rosmarinus officinalis*
  (rosemary) 88
rowan 17, 111
*Rubus fruticosus* 13, 23,
  37, 99
*Rudbeckia fulgida* 39, 79
rush, flowering 11, 43, 116

## S

sage 88
  Russian 96
  wood 79
*Salix caprea* 111
*Salvia nemorosa* 79
*Salvia officinalis* 88
*Sambucus niger* 17, 23, 100
*Satureja montana* 89
savory, winter 89
*Scabiosa caucasica* 80
scabious 80
scorpions 30–1
Scots pine 21, 109
sea holly 73
*Sedum spectabile* 33, 80
*Silene dioica* 80
*Silybum marianum* 60
*Skimmia japonica* 100
slime mould 121
slugs and snails 47
snake's head fritillary 64
snapdragon 53

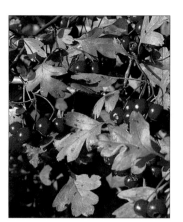

sneezeweed 74
snowberry 100
*Solidago virgaurea* 11, 81
*Sorbus aucuparia* 17, 111
*Sparganium erectum* 43
spearmint 87
speedwell 35, 83
spiders 30–1
  blackthorn 31
  hawthorn 31
  ivy 31
  Lawson cypress 31
spindle tree 102
*Spirodela polyrhiza* 27
squirrels
  English oak 21
  hazel 21
  Scots pine 21
  sweet chestnut 21
*Stachys officinalis* 39, 81
*Sternbergia lutea* 65
stick insects 46
stock, night scented 19
*Stratiotes aloides* 29
strawberries 17
sunflower 15, 56
  prairie 35
swallows 10
sweet chestnut 21, 107
sweet cicely 87
sweet rocket 57
sweet William 54
*Symphoricarpos albus* 100
*Symphytum grandiflora*
  81
*Syringa vulgaris* 101

## T

*Tagetes patula* 35, 60
*Tanacetum vulgare* 11,
  35, 89
tansy 11, 35, 89
*Taraxacum officinale* 15, 82
*Taxus baccata* 105

teasel 15, 55
termites 46
thistle
  globe 72
  milk 60
  plume 71
*Thymus vulgaris* (thyme) 89
tickseed 71
*Tilia cordata* 111
tits, blue 12
toadflax 76
tobacco plant 19, 33,
  59
*Trifolium pratense* 15, 82
*Tropaeolum majus* 61
*Tulipa biflora* (tulip) 65
*Typha minima* 43, 119

## U

*Ulex europaeus* 101
*Ulmus glabra* 103
*Urtica dioica* 82

## V

*Vaccinium myrtillus* 25
*Vaccinium oxycoccos* 25
valerian, red 70
*Verbascum olympicum* 83
*Verbena bonariensis* 33,
  49, 61
*Veronica beccabunga* 43
*Veronica spicata* 35, 83
vervain, purpletop 61
*Viburnum*
  *V. lanata* 103
  *V. opulus* 17
  *V. tinus* 37
  *V. x bodnantense* 101
*Viola odorata* (violet) 83
Virginia creeper 114
*Vitis vinifera* 115

## W

wallflower 55
wasps 36–7
water avens 117
water crowfoot 43
water forget-me-not 43
water horsetail 43
water lily 43
  white 27, 29, 119
water milfoil, Eurasian 43
water mint 27, 29, 43, 118
water smartweed 43
water soldier 29
water starwort 43
wayfaring tree 103
white water lily 27, 29, 119

wild strawberry 17
willow, goat 111
*Wisteria sinensis* 115
wood betony 39, 81
woodlice 47
worms 44–5

## Y

yarrow 11, 35, 39, 66
yellow flag 43
yew 105
Yorkshire fog 74

## Z

*Zinnia elegans* 33, 61

## ACKNOWLEDGEMENTS

The publisher would like to
thank the following for allowing
their photographs to be
reproduced in the book
(t=top, b=bottom, l=left,
r=right, c=centre, f=far):
**Alamy:** 41 panel 2nd from l,
41 panel fr, 121b.
**Charles Lightfoot:** 13tr.
**Corbis:** 25 panel 2nd from r,
41 panel 2nd from r, 43 panel tl.
**Dave Bevan:** 44b, 45b, 68tl,
75b, 97bl, 98tl, 119tl, 120b.
**Garden Picture Library:** 80tl,
81br.
**Garden World Images:**
25 panel fl, 25 panel 2nd from l,
37 panel bl, 41 panel fl, 43
panel cl, 57t, 58tr, 62b, 65tr,
65b, 67br, 68tr, 69bl, 70bl, 74t,
76tl, 77br, 79t, 90bl, 92bl, 94bl,
95b, 96b, 100br, 103tr.
**Michael Lavelle:** 15br, 69br.
**NHPA:** 13tl, 17bl, 46c, 46bl.
**papiliophotos.com:** 10t, 14t,
15tl, 16t, 17br, 19m, 24br.

# PLANT HARDINESS AND ZONES

## HARDINESS SYMBOLS
❀ = half-hardy (down to 0°C)
❀ ❀ = frost hardy (down to -5°C)
❀ ❀ ❀ = fully hardy (down to -15°C)

## ZONE ENTRIES

Plant entries in the directory of this book have been given zone numbers, and these zones relate to their hardiness. The zonal system used, shown right, was developed by the Agricultural Research Service of the United States Department of Agriculture. According to this system, there are 11 zones in total, based on the average annual minimum temperature in a particular geographical zone.

The zone rating for each plant indicates the coldest zone in which a correctly planted subject can survive the winter. Where a plant's hardiness is borderline, the first number indicates the marginal zone and the second the safer zone.

This is not a hard and fast system, but simply a rough indicator, as many factors other than temperature also play an important part where hardiness is concerned. These factors include altitude, wind exposure, proximity to water, soil type, the presence of snow or shade, night temperature, and the amount of water received by a plant. These kinds of factors can easily alter a plant's hardiness by as much as two zones. The presence of long-term snow cover in the winter especially can allow plants to survive in colder zones.

## KEY TO ZONES

These maps show the zones in Europe and the USA. The temperature ranges apply worldwide.

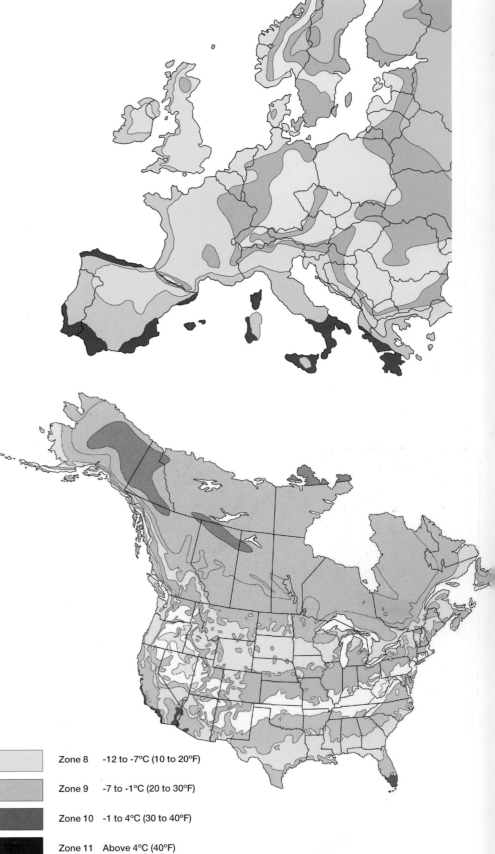

| | | |
|---|---|---|
| ■ | Zone 1 | Below -45°C (-50°F) |
| ■ | Zone 2 | -45 to -40°C (-50 to -40°F) |
| ■ | Zone 3 | -40 to -34°C (-40 to -30°F) |
| ■ | Zone 4 | -34 to -29°C (-30 to -20°F) |
| ■ | Zone 5 | -29 to -23°C (-20 to -10°F) |
| ■ | Zone 6 | -23 to -18°C (-10 to 0°F) |
| ■ | Zone 7 | -18 to -12°C (0 to 10°F) |
| ■ | Zone 8 | -12 to -7°C (10 to 20°F) |
| ■ | Zone 9 | -7 to -1°C (20 to 30°F) |
| ■ | Zone 10 | -1 to 4°C (30 to 40°F) |
| ■ | Zone 11 | Above 4°C (40°F) |